Competitive Diving Illustrated

Coaching Strategies to Perform 134 Dives

Hobie Billingsley
World's Greatest Diving Coach

Trius Publishing
San Diego

Competitive Diving Illustrated
Coaching Strategies to Perform 134 Dives

Illustrated drawings of dive sequences by Hobie
Cover design by Jonatan Azpilcueta
Edited by Peter Andersen, Ph.D.

Copyright © 2018 by Hobart (a.k.a. Hobert) Sherwood Billingsley
Published in the United States of America by:
Trius Publishing, 6382 Lake Dora Ave., San Diego, CA 92119

All rights reserved. No part of this book may be reproduced by any mechanical, photographic, or electronic process, or in the form of an audio recording nor may it be stored in a retrieval system, transmitted, or otherwise be copied for public or private use – other than for "fair use" as brief quotations embodied in articles and reviews without prior written permission of the author and publisher.

The author of this book, and other written materials does not dispense medical advice or prescribe the use of any technique as a form of treatment for physical or mental problems without the advice of a physician, either directly or indirectly. The intent of the author is only to offer information of a general nature to help you in your quest for diving performance improvement. In the event you use any of the information or methods and cues in this book for yourself or to help others is your constitutional right, the author and publisher assume no responsibility for your actions.

This is a how-to learn and perform most often used competitive dives from illustrated sequences of drawings. Each drawing is labeled with a sequence number. Hobie describes the correct method and cue to focus on corresponding to the number so you can efficiently perform each dive.

To learn more, place book orders, find stories and pictures about this sports icon, go to his website: https://HobieBillingsley.com

ISBN: 978-0-9986357-1-2   paperback $29.95
ISBN: 978-1-961817-15-9   e-book .epub $9.97

Order other Hobie Billingsley publications at
https://HobieBillingsley.com

Challenge: How to succeed beyond your dreams

Hobie's autobiography. An entertaining page-turner, his life and worldwide influence on history of competitive diving.

ISBN: 978-0-9986357-0-5 paperback 7x10 375 pages $29.95

Competitive Diving Illustrated – Coaching Strategies to Perform 134 Dives

Illustrated numbered sequence drawings with detailed explanations how to perform 134 of the more common competitive dives.

ISBN: 978-0-9986357-1-2 paperback 7x10 325 pages $29.95

Competitive Diving – The Complete Guide for Coaches, Divers, Judges

The most complete guide for establishing and developing competitive diving programs. You can learn methods and skills to evaluate programs, facilities, coaches, divers, and judges. Mechanical principles and techniques are offered to help teach and judge competitive dives and organize and administer programs. Communication and safety practices are also covered for one and three meter, and tower/platform diving.

ISBN: 978-0-9986357-2-9 paperback 7x10 317 pages $29.95

Hobie's Heroes 25th Anniversary Edition

A film by Steven Montgomery, Barbara Wolver, and Tony Gucchiari. Documents young divers overcoming their fears to learn a full list of new dives on one meter and three-meter for the first time at Hobie's famous summer camps. Updates divers 25 years after the making of the film.
DVD color 29 minutes $19.95

Photo at left shows Hobie coaching on deck at his summer camp

HOBIE BILLINGSLEY, affectionately dubbed the Coach's Coach, presided over diving at Indiana University for 30 years. When he retired, he didn't leave the sport. Instead, he continues to travel around this country and overseas, giving clinics, conducting camps for coaches and assisting with fund raising. During his tenure at IU, Hobie's divers captured an amazing 115 national titles, three Olympic and five Pan American golds, and 22 Big Ten titles. He coached such greats as Cynthia Potter, who won more national titles than any other woman; Olympic gold medalists Ken Sitzberger and Lesley Bush; and Rick Gilbert, winner of 11 national crowns. Hobie also had the daring and foresight to offer a scholarship at Indiana to a brash ex-wrestler named Mark Lenzi, despite Lenzi's brief diving experience. Yes, that's the same Mark Lenzi who won the gold medal at the 1992 Olympic Games. A national champion on both boards at Ohio State, Billingsley one time barnstormed the country as an acrobatic and clown diver. He coached in four Olympics, organized both the World Diving Coaches Association and American Diving Coaches Association (now known as the Professional Diving Coaches Association), was named Diving Coach of the Year in 1964 through 1970, and, in 1982, became the first recipient of the NCAA Coach of the Year Award as well as an inductee into the International Swimming Hall of Fame. *Hobie Billingsley's* **Diving Illustrated,** for which Hobie did both the text and drawings, was first published in 1965 and soon became a classic. This revised edition includes both the latest dives and a new chapter on platform diving.

PREFACE

I present this book with the purpose of providing a guide that can be useful to the coach, diving instructor and others concerned with the development of diving skills.

It portrays an accepted and desirable way of executing standard competitive dives. Each dive is drawn in sequence with corresponding explanations to help in understanding the dive from beginning to end. This type of presentation makes it possible for anyone to form quickly a mental picture of the dive and to develop a basic understanding of what motor skills are needed to execute the dive successfully.

Many of the drawings for this book have been derived from actual movies of the world's finest divers. The author has attempted to illustrate the outstanding dives performed by these divers using their own styles and techniques. He has made no attempt to emphasize any particular style, because the manner in which certain dives are performed depends much upon the physical structure and motor skills of the individual.

The author wishes to pay special tribute to the late Bruce Harlan, his diving companion and closest friend for fifteen years, and to Art Weibel, his high school coach who started him in his career.

HOBIE BILLINGSLEY

Bloomington, Indiana

January 1994

Editor's Note:

I've known Hobie Billingsley since 1961 when I entered Indiana University to swim for Doc Counsilman, and study to be a physical education teacher and swim coach. I knew I would need divers just like I.U. I watched all the diving competitions to learn what I could knowing that not many programs then could afford a diving coach.

I became good friends with all the divers and roomed with Rick Gilbert his first national champion. Since then, I've learned more about the history and application of physics principles and teaching methods Hobie first introduced to coaches all over the world of diving that are still most applicable today. Because of that knowledge I was able to publish Hobie's acclaimed autobiography, and put it on Amazon and his website https://HobieBillingsley.com

Then I learned he had two other competitive diving books that were now out-of-print and in the old formats. Hobie gave me copies and notarized signed permission to republish these books in a new 7x10 paperback with better eye-catching covers and titles. This book is one of two also available on Amazon and his website.

As I started to revise and rework his outstanding books, I realized the amount of quality effort and knowledge of his world-class experience and leadership. These books are a legacy and tribute to help all coaches, divers, and judges continue to improve this sport. He devoted his life to mentor hundreds of divers and was more than a coach. I guarantee any competitive diving coach or diver will shorten their learning curve by reading this book and Competitive Diving – Complete Guide for Coaches, Divers, Judges.

I am proud to say Hobie has been my mentor, too. Over the years we have become very close friends. And I am very proud to reproduce these fine books and preserve his great legacy – a gift to all associated with competitive diving.

Peter Andersen, Ph.D.
Editor and Publisher

CONTENTS

	PAGES
GROUP I—FORWARD DIVES	**1-45**
Forward Approach and Take-Off	2-3
Forward Dive—Tuck (One Meter)	4-5
Forward Dive—Pike (One Meter)	6-7
Forward Dive—Layout (One Meter)	8-9
Forward Somersault—Tuck (One Meter)	10-11
Forward Somersault—Closed Pike (One Meter)	12-13
Forward Somersault—Layout (One Meter)	14-15
Flying Forward Somersault—Tuck (One Meter)	16-17
Flying Forward Somersault—Pike (One Meter)	18-19
Forward 1½ Somersaults—Tuck (One Meter)	20-21
Forward 1½ Somersaults—Open Pike (Three Meter)	22-23
Forward 1½ Somersaults—Layout (Three Meter)	24-25
Flying Forward 1½ Somersaults—Tuck (One Meter)	26-27
Flying Forward 1½ Somersaults—Pike (Three Meter)	28-29
Forward Double Somersault—Tuck (One Meter)	30-31
Forward Double Somersault—Pike (One Meter)	32-33
Forward 2½ Somersaults—Tuck (One Meter)	34-35
Forward 2½ Somersaults—Pike (Three Meter)	36-37
Forward Triple Somersault—Tuck (Three Meter)	38-39
Forward Triple Somersault—Pike (Three Meter)	40-41
Forward 3½ Somersaults—Tuck (Three Meter)	42-43
Forward 3½ Somersaults—Pike (Three Meter)	44-45
GROUP II—BACKWARD DIVES	**47-83**
Back Dive—Tuck (One Meter)	48-49
Back Dive—Pike (Three Meter)	50-51
Back Dive—Layout (One Meter)	52-53
Back Somersault—Tuck (One Meter)	54-55
Back Somersault—Pike (One Meter)	56-57
Back Somersault—Layout (One Meter)	58-59
Flying Back Somersault—Tuck (One Meter)	60-61
Flying Back Somersault—Pike (One Meter)	62-63
Back 1½ Somersaults—Tuck (One Meter)	64-65
Back 1½ Somersaults—Pike (One Meter)	66-67
Back 1½ Somersaults—Layout (Three Meter)	68-69
Flying Backward 1½ Somersaults—Tuck (Three Meter)	70-71
Back Double Somersault—Tuck (One Meter)	72-73
Back Double Somersault—Pike (Three Meter)	74-75
Back Double Somersault—Layout (Three Meter)	76-77
Back 2½ Somersaults—Tuck (Three Meter)	78-79

	PAGES
Back 2½ Somersaults—Pike (Three Meter)	80-81
Back 3½ Somersaults—Tuck (Three Meter)	82-83

GROUP III—REVERSE DIVES **85-119**

Reverse Dive—Tuck (Three Meter)	86-87
Reverse Dive—Pike (One Meter)	88-89
Reverse Dive—Layout (Three Meter)	90-91
Reverse Somersault—Tuck (One Meter)	92-93
Reverse Somersault—Pike (One Meter)	94-95
Reverse Somersault—Layout (One Meter)	96-97
Reverse Flying Somersault—Tuck (One Meter)	98-99
Reverse Flying Somersault—Pike (One Meter)	100-101
Reverse 1½ Somersaults—Tuck (Three Meter)	102-103
Reverse 1½ Somersaults—Pike (Three Meter)	104-105
Reverse 1½ Somersaults—Layout (Three Meter)	106-107
Flying Reverse 1½ Somersaults—Tuck (Three Meter)	108-109
Reverse Double Somersault—Tuck (Three Meter)	110-111
Reverse Double Somersault—Pike (One Meter)	112-113
Reverse 2½ Somersaults—Tuck (Three Meter)	114-115
Reverse 2½ Somersaults—Pike (Three Meter)	116-117
Reverse 3½ Somersaults—Tuck (Three Meter)	118-119

GROUP IV—INWARD DIVES **121-151**

Inward Dive—Tuck (One Meter)	122-123
Inward Dive—Pike (Three Meter)	124-125
Inward Dive—Layout (Three Meter)	126-127
Inward Somersault—Tuck (One Meter)	128-129
Inward Somersault—Pike (One Meter)	130-131
Inward Flying Somersault—Tuck (One Meter)	132-133
Inward Flying Somersault—Pike (One Meter)	134-135
Inward 1½ Somersaults—Tuck (One Meter)	136-137
Inward 1½ Somersaults—Pike (One Meter)	138-139
Inward Flying 1½ Somersaults—Tuck (Three Meter)	140-141
Inward Double Somersault—Tuck (One Meter)	142-143
Inward Double Somersault—Pike (Three Meter)	144-145
Inward 2½ Somersaults—Tuck (Three Meter)	146-147
Inward 2½ Somersaults—Pike (Three Meter)	148-149
Inward 3½ Somersaults—Tuck (Three Meter)	150-151

GROUP V—TWISTING DIVES **153-261**

Forward Dive, Half-Twist—Pike (One Meter)	154-155
Forward Dive, Half-Twist—Layout (One Meter)	156-157
Forward Dive, Twist—Pike (Three Meter)	158-159
Forward Dive, Twist—Layout (One Meter)	160-161
Forward Somersault, Half-Twist—Pike (One Meter)	162-163
Forward Somersault, Half-Twist—Layout (One Meter)	164-165
Forward Somersault, One Twist—Free Position (One Meter)	166-167

PAGES

Forward Somersault, Double Twist—Free Position
  (One Meter) 168-169
Forward 1½ Somersaults, Half-Twist—Tuck (One Meter) 170-171
Forward 1½ Somersaults, Half-Twist—Pike (One Meter) 172-173
Forward 1½ Somersaults, One Twist—Free Position
  (One Meter) 174-175
Forward 1½ Somersaults, Double Twist—Free Position
  (Three Meter) 176-177
Forward 1½ Somersaults, Triple Twist—Free Position
  (Three Meter) 178-179
Forward 2½ Somersaults, One Twist—Pike (Free Position)
  (Three Meter) 180-181
Forward 2½ Somersaults, Double Twist—Pike (Free Position)
  (Three Meter) 182-183
Back Dive, Half-Twist—Pike (One Meter) 184-185
Back Dive, Half-Twist—Layout (Three Meter) 186-187
Back Dive, One Twist—Layout (Three Meter) 188-189
Back Somersault, Half-Twist—Pike (Free Position)
  (One Meter) 190-191
Back Somersault, Half-Twist—Layout (Free Position)
  (Three Meter) 192-193
Back Somersault, One Twist—Pike (Free Position)
  (One Meter) 194-195
Back Somersault, One Twist—Layout (Free Position)
  (One Meter) 196-197
Back Somersault, 1½ Twists—Pike (Free Position)
  (One Meter) 198-199
Back Somersault, 1½ Twists—Layout (Free Position)
  (One Meter) 200-201
Back 1½ Somersaults, Half-Twist—Tuck (Free Position)
  (Three Meter) 202-203
Back 1½ Somersaults, Half-Twist—Pike (Free Position)
  (Three Meter) 204-205
Back 1½ Somersaults, 1½ Twists—Pike (Free Position)
  (One Meter) 206-207
Back 1½ Somersaults, 2½ Twists—Pike (Free Position)
  (Three Meter) 208-209
Back 1½ Somersaults, 3½ Twists—Pike (Free Position)
  (Three Meter) 210-211
Reverse Dive, Half-Twist—Pike (One Meter) 212-213
Reverse Dive, Half-Twist—Layout (Three Meter) 214-215
Reverse Dive, One Twist—Layout (One Meter) 216-217
Reverse Somersault, Half-Twist—Tuck (Free Position)
  One Meter) 218-219
Reverse Somersault, Half-Twist—Pike (Free Position)
  (One Meter) 220-221
Reverse Somersault, One Twist—Tuck (Free Position)
  (One Meter) 222-223
Reverse Somersault, One Twist—Pike (Free Position)
  (One Meter) 224-225
Reverse Somersault, One Twist—Layout (Free Position)
  (One Meter) 226-227

	PAGES
Reverse Somersault, 1½ Twists—Tuck (Free Position) (One Meter)	228-229
Reverse Somersault, 1½ Twists—Pike (Free Position) (One Meter)	230-231
Reverse Somersault, 1½ Twists—Layout (Free Position) (One Meter)	232-233
Reverse 1½ Somersaults, Half-Twist—Tuck (Free Position) (Three Meter)	234-235
Reverse 1½ Somersaults, Half-Twist—Pike (Free Position) (Three Meter)	236-237
Reverse 1½ Somersaults, 1½ Twists—Pike (Free Position) (Three Meter)	238-239
Reverse 1½ Somersaults, 2½ Twists—Pike (Free Position) (Three meter)	240-241
Reverse 1½ Somersaults, 3½ Twists—Pike (Free Position) (Three Meter)	242-243
Inward Dive, Half-Twist—Pike (One Meter)	244-245
Inward Dive, Half-Twist—Layout (One Meter)	246-247
Inward Dive, One Twist—Pike (One Meter)	248-249
Inward Dive, One Twist—Layout (One Meter)	250-251
Inward Somersault, Half-Twist—Tuck (Free Position) (One Meter)	252-253
Inward Somersault, Half-Twist—Pike (Free Position) (One Meter)	254-255
Inward Somersault, One Twist—Pike (Free Position) (One Meter)	256-257
Inward 1½ Somersaults, One Twist—Pike (Free Position) (Three Meter)	258-259
Inward 1½ Somersaults, Double Twist—Pike (Free Position) (Three Meter)	260-261

GROUP VI—TOWER DIVING ... 263-301

Introduction	264-265
Tower Approaches and Take-Offs	266
Standing Forward Take-Off A	267
Standing Forward Take-Off B	268
Running and Walking Forward Take-Off C	269
Running and Walking Forward Take-Off D	270
Walking Approach With One Foot Take-Off E	271
Walking Approach With One Foot Take-Off F	272
Walking Approach, Skip Step, With One Foot Take-Off	273
Backward Take-Off	274
Inward Take-Off	275
Armstand Approaches and Take-Offs	276
One Leg Kick Up	277
Press Up in Tuck Position	278
Press Up in Pike Position	279

CONTENTS

	PAGES
Basic Dives	281
Running Front 1½ Somersaults, Open or Closed Pike	
Figure A	282-283
Standing Front Dive, Layout	
Figure B	284-285
Inward Dive, Pike	
Figure C	286-287
Back Dive, Pike	
Figure D	288-289
Reverse Dive, Pike	
Figure E	290-291
Handstand, Cut Through, Tuck	
Figure F	292-293
Forward Flying 1½ Somersaults, Pike	
Figure G	294-295
Reverse Somersault, Layout	
Figure H	296-297
Inward 1½ Somersaults, Pike	
Figure I	298-299
Things to Remember When Tower Diving	300
Safety Hints for Tower	301

GROUP 1 - FORWARD DIVES

FORWARD APPROACH AND TAKE-OFF

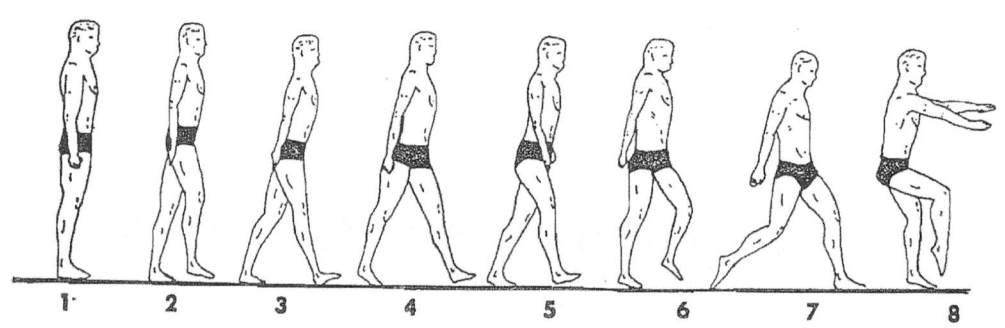

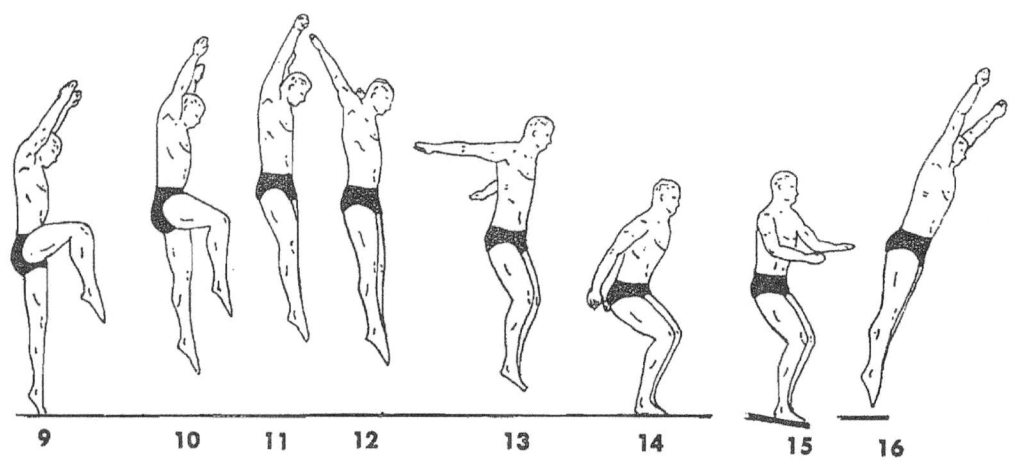

2

FORWARD APPROACH AND TAKE-OFF

1. The diver stands erect with the legs straight but not locked at the knees. The pelvis is pushed slightly forward; the stomach is drawn in but not overly so; and the arms are extended at the sides with the fingers together but not stiff. The shoulders are pulled back slightly, and the eyes are focused on the end of the board.

2-3-4. Most divers use a three- or four-step approach. This illustration demonstrates the latter, which is started with the diver leaning forward slightly before taking the first step, to keep the body weight over the legs. The steps are of normal length, and the arms swing, about half as far as in a normal walk. The length of the steps increases slightly with the forward momentum of the body.

5-6. At the completion of the third step, a coordinated arm movement is started with both arms swinging slightly in front of the body. They then swing behind the body as the fourth step begins.

7. The arms remain straight as they start to swing forward at the completion of the fourth step. The eyes remain fixed on the end of the board.

8. The hurdle is started by lifting one leg, which is bent at the knee to form a right angle, simultaneously with the forward and upward swing of the arms. The arms spread laterally a little as they rise, to provide the diver with better balance.

9. The simultaneous lifting of the arms and knee continues until the arms nearly reach overhead. The knee lifts until the thigh is on a horizontal plane and the toes are pointing straight down at the board. The other leg extends up to the tips of the toes during this entire coordinated action, to lift the body as high as possible.

10-11. The normal length of the hurdle is recognized to be about three feet. The knee lifted in the hurdle extends downward near the peak of the jump while the arms remain overhead slightly in front of the body. The "push off" leg then moves forward to meet the "hurdle" leg. With both legs extended and held slightly in front of the body, the arms are used to balance the body as it reaches the peak of the hurdle. The head tilts down slightly so the eyes can continue to sight the end of the board.

12. The arms extend behind the shoulders and start a downward sweep as the body descends toward the end of the board.

13-14. The legs bend slightly at the knees just before the balls of the feet contact the end of the board. At this moment, the head is brought to an erect position. The arms continue to sweep downward as the feet meet the end of the board.

15. When the weight of the body drops onto the board, the arms sweep past the hips and then bend slightly at the elbow as they move forward and upward. They again straighten as they lift in front of the face. The head remains erect.

16. As the board springs up, the diver extends the legs with the arms completely extended.

FORWARD DIVE - TUCK

(One Meter) 101C

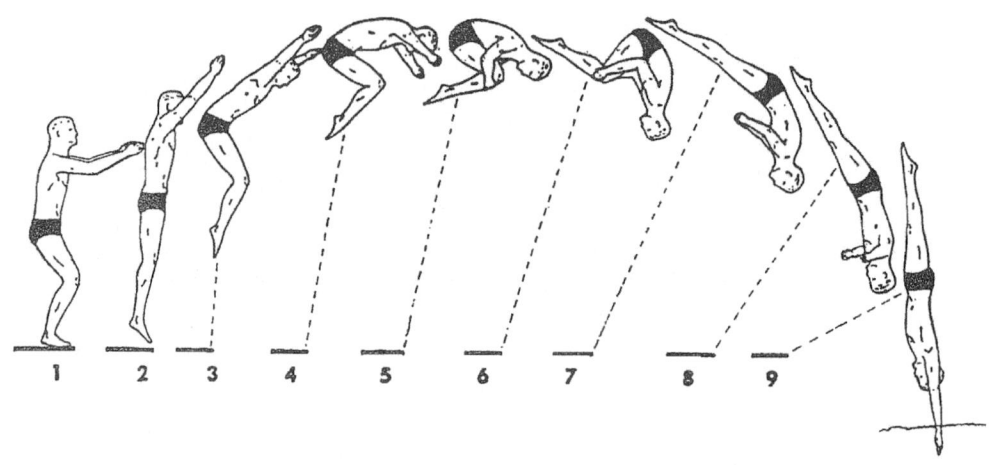

FORWARD DIVE - TUCK

(One Meter)

1. Prior to the take-off, the legs flex as the arms swing forward and upward with the head erect.
2. The body rocks forward slightly while the arms continue to reach over the head. The legs, ankles, and toes then extend to lift the diver from the board.
3-4. When the diver leaves the board, the knees draw up toward the chest. The body bends at the waist as the arms move downward about shoulder width apart toward the knees and with the eyes spotting the water at the approximate point of entry.
5. The hands clasp the legs between the shins and the knees near the peak of the dive. The head is in line with the body, with the eyes spotting the water throughout the entire dive.
6-7. The hands release the knees as the body begins to descend. The legs extend with a snap and aim slightly above the horizontal. The balance of the dive is maintained by leaving the hands near the knees and along the sides of the body as the legs extend. The arms straighten and then begin to move laterally as the body straightens.
8. The arms extend laterally over the head as the diver nears the water for the entry.
9. The entry is made with the body straight and slightly short of vertical.

FORWARD DIVE-PIKE

(One Meter) 101B

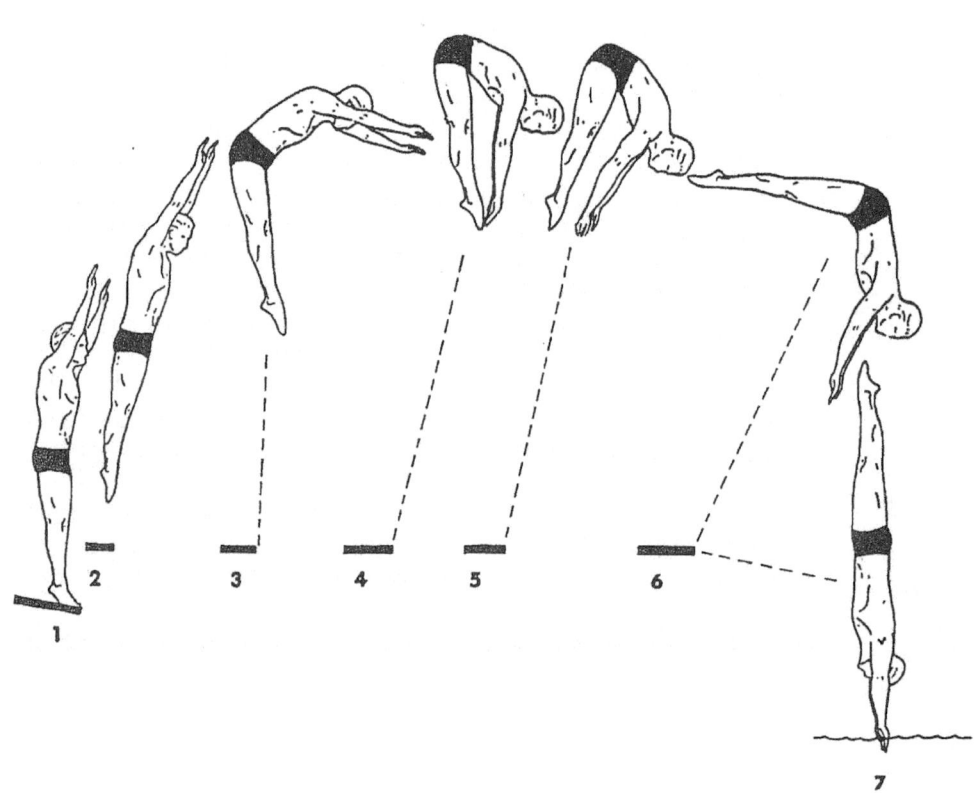

FORWARD DIVE - PIKE

(One Meter)

1. The diver jumps from the board by completely extending the legs and feet while reaching overhead with the arms shoulder width apart and with the head held erect.

2. The diver leaves the board at a slight angle, with the arms continuing to reach upward. The head remains erect with the eyes spotting the water in front of the board.

3. The hips then push upward while the legs pull forward slightly to a vertical position. The extended arms press down toward the legs, and the eyes continue to spot the water at the approximate point of entry.

4. The hands touch the insteps, with the legs in a vertical position at the very peak of the dive.

5. The body starts its descent following the touching of the insteps. After the touch is made, the arms spread about shoulder width apart and begin to reach toward the water. The eyes remain fixed on the approximate point of entry. Immediately following the touch of the toes, the legs begin to push upward behind the body.

6. The arms remain straight as they reach overhead toward the water at a point slightly in front of vertical. The legs continue to press upward, and the body begins to straighten for the entry.

7. The diver enters the water slightly short of vertical with the arms stretched over the head and pressing against the ears. The legs are straight, and the toes are pointed.

FORWARD DIVE-LAYOUT

(One Meter) 101A

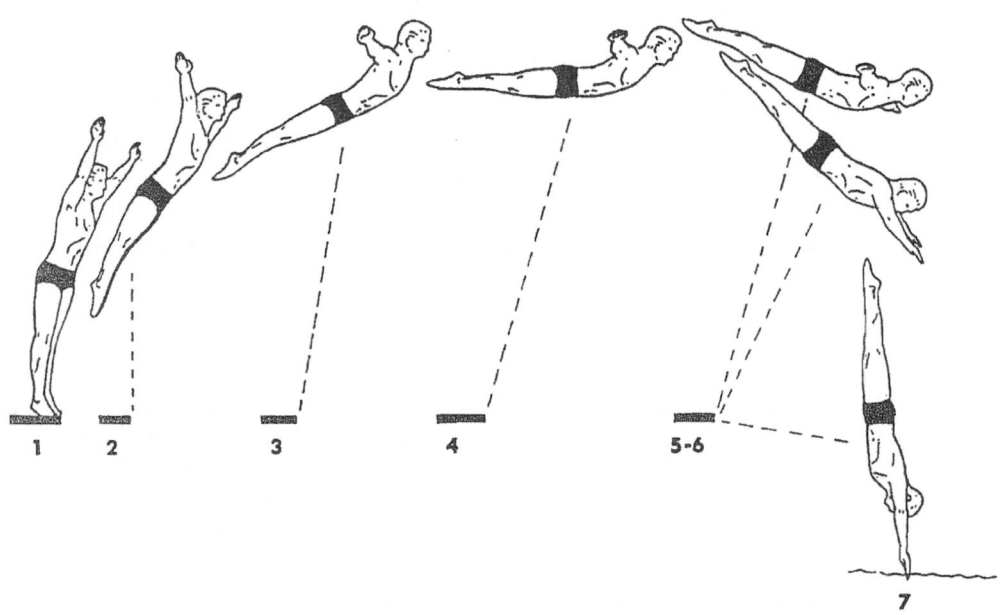

FORWARD DIVE - LAYOUT

(One Meter)

1. The diver leaves the board, with the arms extended over the head. The head is erect with the eyes fixed on a point at the other end of the pool. The body leans slightly forward, and the legs fully extend.

2. As the body rises from the board, the arms pull down laterally toward a position at right angles to the body. The head and eyes remain stationary. Emphasis is placed on lifting the legs upward behind the body without piking.

3. The legs continue to move upward behind the body. When the arms are placed in a position at right angles to the body, they do not move until the reach for the water is made. There is very little arch in the back throughout the execution of the swan dive.

4-5. The legs continue to rise as the body reaches its peak and starts its descent. With the slow rotation of the body, the eyes follow a path from the other end of the pool to the spot in the water where the entry will be made.

6. When a position is reached short of vertical, where the diver can make a head-first entry without piking, the arms quickly extend over the head when the diver nears the water in a position slightly short of vertical. The eyes continue to spot the water where the entry will be made.

7. The entry is made with the arms stretched over the head, pressing against the ears, and with the body straight, slightly short of vertical.

FORWARD SOMERSAULT - TUCK

(One Meter) 102C

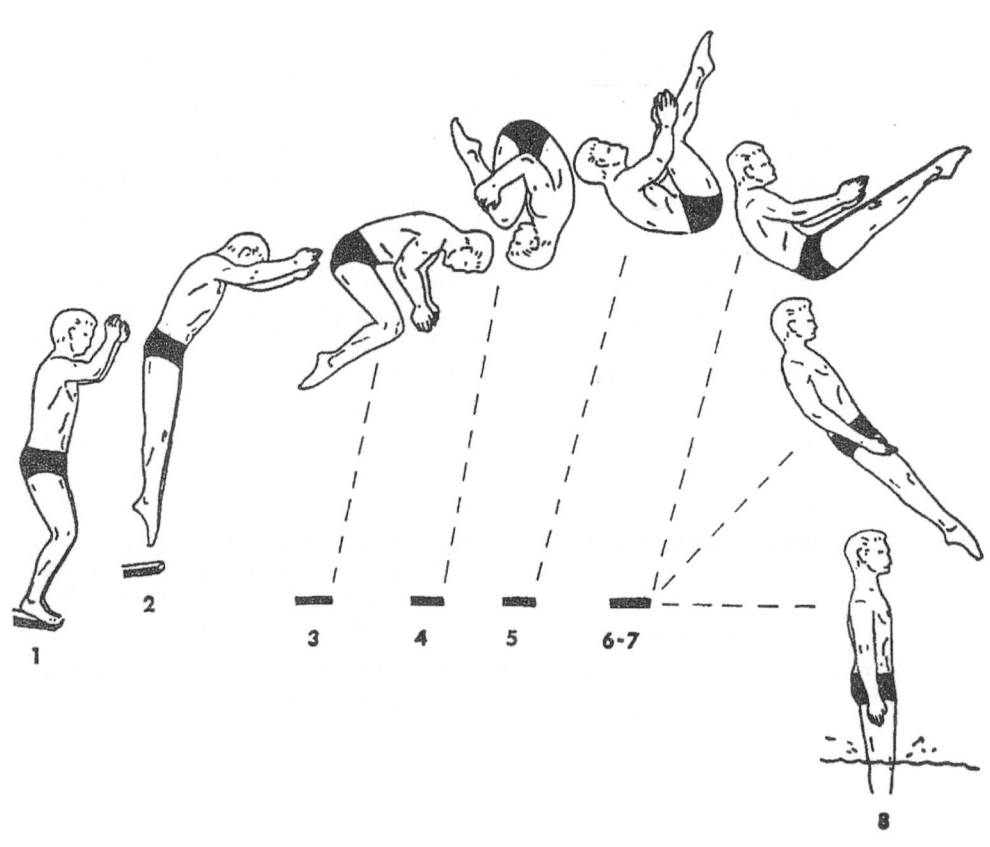

FORWARD SOMERSAULT - TUCK

(One Meter)

1. While on the board ready for the take-off, the diver leans very slightly forward with the knees bent, the hips directly over the feet, the arms bent and held slightly over, and in front of, the head, and the head held erect with the eyes spotting the water in front.

2. Before leaving the board, the diver extends the legs with the arms reaching overhead slightly in front of vertical. The diver then pushes the hips upward with a simultaneous forward and downward movement of the arms and head just prior to leaving the board. These motions continue upon leaving the board.

3. The knees are drawn toward the chest, and the heels are brought up and back toward the hips as the hips begin to move upward. Rotation is generated by moving the arms and head toward the knees. *Caution:* Do not bring the knees to the hands.

4. Holding the elbows against the sides of the body, the diver grasps the shins, pulling the knees into the chest.

5. The diver releases and begins to extend the legs as the trunk approaches a vertical position near the highest point of the dive.

6. When the somersaults near three quarters complete, the legs straighten with the hips slightly bent. The water is spotted some distance out. The arms begin their movement toward the sides of the body.

7. The diver achieves an erect position by aiming the legs toward the water slightly in front of vertical while raising the head and chest. The eyes focus on a point at the other end of the pool. The arms are held close to the sides with the hands near the front of the thighs.

8. Entry into the water is made slightly short of the vertical position.

FORWARD SOMERSAULT - CLOSED PIKE

(One Meter) 102B

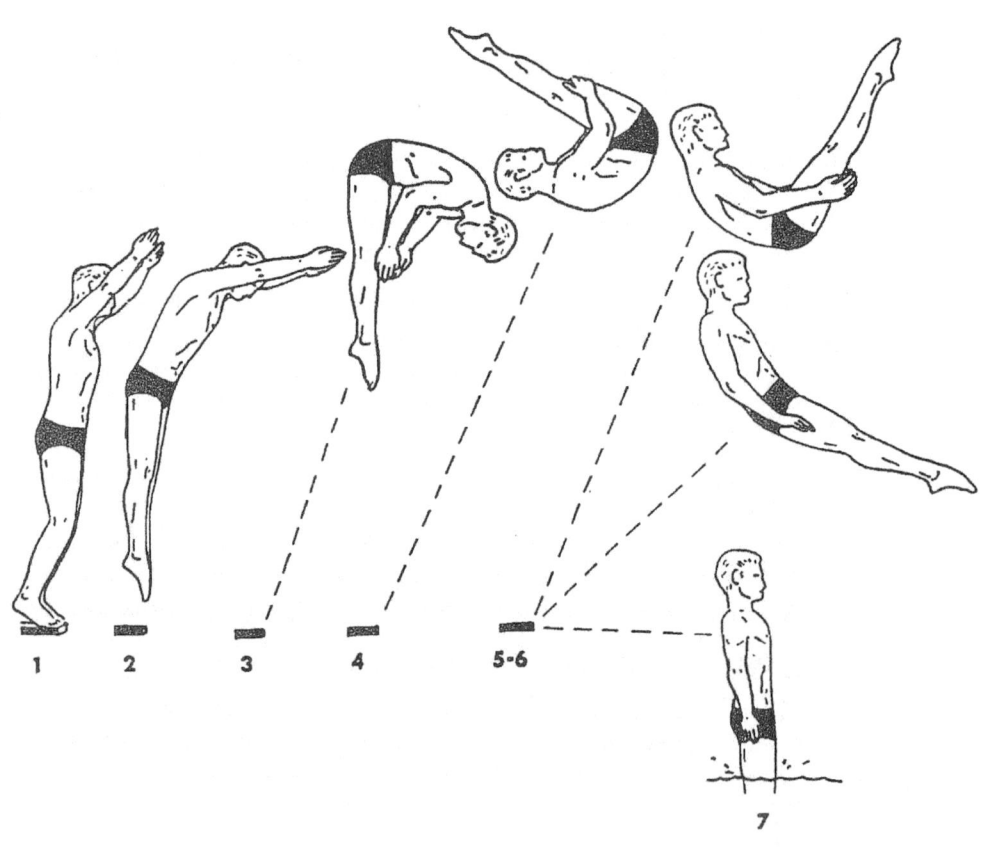

FORWARD SOMERSAULT - CLOSED PIKE

(One Meter)

1. At the take-off, the body tilts slightly forward with the arms extended upward and in front of the head.
2. With the arms in a near straight position, they move in a forward and downward direction. The arms remain over the head until the hips start their upward motion. The eyes spot the water at the approximate spot where the entry will be made.
3. When the hips start upward, the arms and head drive down toward the knees. There is a slight bend in the arms so that the legs can be grasped with the hands.
4. The hands grasp the legs just above and behind the knees with the elbows held close to the sides.
5. As the body rotates to a near "sitting" position, the legs are released by the hands and begin to straighten out.
6. The legs drive down toward the water while the head and shoulders lift to an erect position. The arms are placed at the sides for the entry.
7. The diver enters the water with a straight body slightly short of the vertical position.

FORWARD SOMERSAULT - LAYOUT

(One Meter) 102A

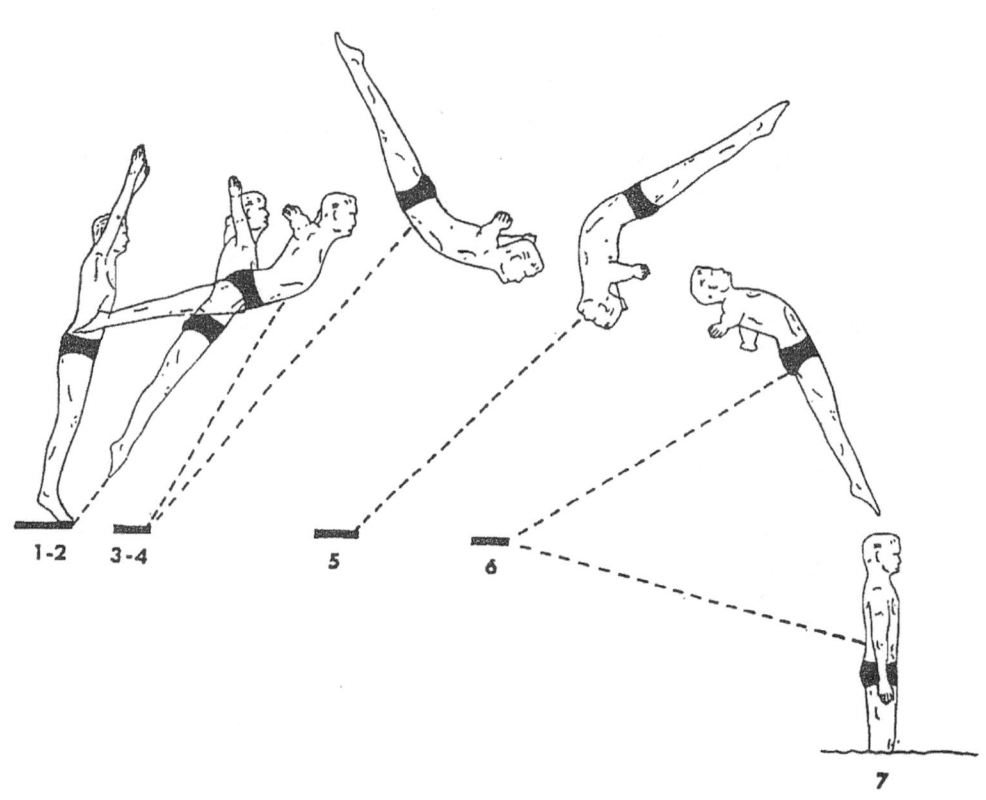

FORWARD SOMERSAULT - LAYOUT

(One Meter)

1. As the diver prepares for the take-off, the head is held erect and the body leans slightly forward. The arms are swept overhead while emphasis is placed on pushing off from the board with the toes.
2. As the diver leaves the board, the head remains up, with the eyes sighting the other end of the pool. The arms begin a forceful lateral movement toward shoulder level to aid in lifting the legs over the head.
3. The body continues its forward rotation as the head remains in a fixed position and the arms continue their lateral movement toward shoulder level.

4-5. Once the arms reach shoulder level, the diver rides the position until the dive is over three-quarters completed.

6. As the diver completes three-quarters of a somersault and the legs descend toward the water, the head is dropped to an erect position in line with the body and the arms are dropped laterally to the sides.
7. The diver enters the water feet first with the body erect and slightly short of vertical.

FLYING FORWARD SOMERSAULT - TUCK
(One Meter) 112C

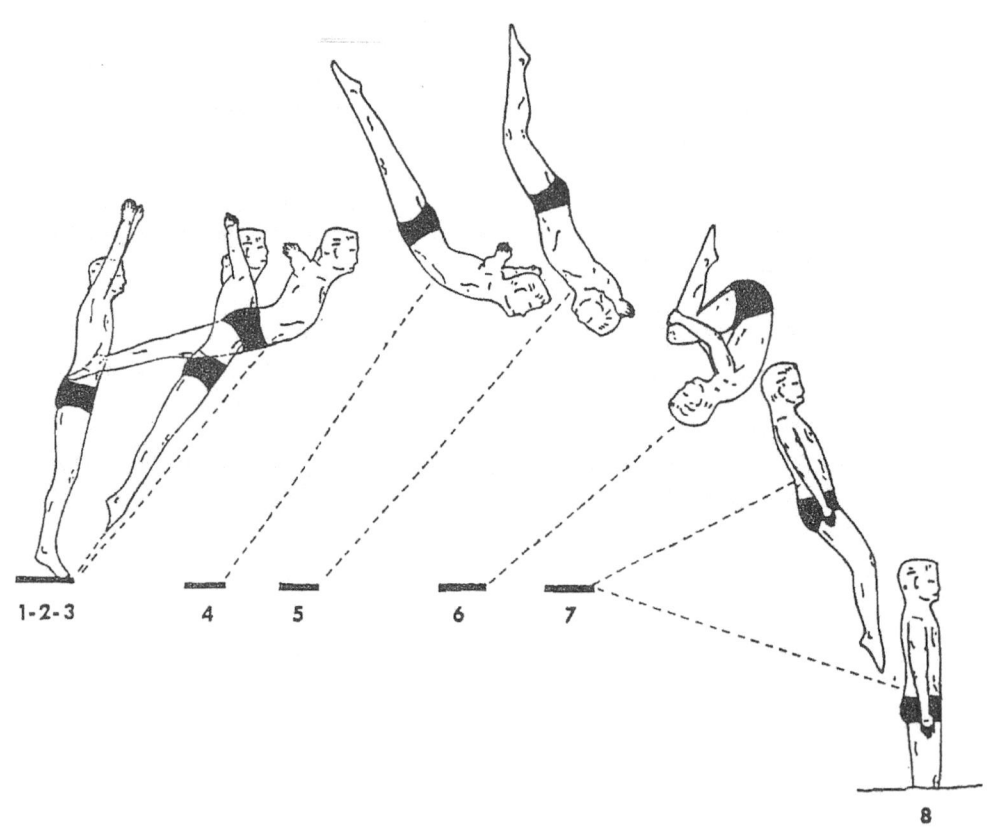

FLYING FORWARD SOMERSAULT - TUCK

(One Meter)

1. As the diver prepares for the take-off, the arms reach forward and upward with the head held erect and the body leaning slightly forward. Emphasis is placed on pushing off from the board with the toes.
2. As the diver leaves the board, the head remains up and the eyes sight the other end of the pool. The arms start a forceful lateral movement toward the level of the shoulders. This aids in lifting the legs.
3. The arms move laterally to a position level with the shoulders. The legs continue to move upward as the body begins to rotate in the layout position. The head remains tilted upward, so the body will remain in the layout position.
4. As the diver approaches the peak of the dive, he is in a near vertical position with the arms at right angles to the body and slightly bowed behind the shoulders.
5. The diver starts to move into a tuck position just as the legs approach a vertical position. The head pulls down with the chin close to the chest; the arms move forward and laterally toward the shins; and the legs begin to bend at the knees as the body bends at the waist.
6. The tuck is completed as the hands grasp the shins and draw the knees in toward the chest and the heels toward the buttocks.
7. When the diver reaches a "sitting" position, the hands release the legs and the body starts to straighten. As the body straightens for the entry, the legs are kept slightly in front, so the entry can be controlled. The head is held erect to help keep the dive from going over. The arms are placed at the sides with the hands on the thighs.
8. The body enters the water feet first and in a straight position slightly short of vertical.

FLYING FORWARD SOMERSAULT - PIKE

(One Meter) 112B

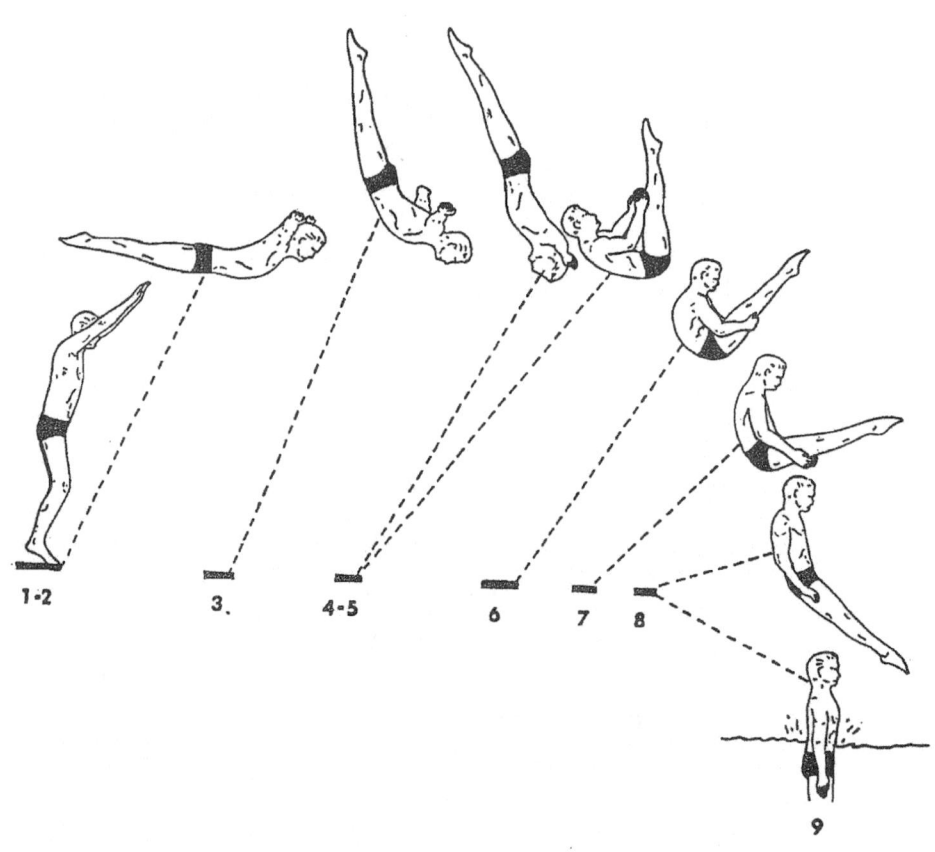

FLYING FORWARD SOMERSAULT - PIKE

(One Meter)

1. As the diver prepares for the take-off, the head is held erect while the arms reach upward in front of the head. The diver leans slightly forward.
2. The diver rotates in a layout position by forcing the legs up and behind the body and vigorously pulling the arms laterally toward shoulder level. The head is tilted up, so the body will remain in a layout position.
3. The diver is in a near vertical position when he reaches the peak of the dive. The arms are at right angles to the body and slightly bowed.
4-5. Approaching the peak of the dive, the diver starts into a pike position by dropping the head, bending at the waist, and drawing the arms for- ward toward the legs.
6. The hands grasp the legs slightly above the knees and draw them toward the chest. The eyes sight the knees in this position.
7-8. When the diver completes three-quarters of a somersault, the hands release the legs and the head and shoulders are lifted to an erect position. The legs are pressed toward the water. The arms are placed at the sides.
9. The diver enters the water in a straight position slightly short of vertical.

FORWARD 1 ½ SOMERSAULTS-TUCK

(One Meter) 103C

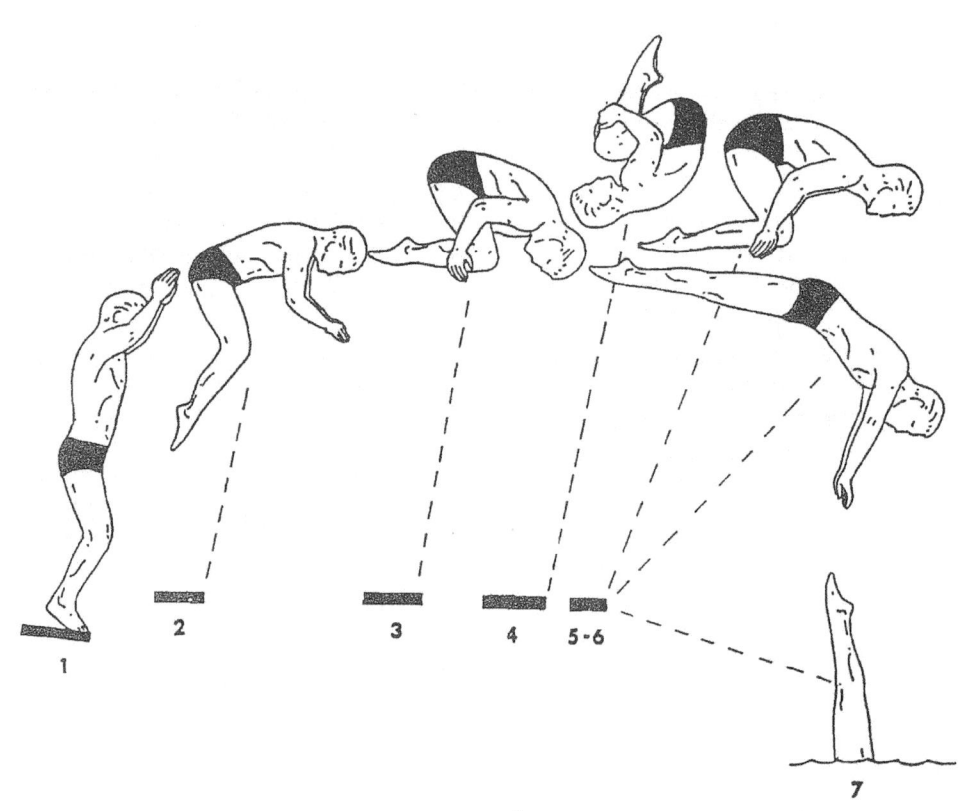

FORWARD 1 ½ SOMERSAULTS - TUCK

(One Meter)

1. At the take-off, the diver leans slightly forward with the arms extended overhead and slightly in front of the head. The head is erect with the eyes sighting the water in front of the board. The knees flex with the weight of the hips over the balls of the feet.
2. The hips push upward as the diver leaves the board. When the hips start their upward movement, the knees draw toward the chest with the heels making an. upward and backward movement toward the buttocks. The spinning motion is also induced by the downward thrust of the arms and head toward the knees.
3-4. The hands grasp the shins and draw the knees tightly against the chest as the head is ducked.
5. The water comes into view when approximately 1 ¼ somersaults are completed. At this point, the eyes spot the water where the entry will be made, and the hands release the knees and begin to extend overhead.
6. The legs extend with a snap and move upward toward a vertical position. Simultaneously, the arms circle slightly as they reach over the head slightly in front of vertical, for the water, with the eyes still fixed on the point where the body will enter the water.
7. The body straightens as the entry is made slightly short of vertical.

FORWARD 1 ½ SOMERSAULTS - OPEN PIKE
(Three Meter) 103B

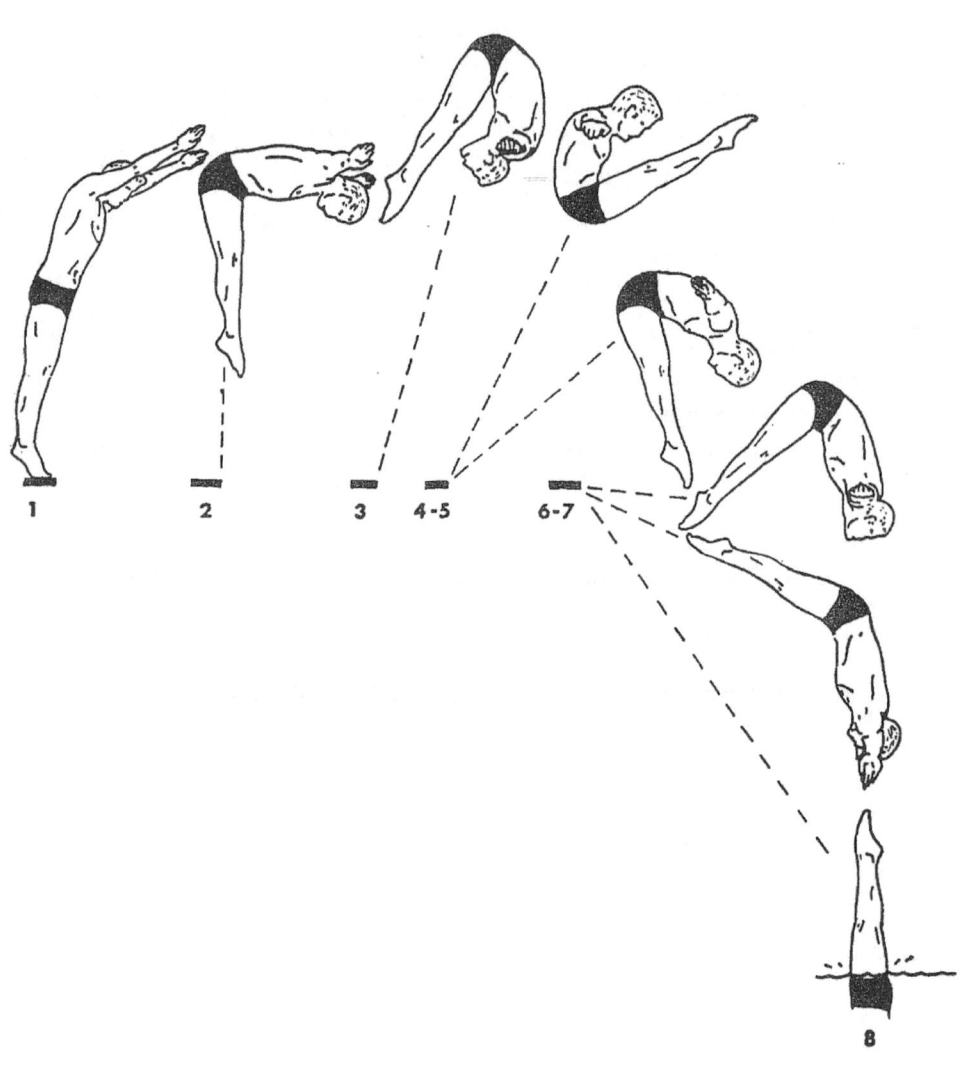

FORWARD 1 ½ SOMERSAULTS - OPEN PIKE

(Three Meter)

1. As the diver takes off from the board, the body tilts slightly forward with the arms extended over the head." The head is kept in line with the body, with the eyes fixed on the water at the approximate place where the entry will be made.
2. The legs extend completely as the diver leaves the board. A sharp, upward thrust of the hips followed immediately by a downward drive of the head and shoulders starts the body rotating. As the head and shoulders drive downward, the arms extend laterally.

3-4. The body attains as deep a pike as possible, with the eyes looking at the knees while the body is rotating. The legs keep straight, and the arms do not change position.

5. When the diver nearly completes one somersault, the water is spotted over the tips of the toes. At this point, the diver concentrates on the entry into the water.
6. The eyes spot the water slightly in front of vertical where the entry is to be made, and the arms begin to move toward that point. The pike is opened by pushing backward and upward with the legs.
7. As the body opens from the pike to a straight position, the arms extend laterally over the head for the entry.
8. The diver enters the water slightly short of a vertical position.

FORWARD 1 ½ SOMERSAULTS - LAYOUT

(Three Meter) 103A

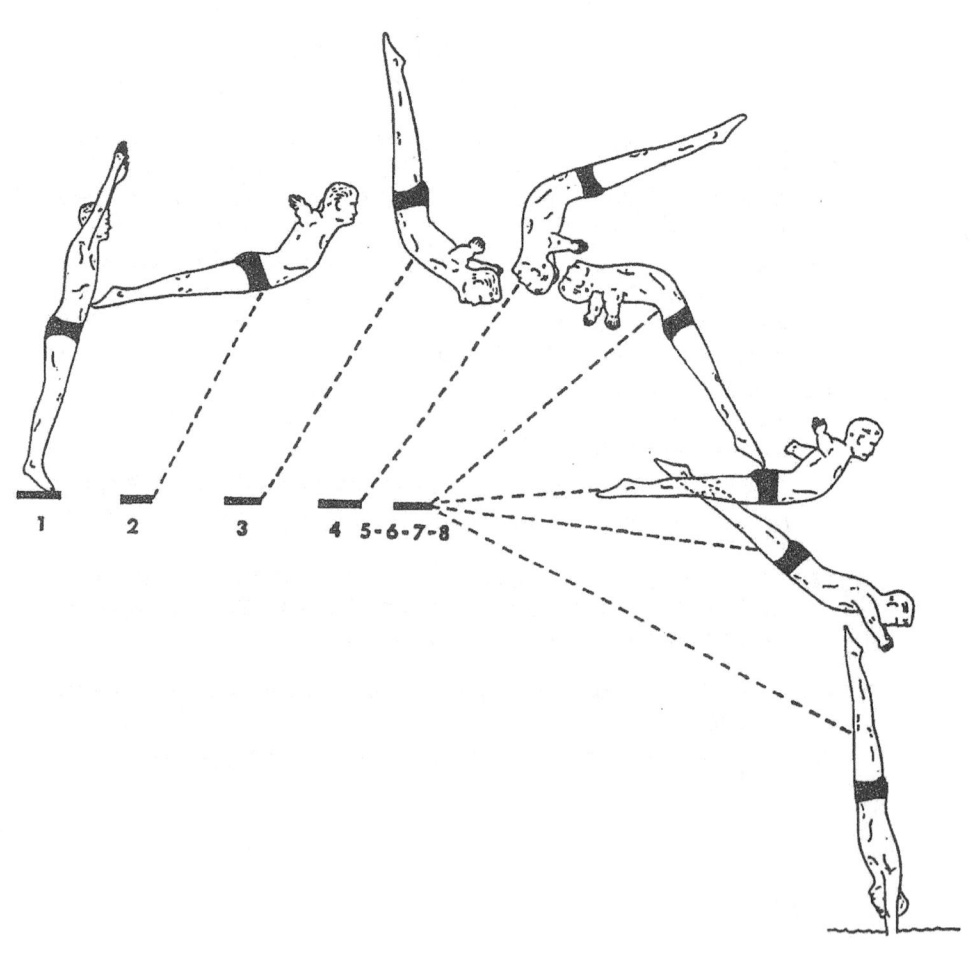

FORWARD 1 ½ SOMERSAULTS - LAYOUT

(Three Meter)

1. The take-off from the board is made with the body tilted slightly forward and with the arms extended overhead. The head is held erect with the eyes focused on the other end of the pool. The arms are then pulled down laterally toward a position even with the shoulders before the feet leave the board.

2. The arms continue to pull down laterally to a shoulder level position. The head remains in a fixed position, with the eyes still fixed on the other end of the pool. This permits the back to arch as the body begins its forward rotation.

3-4-5. As the body continues to rotate in an arched layout position, the head remains tilted back and the arms remain in a fixed swan position. (Note: This dive may also be done with the hands clasped and held close to the body in the lower abdominal area.)

6. The head begins to tilt forward as the body completes 1¼ somersaults. This permits the body to continue its rotation and also allows the diver to sight the water in preparation for the entry.

7. When the diver sights the water, the arms begin to extend over the head laterally, with the eyes sighting the water where the diver will enter.

8. The entry is made slightly short of vertical with the arms completely extended over the head and in line with the body.

FLYING FORWARD 1 ½ SOMERSAULTS – TUCK

(One Meter) 113C

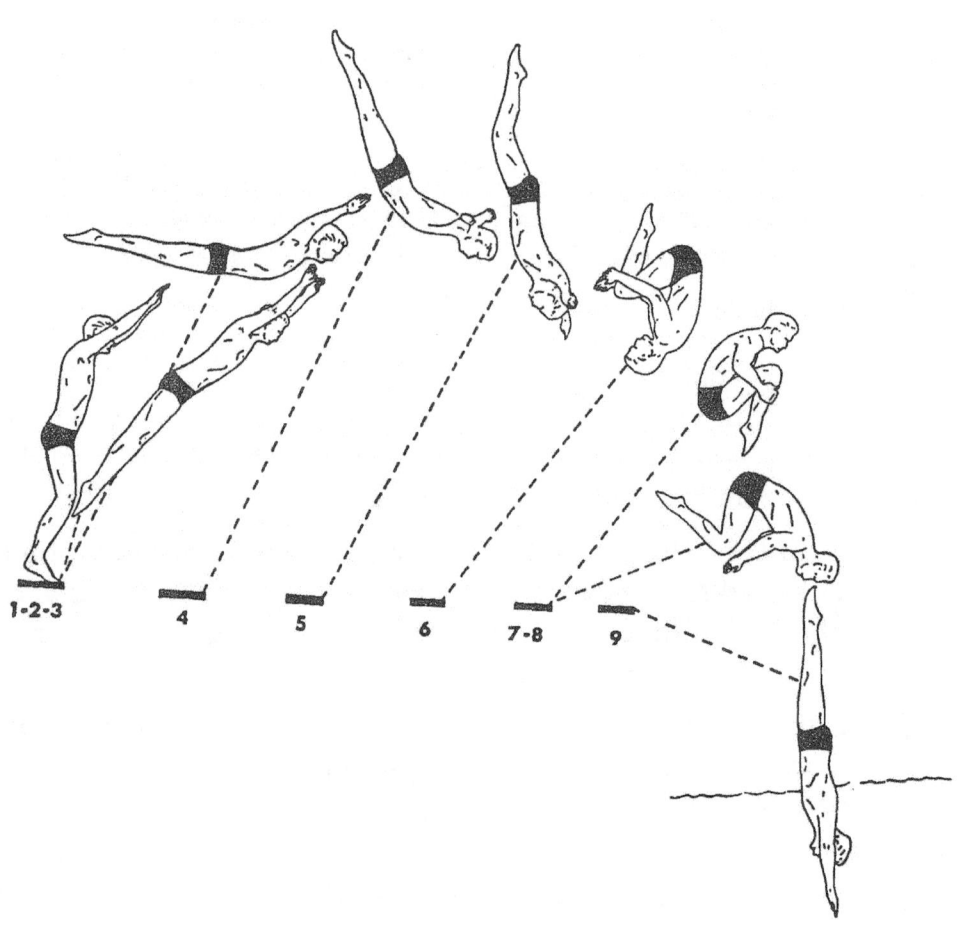

FLYING FORWARD 1 ½ SOMERSAULTS – TUCK

(One Meter)

1. Prior to the take-off, the knees are flexed as the arms reach forward and upward with the head and body erect. The legs then extend with the arms vigorously pulling down laterally toward a shoulder level position before the
feet leave the board.

2. The arms continue to pull down laterally while the head remains vertically erect with the eyes looking toward the other end of the pool.

3. The legs rise as the body begins to rotate in a layout position. The arms continue to pull down laterally until they are at right angles to the body. The head tips back a little to keep the body in the layout position.

4. The legs continue to rise with some arch in the back. The head tipped with the eyes peering down at the water. The arms are placed in a lateral position at right angles to the body.

5-6. The body rotates in the layout position until the legs rise overhead to a near vertical position. At this moment, the body position changes to a tuck. The tuck is initiated by drawing the knees to the chest and the feet toward the buttocks. The hands thrust downward and grasp the legs at the shins while the head is ducked.

7. The tuck is pulled in tight with the hands grasping the shins. This action increases the speed of the somersault. The water comes into view just after the completion of the somersault.

8. The eyes focus on the approximate spot where the diver will enter the water as the hands release the knees and the legs begin to extend.

9. The body assumes a straight position with the legs extending and lifting upward toward a vertical position. Simultaneously, the arms reach overhead for the water, with the eyes still focused on the water. The entry is made slightly short of vertical.

FLYING FORWARD 1 ½ SOMERSAULTS – PIKE

(Three Meter) 113B

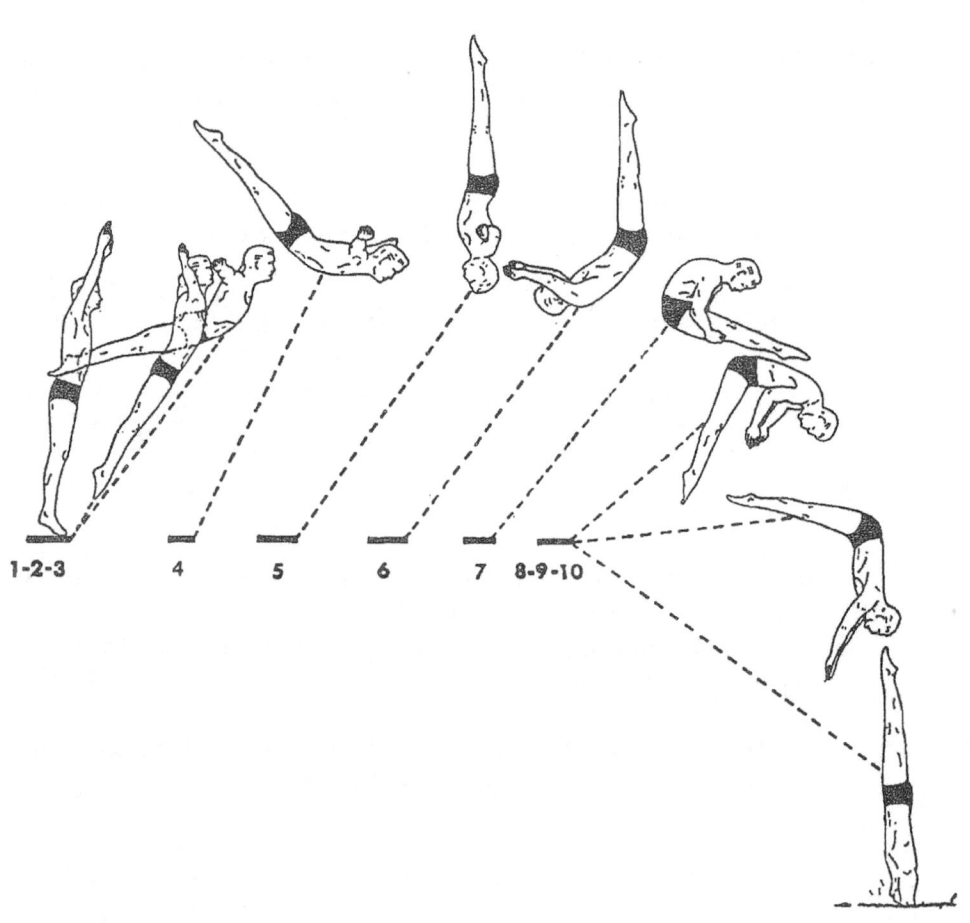

FLYING FORWARD 1½ SOMERSAULTS PIKE
(Three Meter)

1. Prior to the take-off, the diver leans slightly forward with the arms lifted forward and upward in front of the head. The weight of the hips is directly over the feet, and the head is held erect with the eyes spotting the water about five feet from the end of the board. The arms then begin a vigorous lateral movement toward the level of the shoulders before the feet leave the board.

2. As the diver leaves the board, the arms continue a lateral movement downward with the head held in line with the body. The eyes sight the other end of the pool.

3-4. The body continues to rotate as the back begins to arch. The arms continue the lateral movement until they are at shoulder level. The head is tilted back slightly to allow the body to continue rotating in a layout position.

5. As the diver approaches the peak of the dive, the head is tilted forward with the chin moving toward the chest. The arms begin to move toward the front of the body to permit the diver to assume a pike position.

6. The arms continue moving forward toward the legs, and the body continues to bend at the waist.

7. The hands grasp behind the legs slightly above the knees and pull the chest down toward the legs to form a tight pike position. The legs are sighted as the hands reach and grasp the legs.

8-9. As the body passes one somersault, the hands release the legs and begin extending toward the water. The body begins to straighten with the eyes fixed on the water where the diver will enter.

10. The body straightens completely in a near vertical position as the arms extend over the head to make for an aesthetic entry into the water.

FORWARD DOUBLE SOMERSAULT-TUCK
(One Meter) 104C

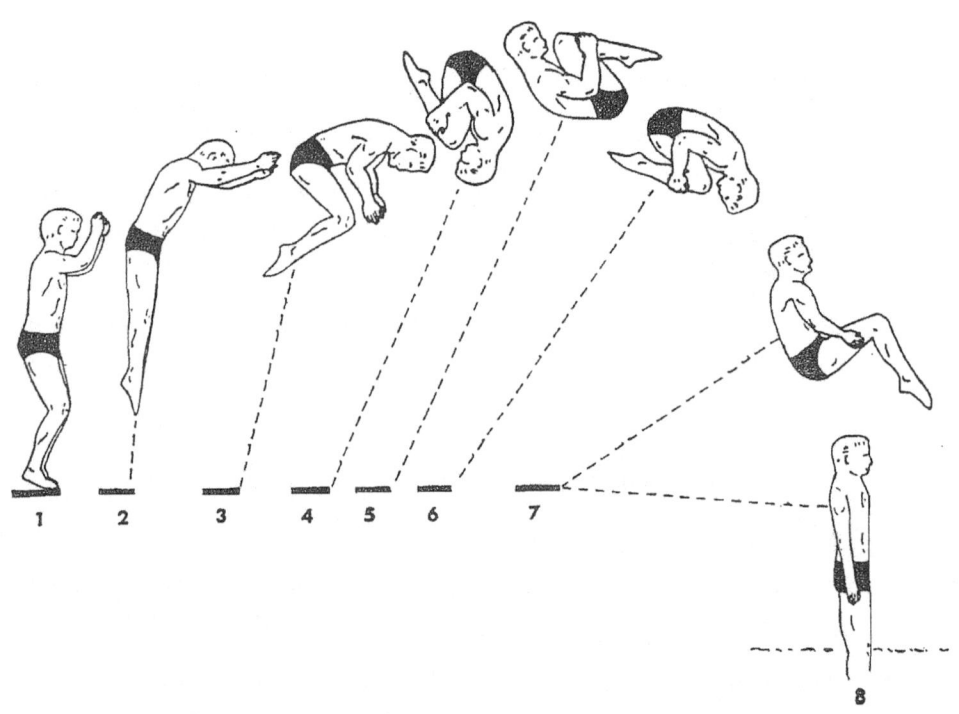

FORWARD DOUBLE SOMERSAULT – TUCK

(One Meter)

1. The take-off from the board is made with the diver leaning slightly forward with the arms lifting forward and upward over the head. The weight of the hips is directly over the feet, and the head is held erect. The arms, head and shoulders start a vigorous forward and downward movement before the feet leave the board.

2. At the take-off, the legs forcefully extend while the hips thrust strongly upward. As the hips begin their upward movement, the arms, head and shoulders continue with a vigorous downward movement.

3. With the upward movement of the hips, the knees immediately draw toward the chest, the heels moving upward toward the buttocks. The arms and head continue their strong forceful movement in chase of the knees.

4-5-6. The hands grasp the shins and pull the knees in tightly while the head continues to duck hard. As the body rotates, the speed of the somersault is increased with the tightening of the tuck.

7. The diver anticipates opening for the entry as the body approaches the "sitting" position of the second somersault. When this position is reached, the legs are released and thrust down toward the water. At the same movement, the head and shoulders lift to an erect position and the arms are placed at the sides. At this point, the water can be seen at a distance. *Caution:* Do not drop the head or look down at the water when coming out of this dive for the tendency will be to go over.

8. The diver enters the water in a near vertical position. The body is straight with the head erect and the arms at the sides with the hands on the thighs.

FORWARD DOUBLE SOMERSAULT - PIKE

(One Meter) 104B

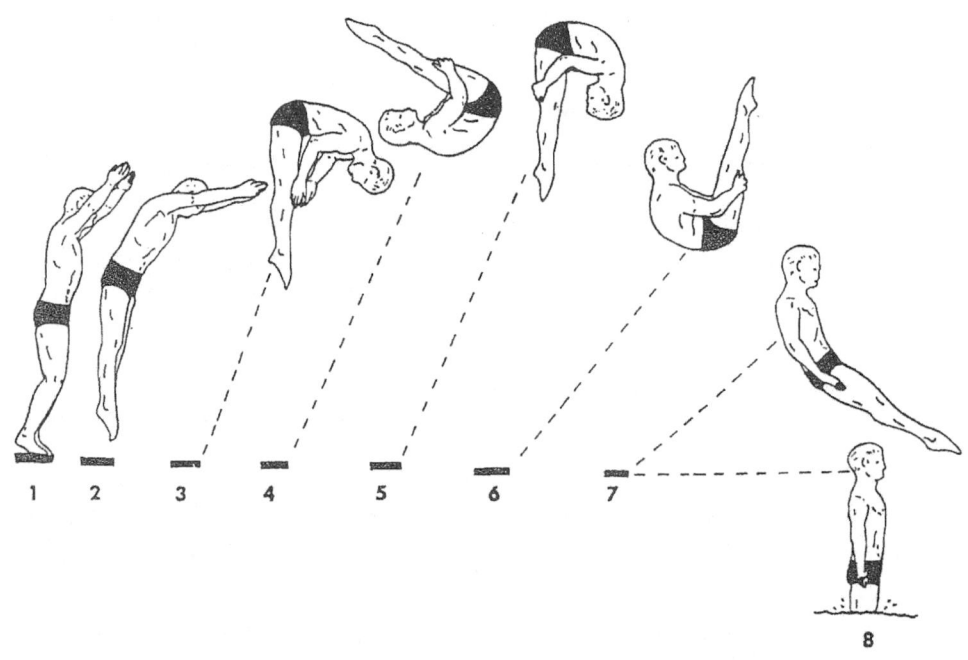

FORWARD DOUBLE SOMERSAULT – PIKE

(One Meter)

1. The diver leans slightly forward at the take-off, with the arms extended above and in front of the head. The head is held erect with the eyes fixed on the water in front of the board.
2. Before the diver's feet leave the board, the legs quickly extend with a vigorous upward lift of the hips. The body bends at the waist as the arms, shoulders and head thrust down toward the legs.
3. As the body begins to rotate, the arms, shoulders and head continue to drive down toward the legs. The body continues bending at the waist.
4. The spin of the somersault is increased as the hands clasp behind the legs slightly above the knees. The upper part of the body is then pulled close to the legs.

5-6. The pull of the upper part of the body toward the legs is continued as the body rotates.

7. The hands release the legs when the body passes $1\frac{3}{4}$ somersaults. The body then begins to straighten as the legs are pushed down toward the water.
8. The body completely straightens as the diver approaches the water. The arms are placed on the thighs, and the head is held. erect. The body enters the water slightly short of vertical.

FORWARD 2½ SOMERSAULTS – TUCK

(One Meter) 105C

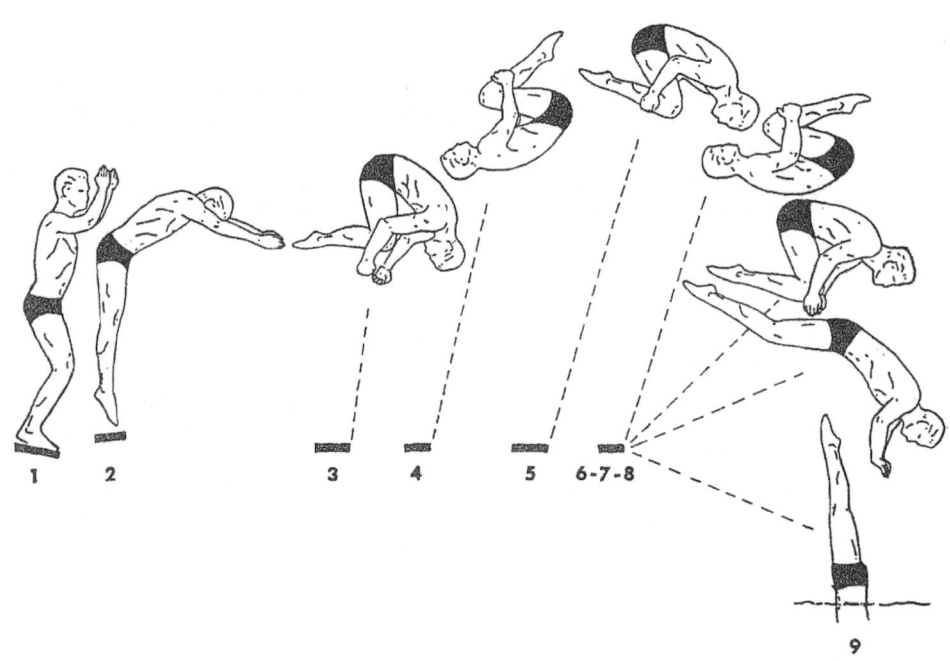

FORWARD 2½ SOMERSAULTS - TUCK

(One Meter)

1. At the take-off from the end of the board, the diver rocks slightly forward and lifts the arms forward and upward over the head. The head is erect with the eyes spotting the water in front of the board.

2. The body leaves the board with a full extension of the legs, ankles, and toes and a vigorous lift of the hips. As the hips begin their upward movement, the arms and head whip downward in chase of the legs.

3. The knees then draw in toward the chest, with the feet moving up to- ward the buttocks. The hands grasp the shins and pull the knees in tightly while the head continues to duck hard.

4-5-6. The speed of the somersault is increased by using the hands to pull the tuck in tighter with the elbows close to the sides.

7. The water comes into view at. the completion of approximately 2¼ somersaults. At this moment, the eyes spot the approximate point of entry while the hands release the knees.

8. The legs extend with a snap and rise toward a vertical position. Simultaneously, the arms reach over the head for the water, and the eyes remain fixed on the point of entry.

9. The body enters the water slightly short of vertical.

FORWARD 2½ SOMERSAULTS-PIKE

(Three Meter) 105B

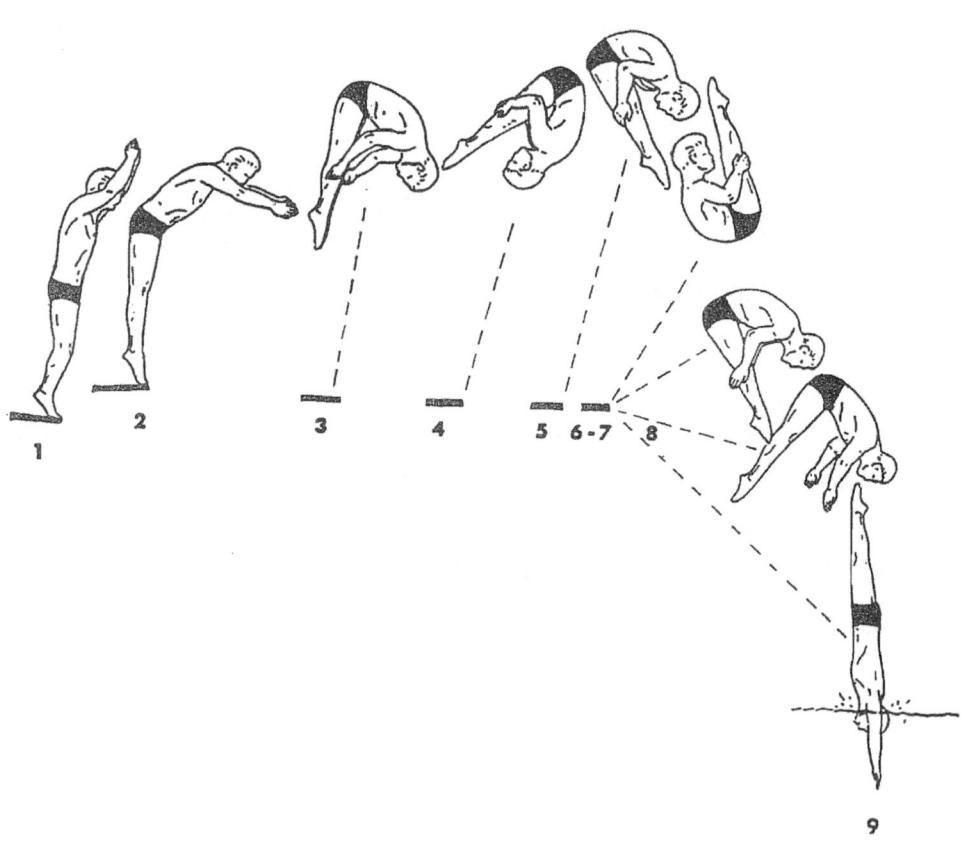

FORWARD 2½ SOMERSAULTS - PIKE

(Three Meter)

1. At the take-off from the end of the board, the diver rocks slightly forward, lifts the arms swiftly in front of, and over, the head, and keeps the head erect with the eyes spotting the water in front of the board.
2. Before the diver lifts from the board, there is a quick extension of the legs, giving a vigorous upward lift of the hips. During this motion, the arms, head and shoulders push downward toward the legs.
3. With the rise of the hips, the arms and head continue to drive downward in chase of the legs. As the body begins to rotate, the hands clasp behind the legs slightly above the knees.
4. The spin in the somersault is initiated by pulling the head down to the knees, while keeping the elbows close to the sides.

5-6. A continuous pull of the head toward the knees is sustained during the somersaults.

7. The water is spotted over the feet as the body completes the second somersault. When the water is spotted; the hands release the legs in anticipation of the reach for the water.
8. With the eyes fixed on the entry slightly in front of vertical, the diver reaches for the water by circling the arms slightly outside the width of the shoulders.
9. The entry is made with the arms fully extended over the head and completely straight. The entry is slightly short of the vertical position.

FORWARD TRIPLE SOMERSAULT - TUCK

(Three Meter) 106C

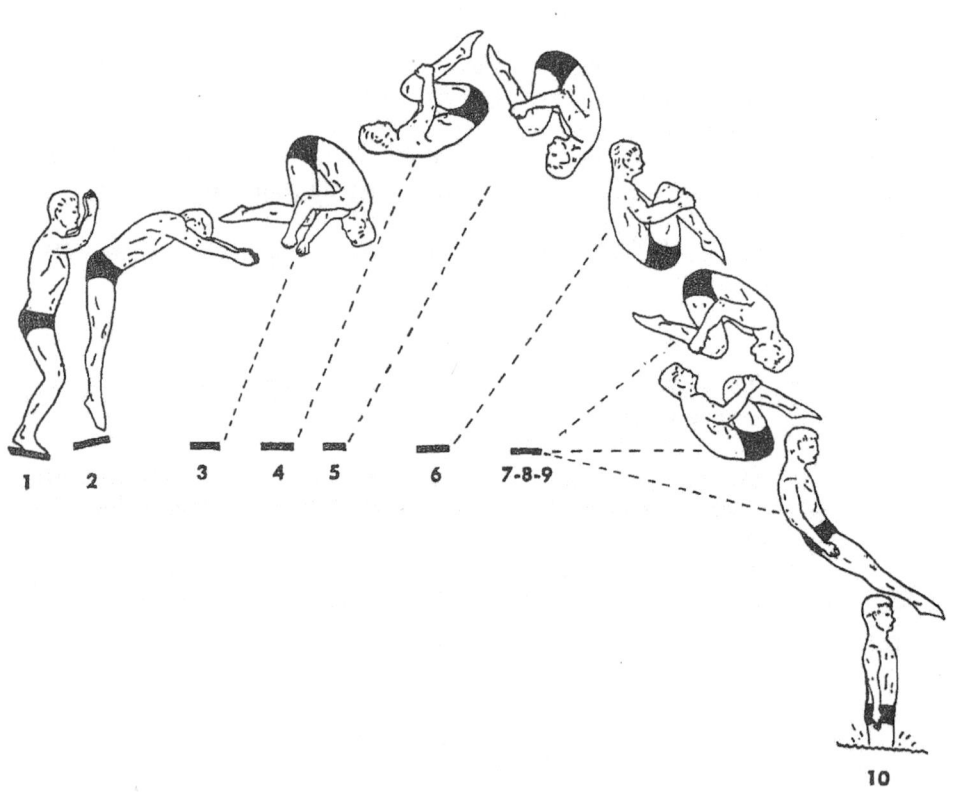

FORWARD TRIPLE SOMERSAULT – TUCK
(Three Meter)

1. The take-off from the board is made with the diver rocking slightly forward and the arms lifting forward and upward over the head. The head remains erect with the weight of the hips directly over the feet.

2. With a slight lean forward before 'leaving the board, the diver's hips are vigorously pushed upward with the quick extension of the legs, ankles and toes. The body begins to bend at the waist as the arms, shoulders and head begin a downward movement.

3. The upward movement of the hips, along with the downward action of the arms, shoulders, and head in chase of the legs, starts the body rotating. The knees then draw in toward the chest, with the feet moving up toward the but tocks.

4. The hands clasp the shins and pull the knees in toward the chest tightly while the head continues to duck toward the knees.

5-6-7. The speed of the somersault is increased by pulling the knees as close to the chest as possible.

8. As the diver approaches the "sitting" position of the third somersault, he should anticipate opening for the entry.

9. When the diver reaches the "sitting" position of the third somersault, the legs are released by the hands. The legs are then extended quickly down toward the water. In the same movement, the head and shoulders lift to an erect position with the arms placed at the sides. The water can be seen at a distance when the body has reached this point. These coordinated movements stop the momentum of the somersault, making for a clean entry into the water.

10. The body is completely extended with the head erect as the diver makes the entry into the water slightly short of the vertical position.

FORWARD TRIPLE SOMERSAULT - PIKE

(Three Meter) 106B

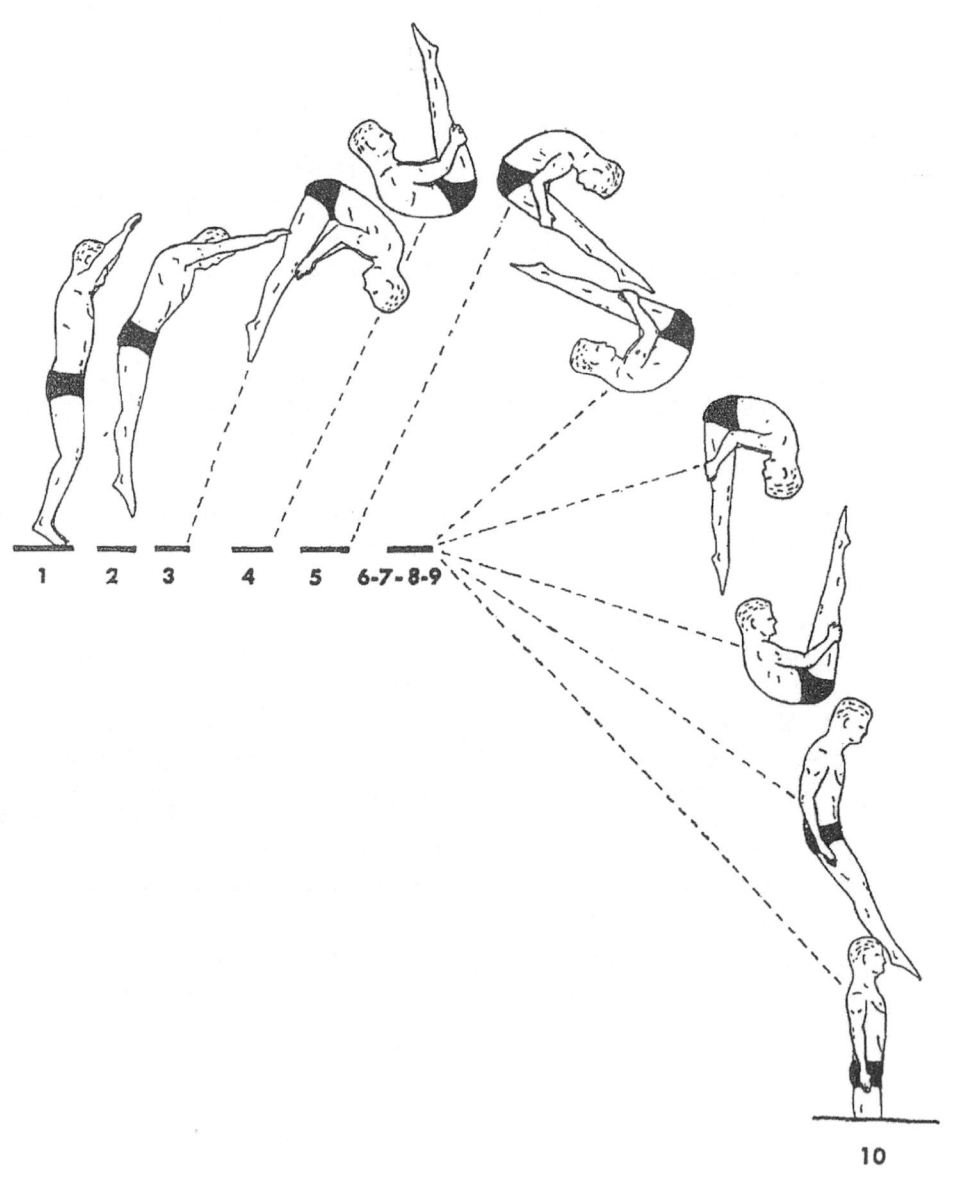

FORWARD TRIPLE SOMERSAULT - PIKE

(Three Meter)

1. The diver lifts the arms overhead and slightly in front of the face as he attempts to stand up at the take-off. This is necessary to obtain the maximum height and the right distance from the board. The head is tilted slightly forward with the eyes spotting the water in front of the board.

2-3. While still in contact with the board, the diver's arms, shoulders and head are thrust downward as the legs extend and the hips move upward. The arms move toward the closed pike position as the body begins to bend at the hips.

4-5. As the hands grasp the legs behind, and slightly above, the knees, the head is pulled in as close to the knees as possible, to increase the spin of the somersault.

6-7. A continuous pull of the head toward the knees is sustained during the somersaults and the arms are kept close to the sides of the body.

8-9. The legs are released as they pass the horizontal at $2\frac{3}{4}$ somersaults. The head is lifted to an erect position as the legs move down toward the water. The arms move toward the sides in readiness for the feet-first entry. The water can often be sighted far down the pool as the legs are released for the entry, which allows for adjustment of the shoulders, head, legs, etc.

10. The body is completely erect with the head in line and the arms at the sides, close to the thighs. The entry is slightly short of vertical.

FORWARD 3½ SOMERSAULTS – TUCK

(Three Meter) 107C

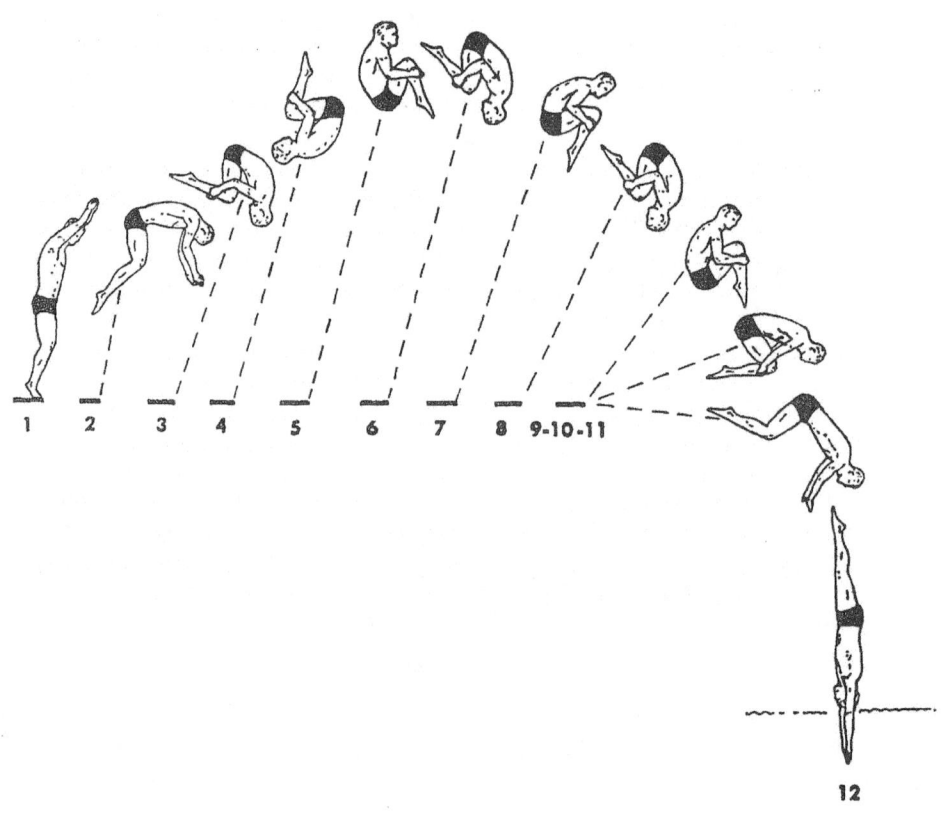

FORWARD 3½ SOMERSAULTS - TUCK

(Three Meter)

1. At the take-off from the end of the board, the diver rocks slightly forward and lifts the arms straight over the head, which remains in line with the body.
2. The legs, ankles and toes fully extend as the arms, shoulders and head push downward before the feet leave the board.
3. As the hips begin their upward movement, the arms and head whip downward in chase of the legs. The knees then draw in toward the chest, with the feet moving up toward the buttocks.
4. The hands grasp the legs at the shins and pull the knees tight to the chest while the head continues to duck hard.

5-6
7-8-9. The speed of the somersault is increased by pulling the tuck in tighter with the elbows close to the sides.

10. The water comes into view just as the body passes 3/4 somersaults. At this moment, the eyes spot the approximate point of entry, slightly in front of vertical, as the hands release the legs.
11. The legs begin to quickly extend as they rise toward a vertical position. Simultaneously, the arms circle just outside the width of the shoulders a they reach for a point of entry slightly in front of vertical. The eyes focus on the point of entry as the legs are released.
12. The straight body enters the water slightly short of vertical.

FORWARD 3½ SOMERSAULTS-PIKE

(Three Meter) 107B

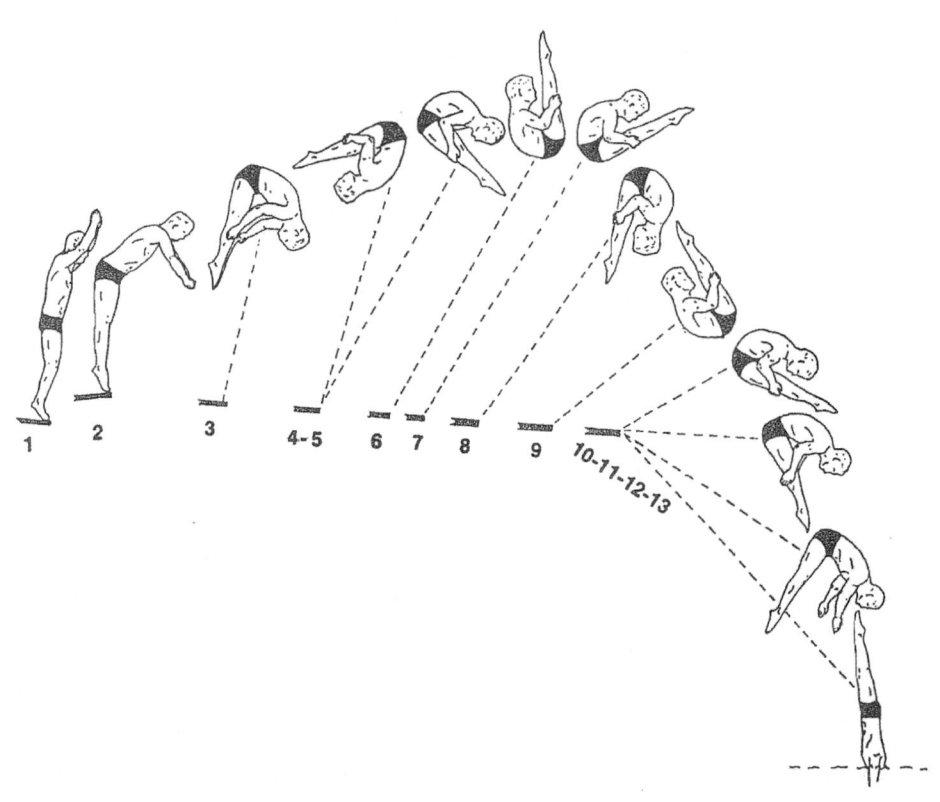

FORWARD 3½ SOMERSAULTS - PIKE

(Three Meter)

1. Before the takeoff, the diver leans slightly forward of vertical with the arms extended overhead and the legs beginning to extend. The diver then extends the legs as the hips thrust upward and the arms, shoulders and head begin a forward and downward movement.
2. As the diver leaves the board, the arms, shoulders and head continue in a downward motion bending at the waist.
3. The arms, shoulders and head continue to move downward until the diver is in a position to grasp the legs from behind with the hands at the knee level.

4-5-6-7
8-9-10. The hands grasp the legs at knee level and pull the chest in as close to the knees as possible to increase the velocity of the somersault. The arms are kept close to the sides and the head is kept in close to the knees.

11. The legs are released as the diver completes three somersaults and the diver sights the water at a point slightly in front of vertical.
12. The arms then begin to circle outward toward the width of the shoulders, then reach for a point on the water slightly in front of vertical.
13. The diver enters the water with the arms extended over the head in line with the body, with the entry slightly short of vertical.

GROUP 11 - BACKWARD DIVES

BACK DIVE - TUCK

(One Meter) 201C

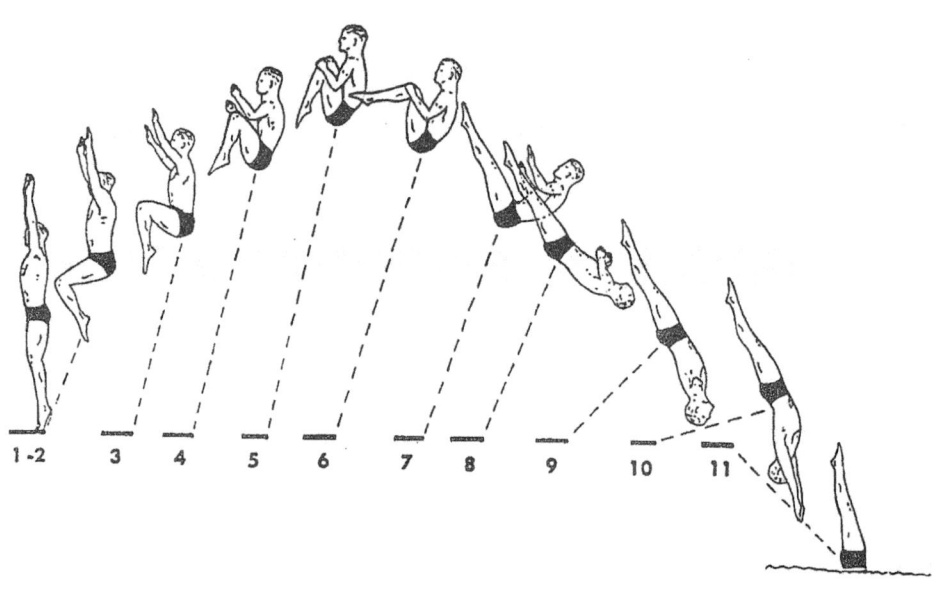

BACK DIVE - TUCK

(One Meter)

1. At the take-off, the body leans back slightly, and the arms extend overhead with the head erect. The legs, ankles, and toes extend to lift the body from the board.

2. As the diver leaves the board, the legs drive toward the chest and the body bends forward slightly at the waist, with the arms fully extended over the head.

3-4-5. The arms drop to a position in front of the face, and the hands grasp the knees above the shins as the knees draw in toward the chest. This action is made at the peak of the dive, with the head remaining straight.

6-7-8. As the body descends, the hands release the knees and the legs quickly extend in a near upward direction. The arms extend laterally as the body begins to straighten. The head is held in line with the body.

9-10. The arms extend laterally over the head for the entry as the body completely straightens.

11. The entry is made slightly short of vertical.

BACK DIVE - PIKE
(Three Meter) 201B

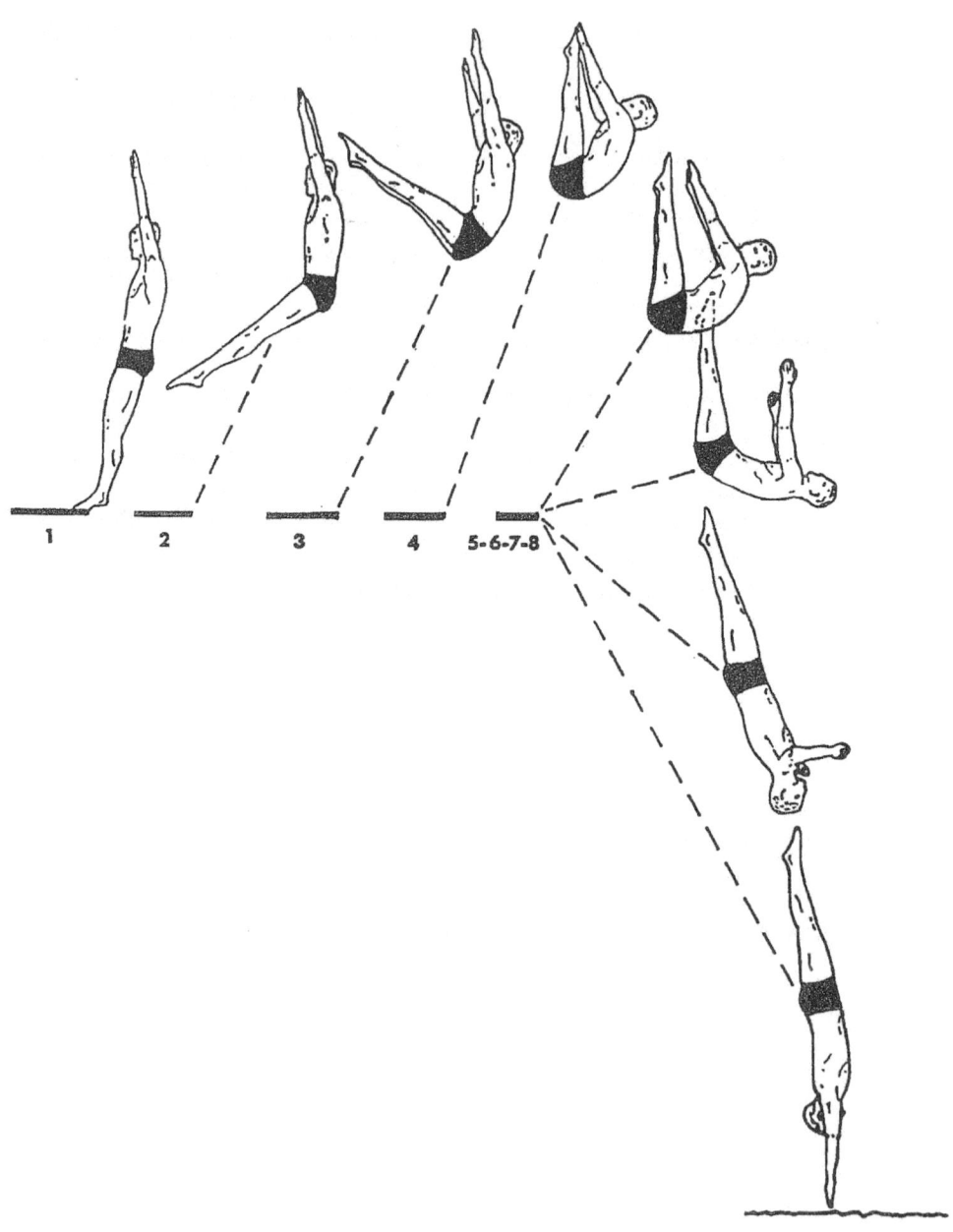

BACK DIVE - PIKE

(Three Meter)

1. Prior to the take-off, the diver assumes an upright position with the knees flexed and with the weight of the hips over the heels. The head is held erect while the arms swing forward and upward. The diver jumps straight up from the board by completely extending the legs, ankles, and toes and lifting the arms directly overhead with the head erect.
2. The legs begin to rise toward the hands as the toes leave the board. This is done by strongly contracting the stomach and thigh muscles. The upper part of the body remains in a fixed upright position.
3. The arms reach forward slightly as the legs continue to rise toward the vertical.
4. The legs draw up to a near vertical position at the peak of the dive, and the eyes watch the hands touching the toes.
5. The upper body pushes away from the legs after the touch is made. The legs remain in a fixed vertical position.
6-7. As the body drops away from the legs, the arms remain straight and move laterally for the extension over the head. The head is gently tilted back until the water comes into view.
8. The arms continue their lateral extension over the head while the stomach muscles relax, and the thigh muscles tighten to allow the body to straighten for a vertical entry.

BACK DIVE - LAYOUT
(One Meter) 201A

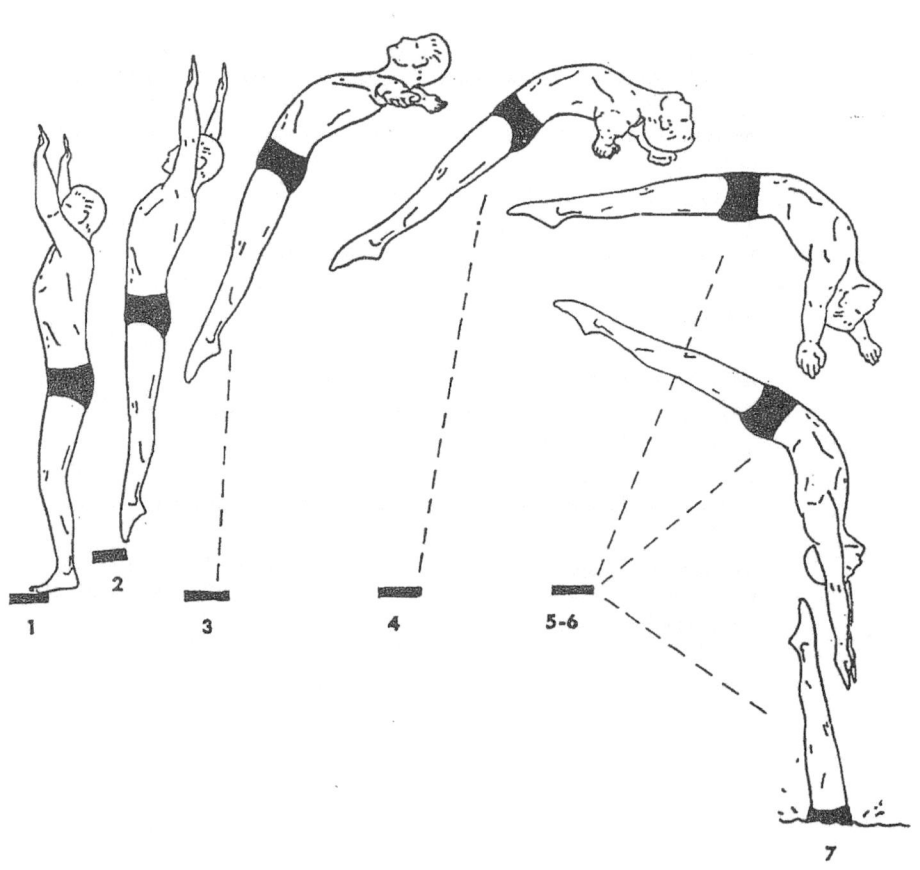

BACK DIVE - LAYOUT

(One Meter)

1. While on the board, the arms sweep forward and upward to a near vertical position above the head, which is held erect. During this motion, the legs extend with the hips directly above the heels.

2. While still on the board, the diver leans back slightly, keeping the head erect. The arms then swing forward and upward to an extended position above the head just short of vertical. From this position, the arms begin a downward lateral movement toward the level of the shoulders.

3. As the body starts its upward flight, the arms extend laterally at right angles to the body. The head is brought into direct line with the body as the hips and legs rise to a horizontal position.

4. With the body in a near horizontal at the peak of the dive, the head gracefully tips back, and the eyes look down at the water. The shoulders
rotate laterally and the back arches while coming over the top of the dive.
The rms do not change position during this movement.

5. While the eyes are fixed on the point where the body will enter the water, the arms begin to extend laterally over the head. The hips are tightened to help reduce the arch in the back.

6. The arms extend directly over the head, with the eyes remaining fixed on the water.

7. The body enters the water with very little arch, and the entry is slightly short of vertical.

BACK SOMERSAULT - TUCK

(One Meter) 202C

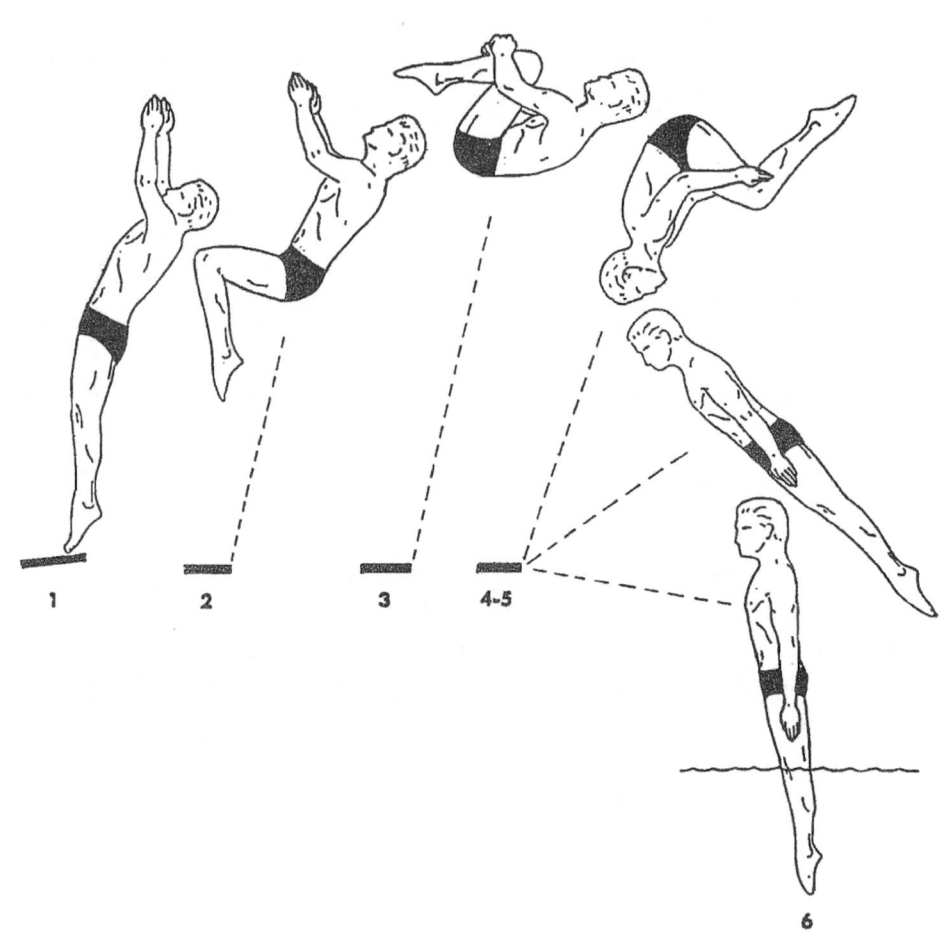

BACK SOMERSAULT - TUCK

(One Meter)

1. On the backward take-off, the diver leans back slightly, and the arms sweep forward and upward to a vertical position. The head lifts with the arms and the eyes sighting the hands as they reach the vertical point. Meanwhile, the legs extend, lifting the body from the board.

2. As the feet leave the board, the legs bend, and the knees lift upward toward the arms, which remain stationary in a vertical position.

3. When the knees reach the hands, they are drawn into the chest. The head then begins to tilt in toward the knees.

4. As the body rotates, the position of the head allows the eyes to sight the board and water. At this point in the dive, the knees are released so the legs can be extended. The hands move up along the legs to the sides in preparation for the entry.

5. The body straightens by quickly extending the legs and gently lifting the head to an erect position.

6. The momentum of the somersault carries the body around to a near vertical entry.

BACK SOMERSAULT - PIKE

(One Meter) 202B

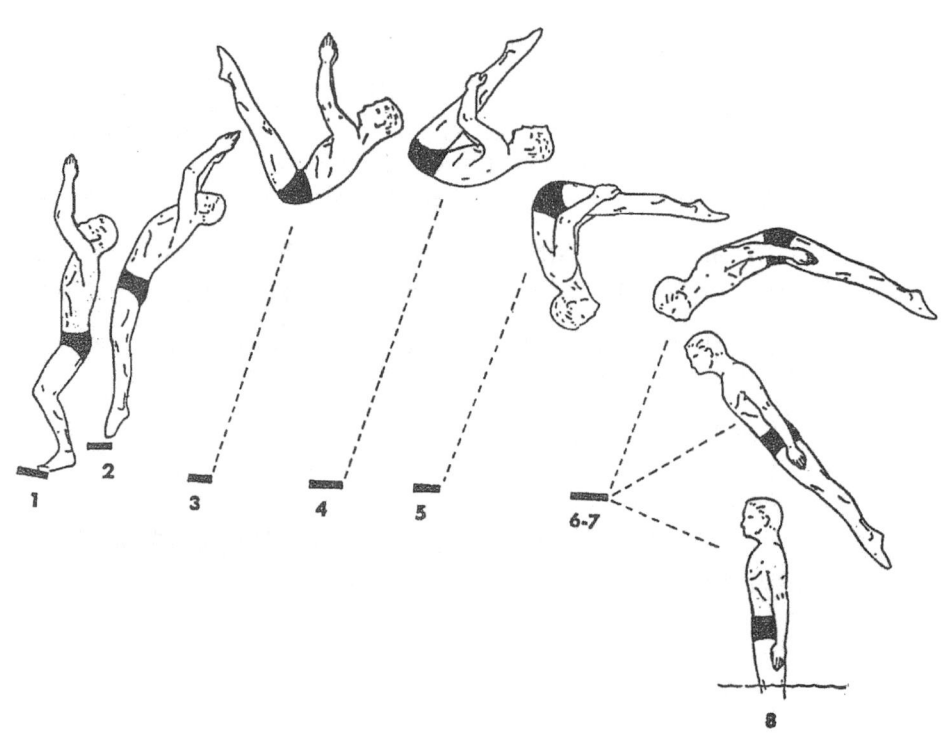

56

BACK SOMERSAULT - PIKE

(One Meter)

1. Prior to the take-off, the body is erect with the hips just off the-tip of the board and directly above the heels. The arms swing forward and upward to a near vertical position above the head and the head tilts upward to look at the hands.

2. The body leans back slightly, and the diver jumps nearly straight up by extending the legs. The chest rises immediately following the rise of the head and arms.

3. The legs then lift toward the hands by contracting the stomach and thigh muscles. During this motion, the head begins to tilt in towards the legs.

4. When the legs reach the arms, which have remained vertical, the hands clasp behind the legs just above the knees and pull the legs toward the chest.

5. The water comes into view when the body has rotated approximately three-quarters of a somersault.

6. The head and shoulders lift to an erect position with the eyes sighting over the board, as the body drops toward the water. The hands remain at the sides after releasing the legs.

7. The body extends to a straight position short of vertical. The momentum of the somersault carries the body around to an upright position for the entry.

8. With the body erect, the entry is made just short of the vertical line.

BACK SOMERSAULT - LAYOUT

(One Meter) 202A

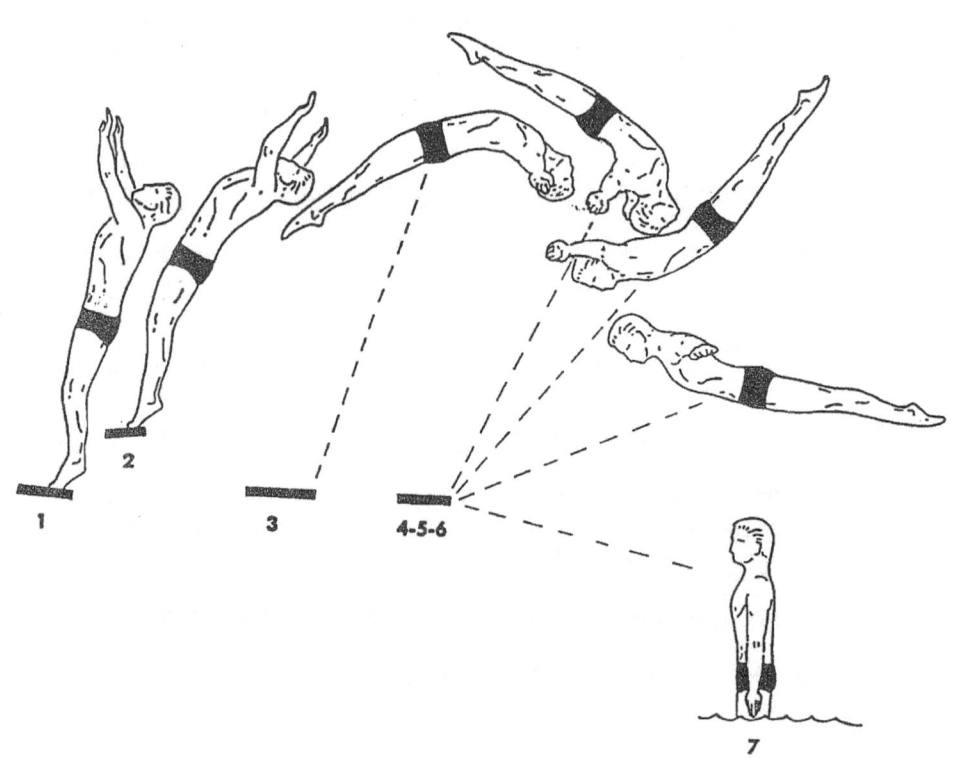

BACK SOMERSAULT - LAYOUT

(One Meter)

1. Prior to the take-off, the diver leans back slightly and lifts the chest along with the forward and upward swing of the arms and the upward tilt of the head.

2. The arms, chest and head continue to rise upward as the diver leaves the board by extending the legs, ankles and toes.

3-4. As the body begins to rotate, the arms pull down laterally to a shoulder level position while the head and shoulders continue to pull back to create an arch in the back.

5. The diving board and water come into view when the somersault has been nearly three-quarters completed. At this point, the diver can adjust for the entry by increasing or decreasing the arch of the back.

6. The head and shoulders pull up and back to an erect position as the legs press down toward the water and the arms drop laterally to the sides.

7. The entry is made slightly short of vertical, with the body straight and the head erect.

FLYING BACK SOMERSAULT - TUCK

(One Meter) 212C

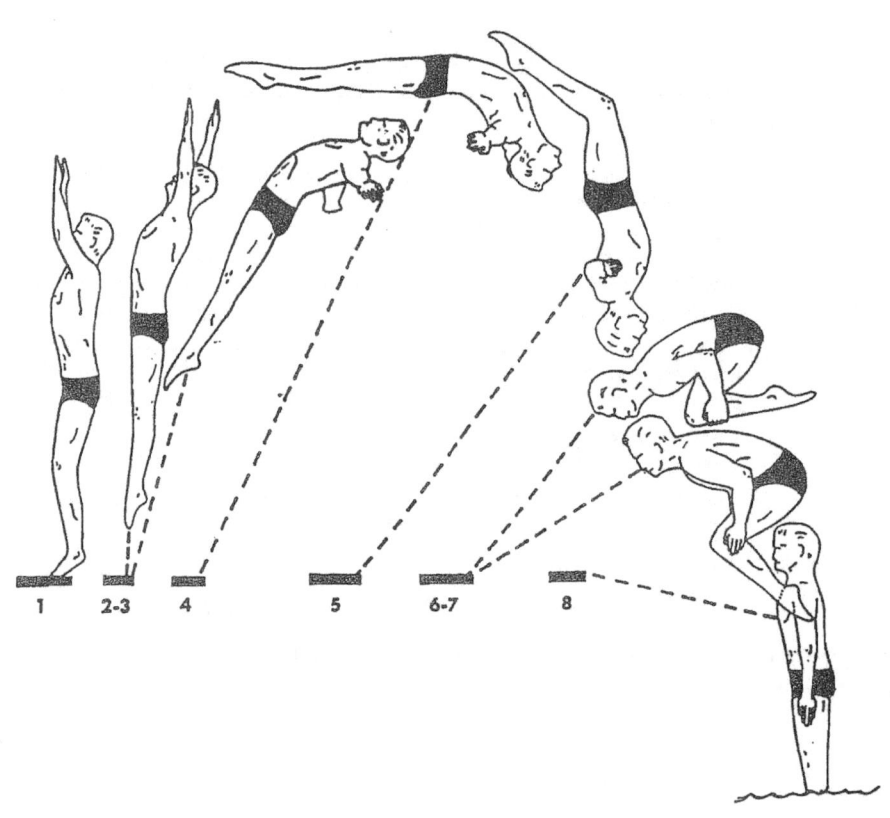

FLYING BACK SOMERSAULT - TUCK

(One Meter)

1. The take-off is made by sweeping the arms forward and upward. As the arms rise overhead, the head tilts upward and the chest is lifted. The legs completely extend as the body leaves the board.

2-3. As the diver leaves the board, the arms pull down laterally to a shoulder level position. The head continues to pull back and the back arches.

4-5. As the diver approaches a vertical position in an arched and layout position, the water can be sighted. The arms then move forward and down toward the waist as the knees bend and are drawn toward the chest. The diver continues to sight the water during this action.

6-7. The legs continue to draw in toward the chest, and the hands grasp high on the shins. A tight tuck position is achieved by pulling the knees in tight against the chest. As soon as the knees are drawn in tight, they are quickly released to prevent the diver from passing one somersault. At the release of the legs, the head and shoulders pull back slightly, and the legs extend toward the water to place the body in a straight and upright position.

8. As the body straightens for a near vertical entry into the water, the arms are placed at the sides, close to the thighs, to prevent the body from arching as it passes through the surface of the water. The head is erect during the entry, and the board may be sighted as the diver enters the water.

FLYING BACK SOMERSAULT – PIKE

(One Meter) 212B

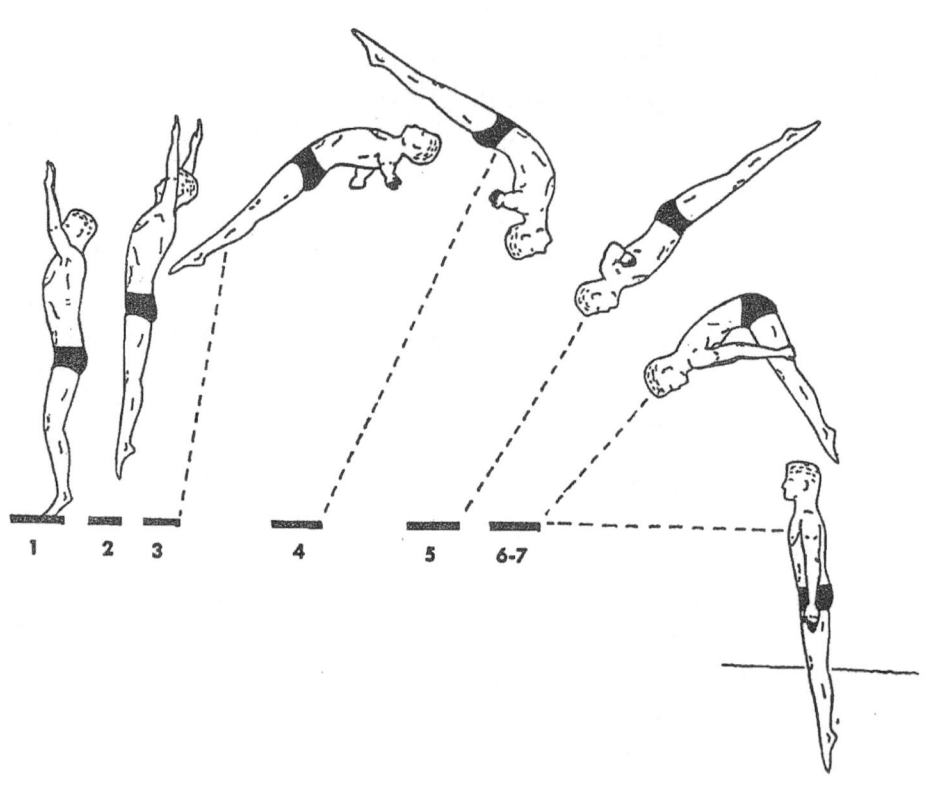

FLYING BACK SOMERSAULT - PIKE

(One Meter)

1. The diver rises from the board by sweeping the arms forward and up-ward to a position above the head. The head and chest lift as the arms pass the horizontal plane at shoulder level. The body leans back slightly.

2-3. As the diver leaves the board, the legs, feet, and toes extend completely. The diver begins to somersault in the layout position as the arms pull laterally to a shoulder level position and as the head and shoulders pull back to arch the back.

4-5-6. The water is sighted as the diver reaches a near vertical position. At this moment, the arms move semi-laterally down toward the legs and the diver pikes by pulling the legs toward the chest and bending at the waist. The arms continue toward the legs until the hands are able to grasp behind, and slightly above, the knees to pull the legs closer to the body. The diver continues to sight the water during these movements.

7. As the legs reach a near vertical position the hands release them, and the head and shoulders pull back slightly to place the body in an upright position. The hands move to a position close to the sides of the body as the diver enters the water at a slightly short of vertical angle.

BACK 1 ½ SOMERSAULTS – TUCK

(One Meter) 203C

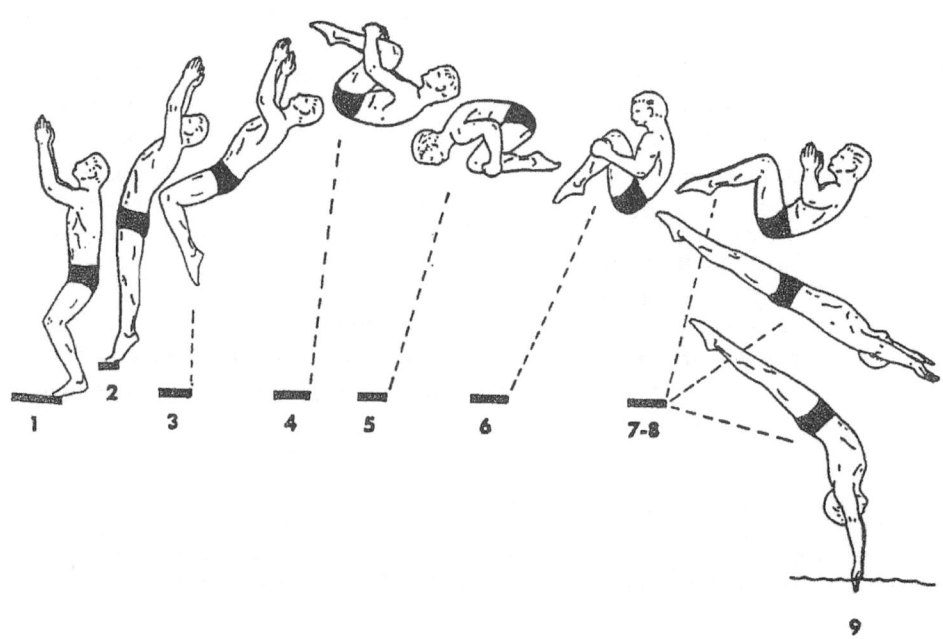

BACK 1½ SOMERSAULTS - TUCK

(One Meter)

1. Prior to the take-off, the body is erect with the knees flexed and the weight of the hips over the heels. The arms swing forward and upward toward a vertical point.
2. The legs fully extend as the diver leaves the board. The chest pushes upward, and the arms swing to a position overhead.
3. The knees move upward toward the hands as soon as the feet leave the board. The arms remain in a vertical position until the knees reach the hands.
4. In this dive, the eyes continue to watch the hands until the knees are grasped by the hands. The hands grasp the legs just above the shins and pull the knees in toward the chest. The somersault is facilitated by pulling the head in toward the knees.

5-6. The hands continue to pull the tuck tight to increase the speed of the spin. The elbows are held close to the sides. The diver can spot the diving board at the completion of the somersault.

7. The hands release the legs as they pass the horizontal level. The legs quickly begin to extend as the shoulders and head pull back toward the water. With the extension of the legs, the arms start to reach overhead in a lateral or semi-lateral direction.
8. The legs fully extend, and the arms continue to reach overhead as the body straightens completely. During this motion, the head tilts back to sight the water at the point of entry or just short of the entry point.
9. The diver stretches for a clean entry with a slight arch in the back just short of the vertical angle.

BACK 1½ SOMERSAULTS – PIKE

(Three Meter) 203B

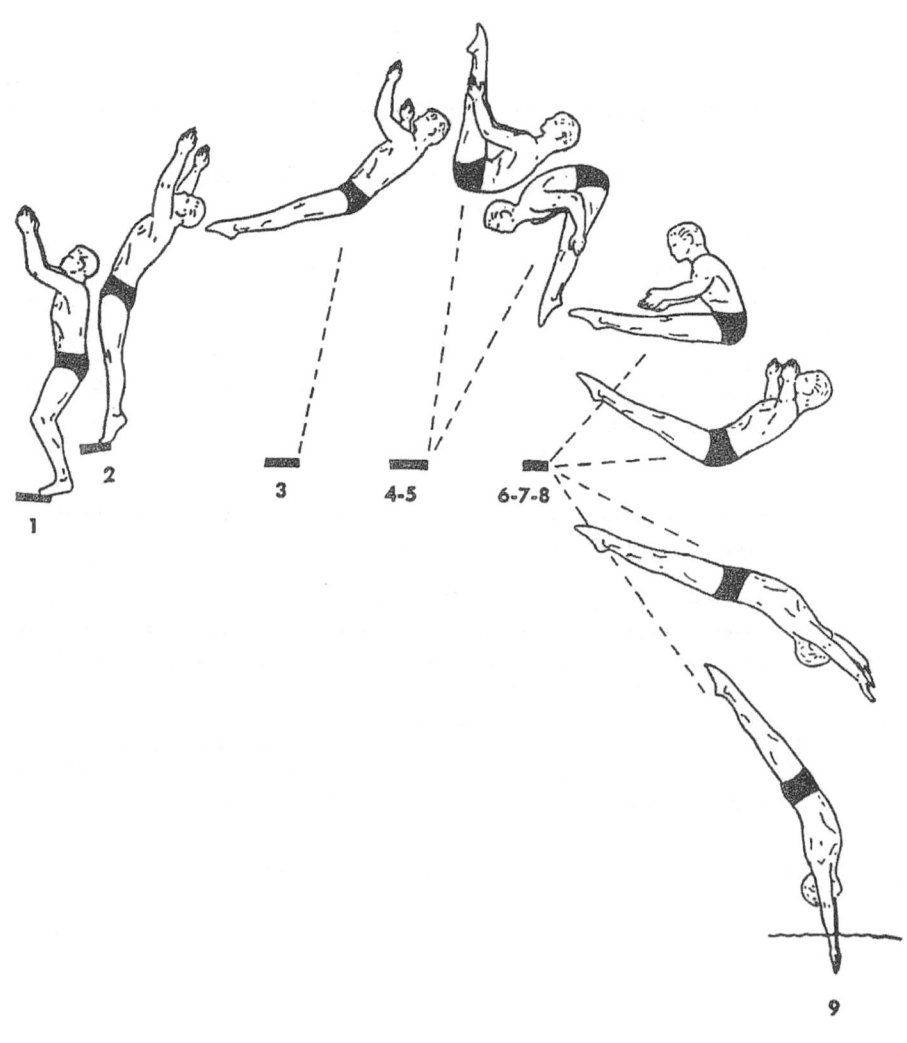

BACK 1½ SOMERSAULTS - PIKE

(Three Meter)

1. Before the take-off, the diver assumes an erect position with the knees flexed, the weight of the hips over the heels, the arms swinging forward and upward to a point near vertical and the eyes sighting the hands as they pass overhead.
2. The body leans back slightly as the legs, ankles, and toes extend to lift the diver into the air. At the same time, a slight arch in the back is created with the lift of the chest. The arms continue to swing upward to a near vertical position.
3. Once off the board, the legs begin to draw upward toward the hands while the body pikes and the head remains in a fixed erect position.
4. Once the legs reach the hands, they clasp the legs from behind at the knee level. The head is pulled in toward the knees to help close the pike and increase the speed of the somersault.
5. The legs then pull toward the chest, with the elbows held close to the sides. The head is brought erect in anticipation of seeing the board.
6. When the board comes into view, the legs pull up parallel with the board and the hands release the legs.
7. The body begins to straighten as the shoulders and head pull back toward the water and the arms begin to reach overhead in a lateral or semi-lateral direction.
8. Coordinating with the movement of the arms, the head tilts back far enough for the water to come into view. This action permits the body to straighten completely with a slight arch in the back.
9. As the arms extend completely over the head, the body stretches for the entry, which is slightly short of vertical.

BACK 1 ½ SOMERSAULTS – LAYOUT

(Three Meter) 203A

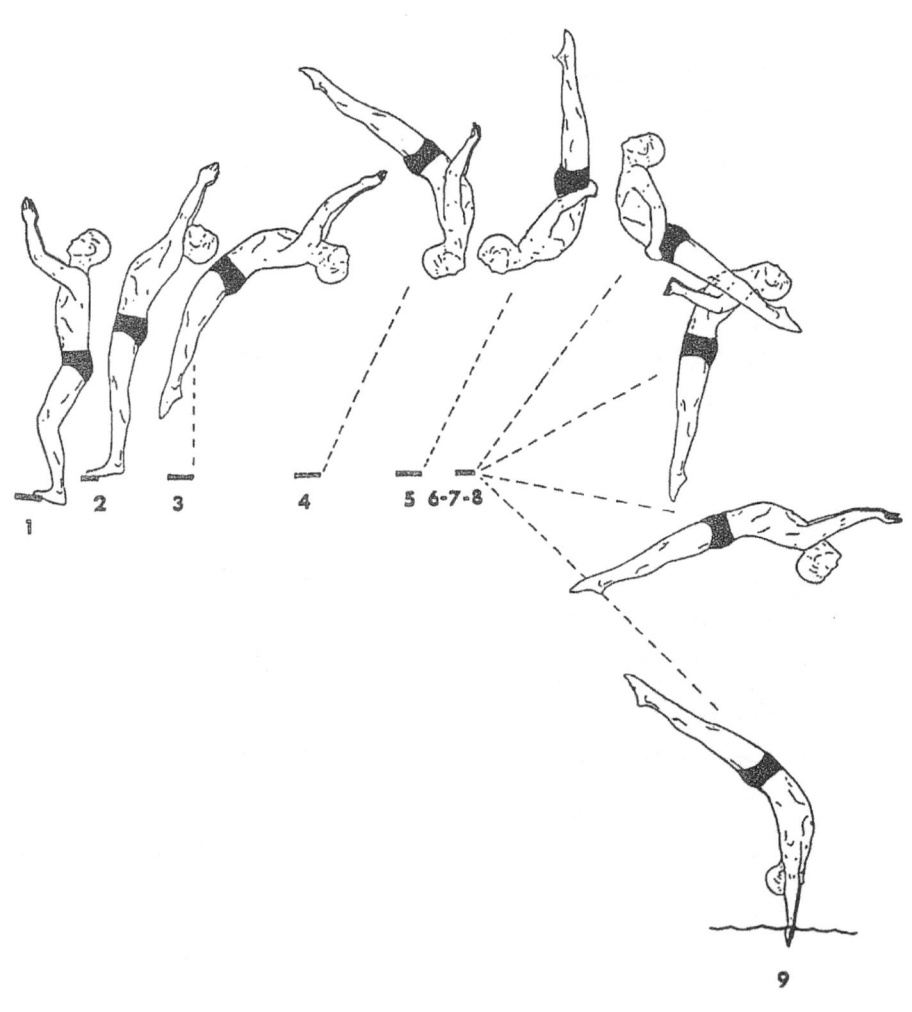

BACK 1½ SOMERSAULTS - LAYOUT

(Three Meter)

1. Prior to the take-off, the body leans back slightly with the knees flexed and the weight of the hips over the heels. The arms circle downward behind the body, passing the hips, and then rise upward over the head.

2. The take-off is initiated by the forceful extension of the legs, ankles, and toes along with the lift of the hips and chest. The arms and head also continue to rise past the vertical.

3. As the diver leaves the board, the legs fully extend and move upward with the back arching and the head and arms pulling back hard.

4. While the legs and hips continue to move upward, the arms reverse their direction and push back toward the hips. The body, however, continues to rotate backward with a deep arch in the back and with the head pulling back.

5. The hands clasp and press against the front of the hips while the body continues to somersault. The diving board comes into view when over half of a somersault has been completed. This gives the diver an opportunity to adjust the speed and action of the dive.

6. As the first somersault nears completion, the diver increases his efforts to continue somersaulting by lifting more with the chest, making a deeper arch in the back, and tightening the legs.

7. At about 1¼ somersaults, the water comes into view. The arms, bent at the elbow, then begin to extend and reach over the head for the entry.

8. As the arms begin to extend overhead, the diver is in a position to adjust the body for the entry by increasing or decreasing the arch in the back.

9. The entry is made with the arms extended over the head, the back slightly arched, and the body a little short of vertical.

FLYING BACKWARD 1 ½ SOMERSAULTS - TUCK

(Three Meter) 213C

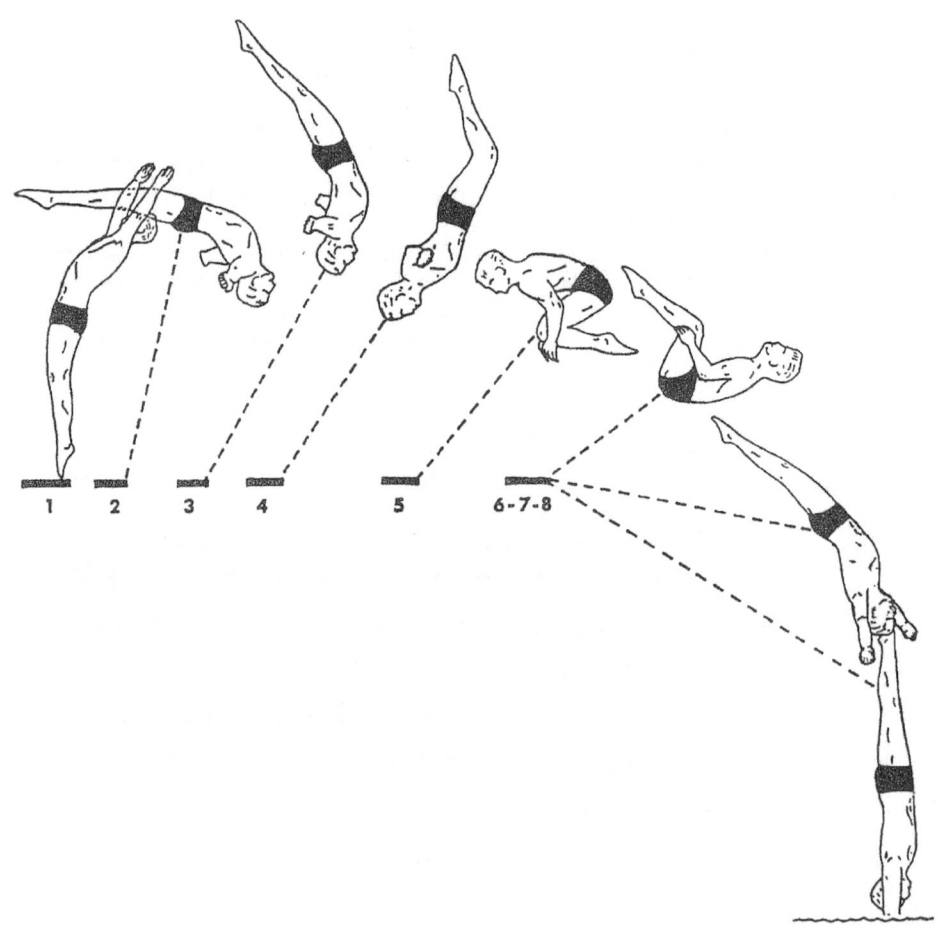

FLYING BACKWARD 1½ SOMERSAULTS - TUCK

(Three Meter)

1. The take-off is made with the arms swung forcefully over the head in front of the face. The back arches as the chest rises. The head is tilted back slightly with the eyes looking at the hands.

2-3. As the feet leave the board, the arms are pulled down laterally to a position level with the shoulders. The body begins to rotate in the layout position with the back arched and the head tilted back slightly.

4. The body changes from a layout to a tuck position as the diver reaches a near vertical position at the peak of the dive. This change is made by drawing the knees toward the chest, pulling the head toward the chest, and drawing the arms semi-laterally toward the legs.

5. When the knees come close to the chest, the hands grasp them just above the shins and draw them still closer. The head tilts slightly in toward the knees, and the eyes sight the board.

6. As the diver completes 1¼ somersaults, the hands release the legs and the body begins to extend to a layout position. As the hands release the legs, they begin to extend overhead in a lateral or semi-lateral direction to control the spin of the somersault. This action, plus the forceful extension of the legs, stops the rotation of the body.

7. The arms continue to extend laterally over the head and reach for the water as the body completely straightens. The head is tilted back so that the eyes may sight the water for the entry. The back is slightly arched.

8. The entry is made with the diver slightly short of vertical. The arms are extended over the head, with the hands clasped and the head in line with the body.

BACK DOUBLE SOMERSAULT – TUCK

(One Meter) 204C

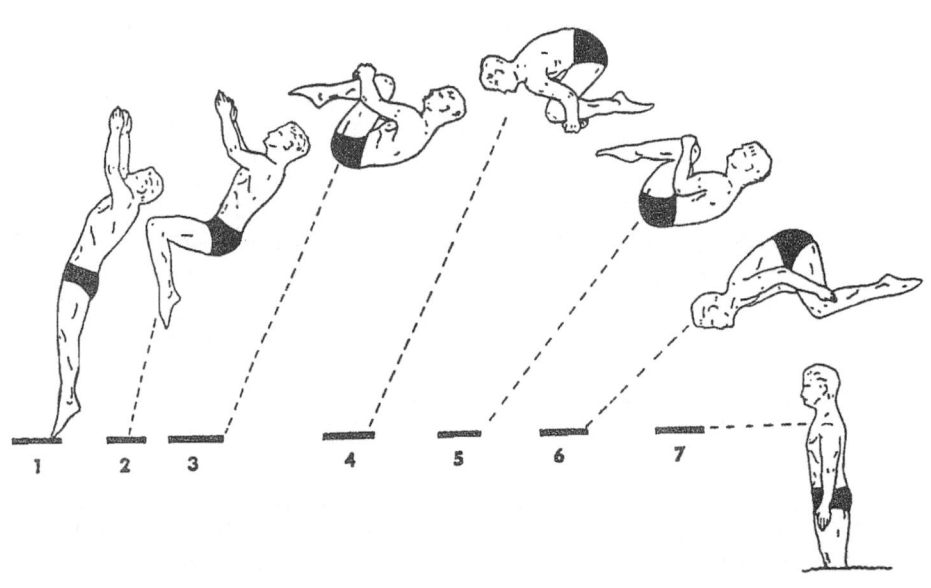

BACK DOUBLE SOMERSAULT - TUCK

(One Meter)

1. In taking off from the board, the diver leans slightly backward as the arms sweep forward and upward to a vertical position. The head is held in line with the body and the eyes sight the hands when the latter reach the vertical point.
2. Upon leaving the board, the knees bend and lift immediately toward the hands, which remain in a near vertical position.
3. When the knees reach a near vertical position, the arms move forward a short distance and grasp high on the shins. The knees are drawn in toward the chest tightly and the head tilts in toward the knees near the completion of the first somersault.

4-5. The hands continue to pull the tuck tight to increase the speed of the somersault. The elbows are held in close to the sides. The diver can spot the board near the completion of the first somersault.

6. As the diver passes 1¾ somersaults, the hands release the legs and the body begins to straighten by quickly extending the legs and lifting the head and shoulders. The diver can sight the water when he releases his legs.

7. As the body straightens for the feet-first entry, the head is brought into an erect position and the eyes look directly at the board. The arms are placed at the sides, with the hands placed slightly toward the front of the thighs.

BACK DOUBLE SOMERSAULT - PIKE

(Three Meter) 204B

BACK DOUBLE SOMERSAULT - PIKE

(Three Meter)

1. As the diver prepares for the take-off, the legs flex at the knees and the body leans back slightly. The arms sweep forward and upward to a vertical position. The head is lifted with the arms, and the eyes sight the hands as the arms reach the vertical position.

2. The legs, ankles, and toes extend as the diver leaves the board. The chest rises immediately following the raising of the arms and head. This creates a slight arch in the back for a split second.

3. As the diver ascends from the board, the legs lift immediately toward the hands by contracting the stomach and thigh muscles. The arms and head remain in a fixed position during the lifting of the legs.

4. The legs continue to drive upward until they reach the position where the hands clasp behind, and just above, the knees. The head pulls in slightly to aid in the spin and the board can be spotted near the completion of the first somersault.

5. The legs continue to be pulled toward the chest with the arms close to the sides as the body rotates backward.

6-7. The water is sighted when the diver completes about 1¾ somersaults. At this time, the hands release the legs, and the head and shoulders rise toward an erect position. The legs continue to move downward so the body can attain an erect position. The arms slide to a position alongside the legs.

8. The body straightens completely just above the water. The diver then enters the water slightly short of vertical.

BACK DOUBLE SOMERSAULT – LAYOUT

(Three Meter) 204A

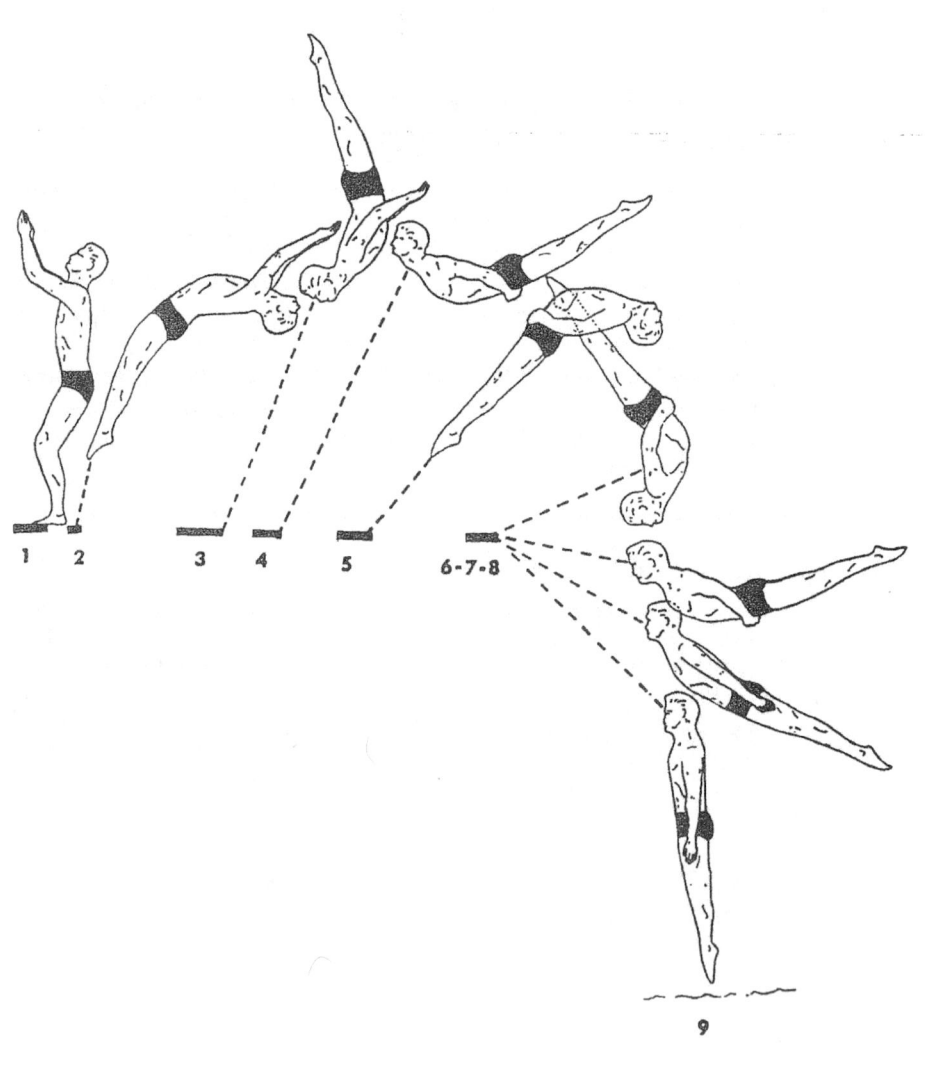

BACK DOUBLE SOMERSAULT - LAYOUT

(Three Meter)

1. The take-off is made with a vigorous swing of the arms forward and upward above the head along with a lifting of the chest and head. The diver rises from the board with a very slight lean.

2. As the diver leaves the board, the back is arched, the chest continues to rise, and the head is pulled back as far as possible. However, the arms begin to move forcefully in the opposite direction, that is toward the waist, to increase the rotation of the body.

3-4
5-6-7. The arms keep moving until they are pressed against the waist with the hands clasped. The diver can sight the board at the completion of the first half somersault and also spot the water at approximately 1¾ somersaults.

8. As 1¾ somersaults are completed, the arms begin to move to the sides of the body, with the hands being placed on the thighs. The head remains up, so the body can stay in the layout position.

9. The entry into the water is slightly short of vertical, with the back having very little arch. The head is in line with the body.

BACK 2 ½ SOMERSAULTS - TUCK
(Three Meter) 205C

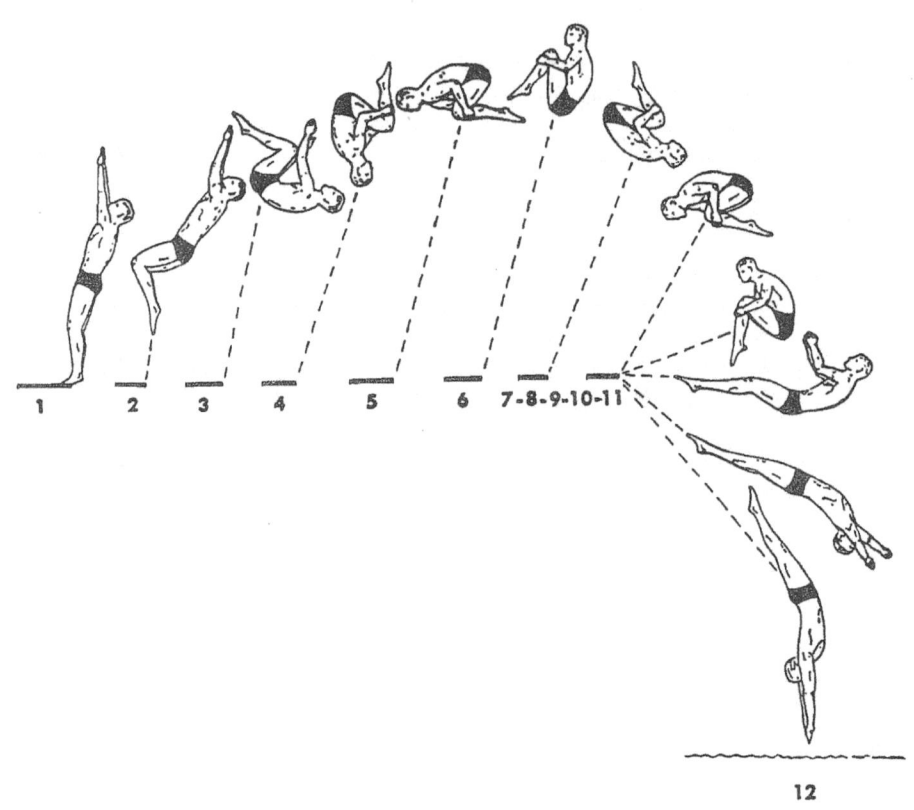

BACK 2½ SOMERSAULTS - TUCK

(Three Meter)

1. For the backward take-off, the body leans back slightly with the hips weighted over the heels. The arms swing forward and upward as the chest and head lift upward. In the same motion, the legs, ankles and toes extend.

2. With the arms and head continuing to move upward, the legs bend, and the knees draw toward the hands.

3. When the knees reach a near vertical position, the arms thrust forward a short distance to grasp them. This reverse action increases the speed of the somersault. The head pulls in slightly during this motion.

4-5

6-7-8. The hands grasp the knees just above the shins and pull them in tight. The elbows are held close to the sides. An effort is made to pull the knees closer to the chest as the body somersaults. The board or the water can be spotted near the completion of the first and second somersault.

9-10. The hands release the knees and the legs quickly extend when approximately 2¼ somersaults have been completed. The moment the hands release the knees, the legs are quickly extended while the upper part of the body pulls back toward the water with the head tilting back for the diver to see the water.

11. The arms extend and rapidly reach, in a narrow position, over the head as the body straightens for the entry.

12. The diver enters the water in a near vertical position. The arms extend completely over the head with a slight arch in the back.

BACK 2½ SOMERSAULTS - PIKE

(Three Meter) 205B

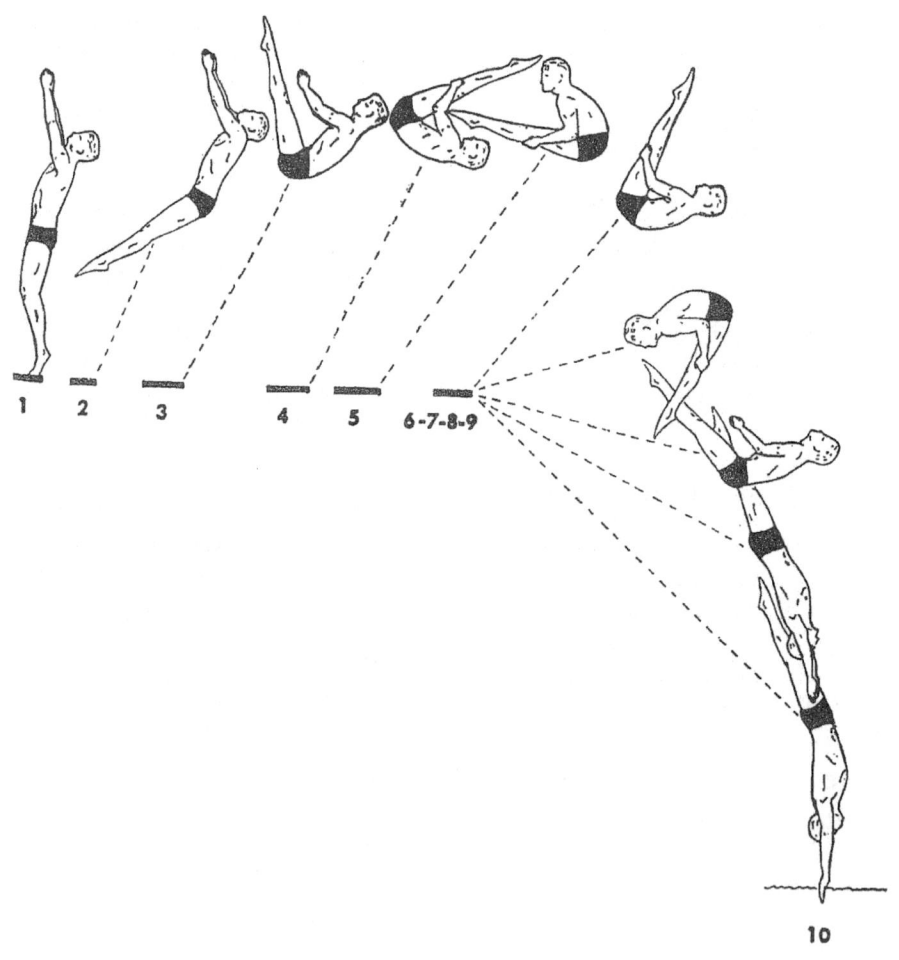

BACK 2½ SOMERSAULTS - PIKE

(Three Meter)

1. The diver leaves the board with a vigorous upward thrust of the arms overhead, along with a lifting of the head and chest. The legs, feet, and toes extend completely, and the body leans very slightly.

2. The eyes sight the hands overhead as the legs immediately draw upward with the body bending at the waist.

3-4. The arms move slightly toward the legs as the legs continue to move upward and the body begins to somersault backward. As the legs near a vertical position, the hands grasp behind, and slightly above, the knees and pull the legs toward the chest. This increases the speed of the somersault.

5-6. The spin of the somersault increases as the diver continues to pull the legs toward the chest as close as possible with the arms close to the body. The head tilts toward the knees to help close up the pike position. The board can be spotted as the diver passes the first somersault and the water can be sighted just after completing the second somersault.

7-8-9. As the diver reaches a "sitting" position at 2¼ somersaults, the legs are released, and the body is straightened by sweeping the arms overhead in a narrow position. The head tilts back in search of the water before the arms pass the level of the shoulders.

10. The arms continue to reach overhead, and the head remains back as the body completely straightens for the entry into the water. The back arches as the diver approaches the water, but an attempt should be made to keep the arch controlled. The diver enters the water at slightly short of a vertical position.

BACK 3½ SOMERSAULTS - TUCK

(Three Meter) 207C

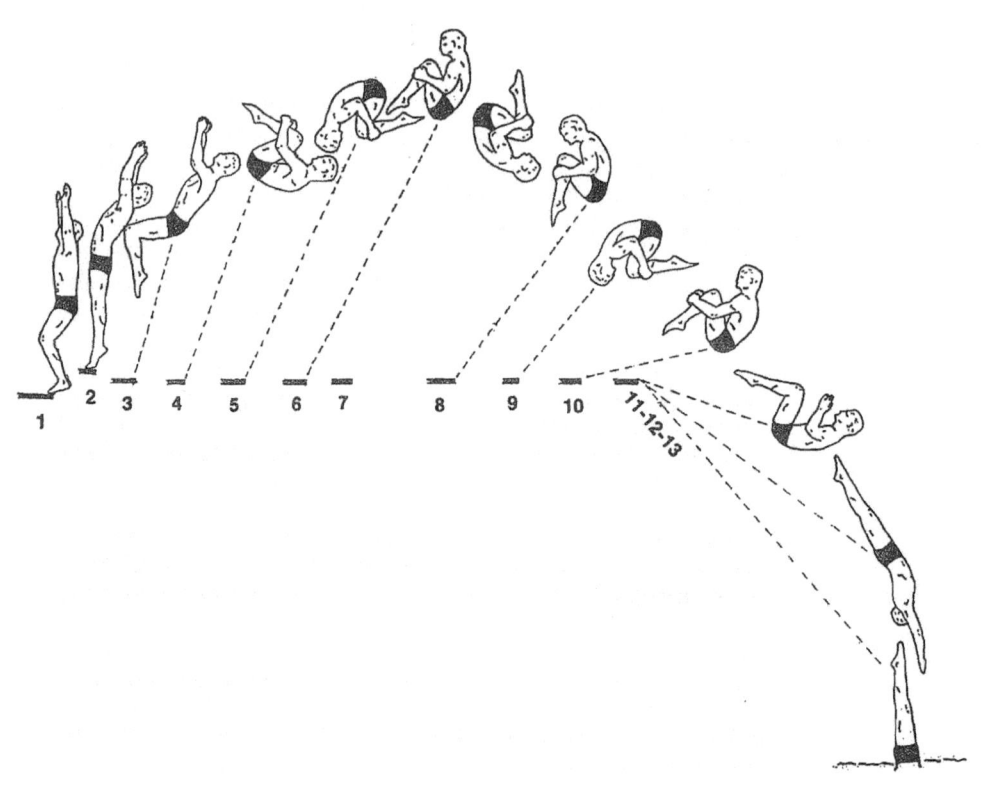

BACK 3½ SOMERSAULTS - TUCK

(Three Meter)

1-2. While on the board, the diver stands erect with the hips over the heels. With the head erect, the arms swing forward and upward to a near vertical position as the legs, ankles and toes extend.

3. Upon leaving the board, the eyes sight the hands overhead and the legs bend, drawing the knees up toward the hands.

4. When the legs meet the hands, they grasp the legs just above the shins and pull the knees in close to the chest. The head draws in toward the legs to aid in a tighter tuck position.

5-6

7-8-9. The diver continues to pull the legs in tight with the arms close to the sides. The board can be spotted at the completion of the first two somersaults and the board or water can be sighted at the completion of the third somersault.

10-11. The legs are released when the diver approaches 3¼ somersaults. The legs then quickly extend, and the head and shoulders pull back toward the water as the arms start to extend in a narrow fashion.

12-13. As the arms con tin u-e to reach overhead narrowly, the head tilts back in search of the water as the body straightens with a slight arch in the back for an entry just slightly short of vertical.

GROUP III - REVERSE DIVES

REVERSE DIVE – TUCK

(Three Meter) 301C

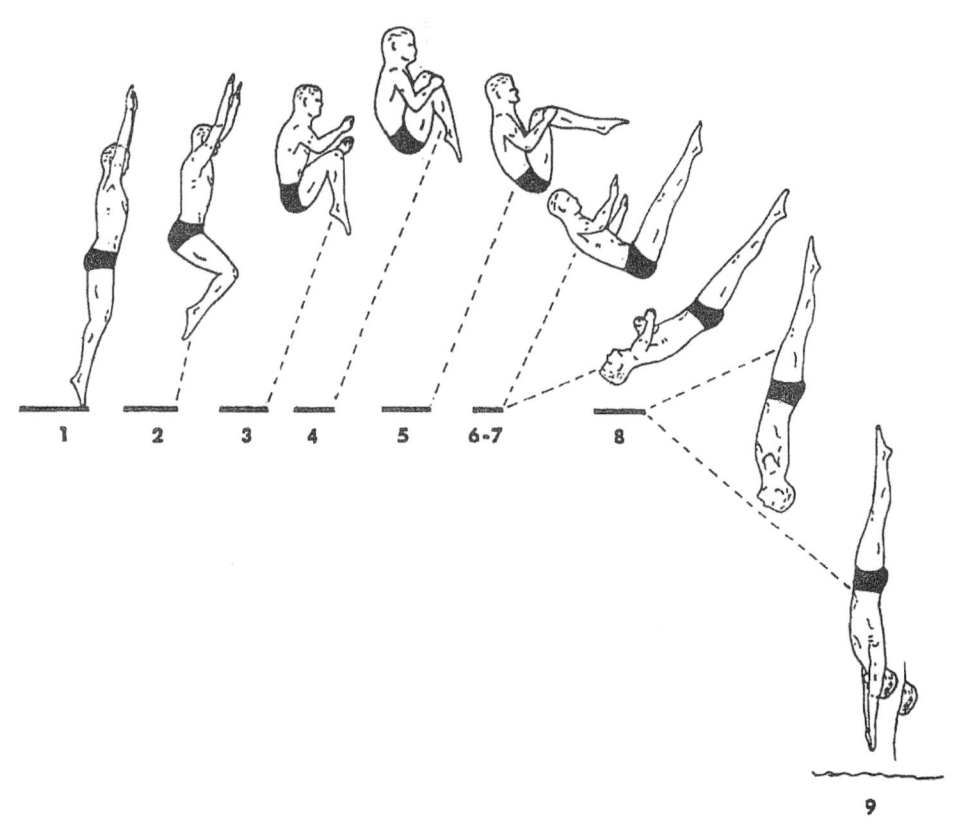

REVERSE DIVE - TUCK

(Three Meter)

1. At the take-off, the diver jumps nearly straight up with the arms swinging in front of the body and over the head. The head is erect as the legs, ankles, and toes extend to lift the diver from the board.

2. As the diver leaves the board, the legs drive quickly up toward the chest while the body bends slightly at the waist, with the arms fully extended over the head.

3-4. The arms drop to a position in front of the face, and the hands grasp the knees above the shins as the knees draw in toward the chest. This is done at the peak of the dive, with the head remaining erect.

5-6. The hands release the knees, and the legs extend slightly upward with a snap as the body descends. The arms begin to straighten in a lateral direction as the body begins to straighten. The head is held in line with the body during these movements.

7-8. The body straightens completely, and the head then tilts back toward the water just before the arms pass the shoulder level as they extend overhead for the entry.

9. The entry is made with the diver slightly short of vertical.

REVERSE DIVE – PIKE

(One Meter) 301B

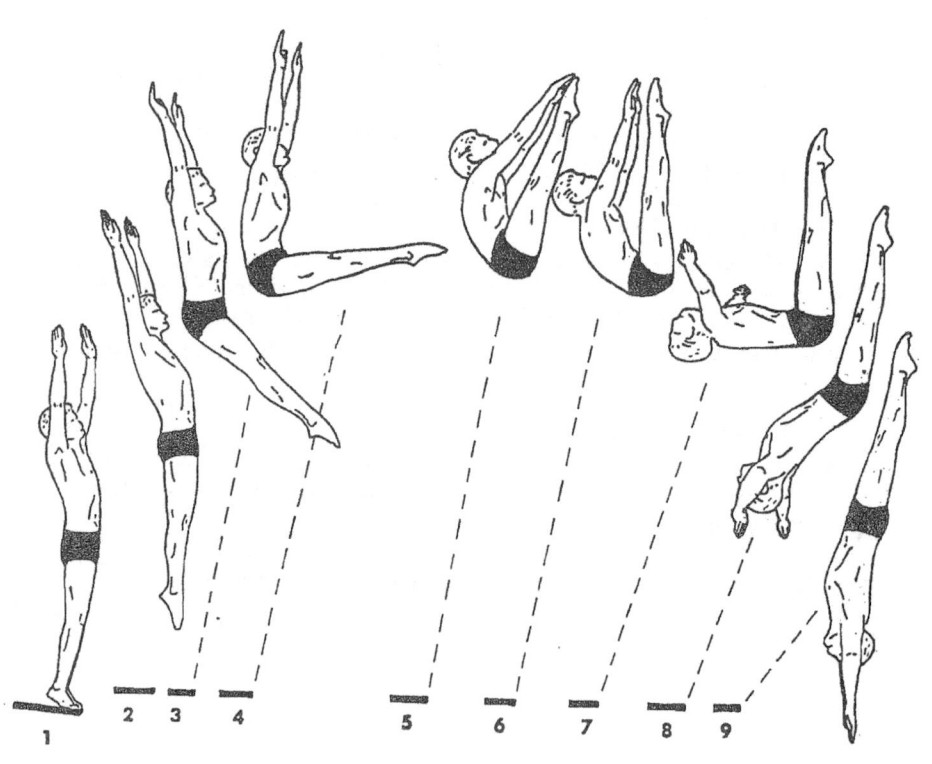

REVERSE DIVE - PIKE

(One Meter)

1. As the feet leave the board, the legs lift quickly by contracting the stomach and leg muscles. The upper part of the body remains in a fixed position as the legs lift upward.

2-3-4. As the feet leave the board, the legs are lifted quickly using a strong contraction of the stomach and thigh muscles. While the legs rise, the upper part of the body remains in a fixed position.

5. At the peak of the dive, the legs assume a position just short of the vertical and the arms reach slightly forward as the hands touch the toes. The eyes watch the hands and toes touch.

6. After the touch is made, the head begins to tilt backward, and the upper body begins to fall away from the legs, which remain stationary in a vertical position.

7. As the body drops away from the legs, the arms move laterally for the extension over the head. The head tilts back in search of the water

8. The arms continue their lateral extension over the head while the stomach muscles relax, and the thigh muscles tighten to allow the body to straighten for the entry.

9. With the eyes fixed on the point of entry, the arms extend overhead, and the body is stretched for a vertical entry.

REVERSE DIVE – LAYOUT

(Three Meter) 301A

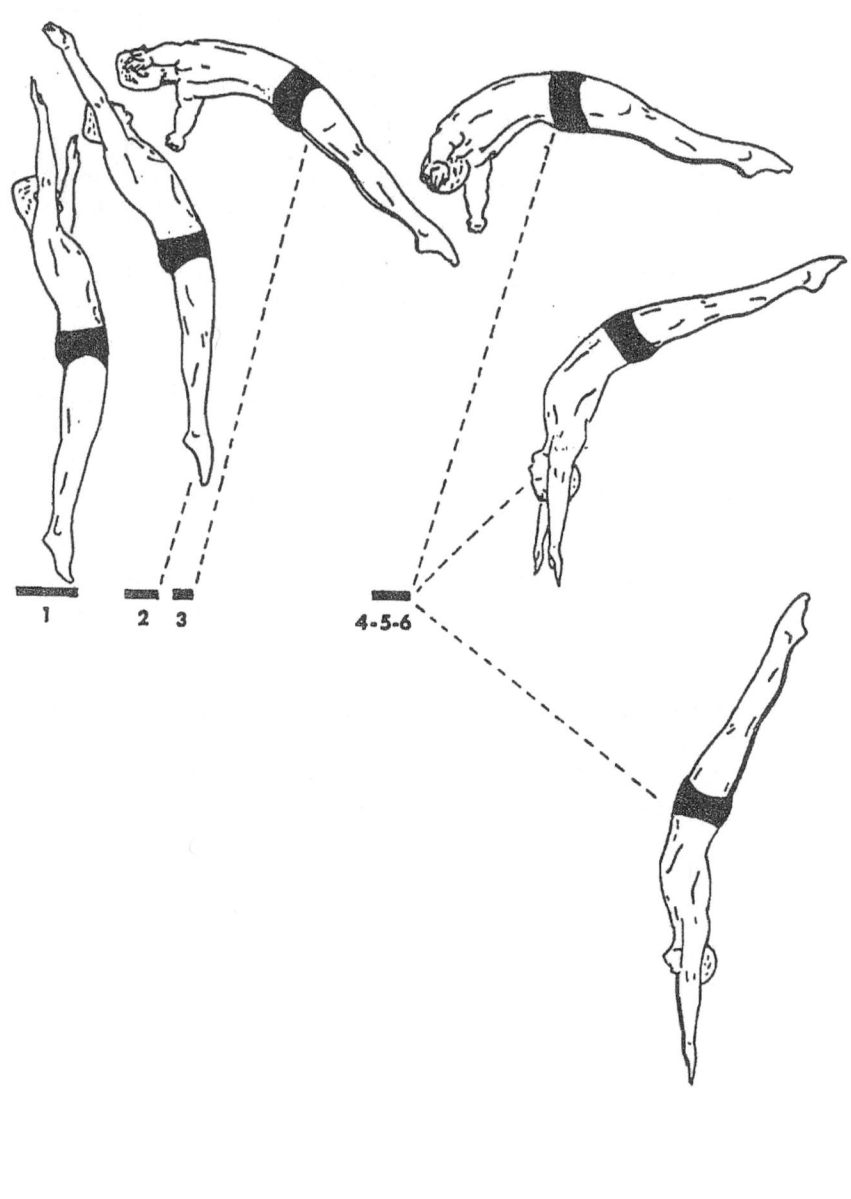

REVERSE DIVE - LAYOUT

(Three Meter)

1. The arms sweep forward and upward to a near vertical position as the diver leaves the board. The head is allowed to rise with the arms. The diver fully extends the legs by pushing off from the end of the board with the feet to the tips of the toes.
2. As the body starts its upward motion, the chest rises, and the arms spread laterally at right angles to the body. At the same time, the head is set in a fixed position with the eyes focused on an imaginary object high in the air and in front of vertical.
3. The upward motion of the arms, head, and chest from the point of take-off allows the hips and legs to move forward and upward until the body is in a horizontal position. The arms remain in a fixed position at shoulder level.
4. At the peak of the dive, the back is arched by a lateral rotation of the shoulders, and the head gracefully tips back until the water *is* sighted.
5. The arms extend over the head as the body approaches the entry into the water.
6. When the arms become fully extended overhead, the head remains in a position where the water can be seen. The arch in the back is reduced to near normal posture as the body approaches the water for a vertical entry.

REVERSE SOMERSAULT - TUCK

(One Meter) 302C

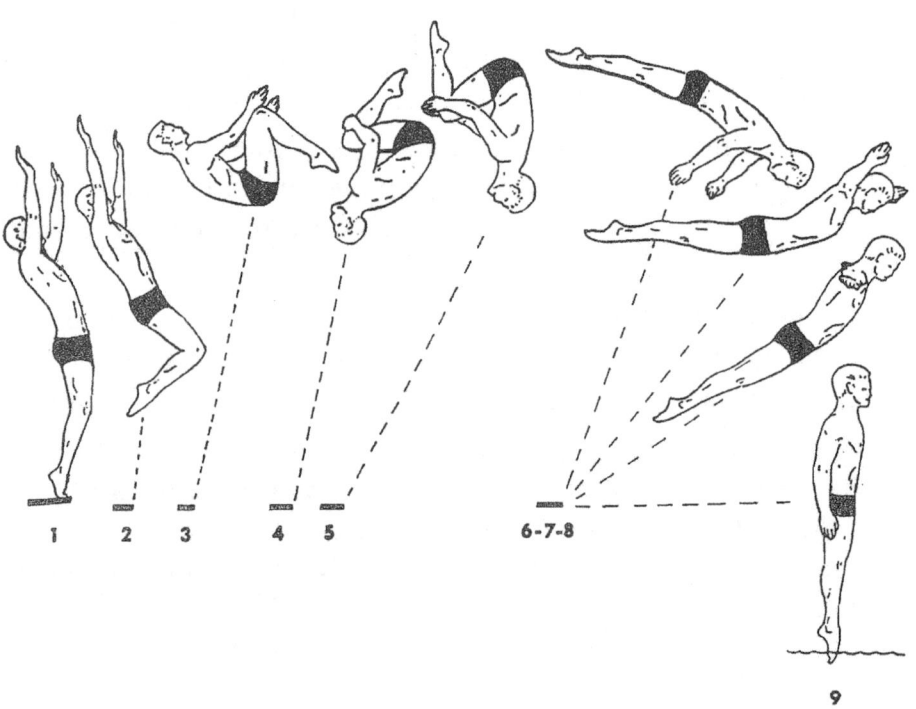

REVERSE SOMERSAULT-TUCK

(One Meter)

1. As the diver is about to leave the board, the legs extend, and the arms rise to a near vertical position in front of the head. The eyes look at the hands when the arms are placed overhead.
2. As the feet leave the board, the legs bend, and the knees quickly draw up toward the hands, with the arms remaining in a fixed position.
3. The head remains in line with the body as the knees approach the hands.
4. The hands grasp the legs just above the shins, and the knees are pulled toward the chest. The head tilts in toward the knees during this action.
5. As the body rotates, the position of the head allows the eyes to sight the board and water. At this point in the dive, the knees are released, and the body begins to straighten.
6. The body is straightened by driving the legs back toward the board. The arms begin a lateral movement and are slightly in front of the chest for balance.

7-8. The head and shoulders rise to make the body erect. The arms are placed in a lateral position to permit the back to arch slightly, so the legs can be brought into position for the entry.

9. The feet-first vertical entry is made with the hands at the sides and the body straight.

REVERSE SOMERSAULT – PIKE

(One Meter) 302B

REVERSE SOMERSAULT - PIKE

(One Meter)

1. The diver rises from the board with the arms reaching overhead and the eyes looking up at the hands. The head also lifts as the legs, ankles, and toes extend and the diver jumps nearly straight up.
2. As the feet leave the board, the legs lift toward the hands by contraction of the stomach and thigh muscles. Care is taken *not* to push outward with, the stomach or hips.
3. When the legs reach the arms, which have remained vertical, the hands grasp behind the legs just above the knees and pull the legs toward the chest. The head pulls in slightly to aid in the spin of the somersault.
4. The water comes into view when the body has rotated through approximately three-quarters of a somersault.
5. The hands release the legs as the water is spotted. The head and shoulders then rise while the legs push down, to place the body in an erect position. The hands remain at the sides after releasing the legs.
6. The body extends and enters the water in a straight vertical position.

REVERSE SOMERSAULT – LAYOUT

(One Meter) 302A

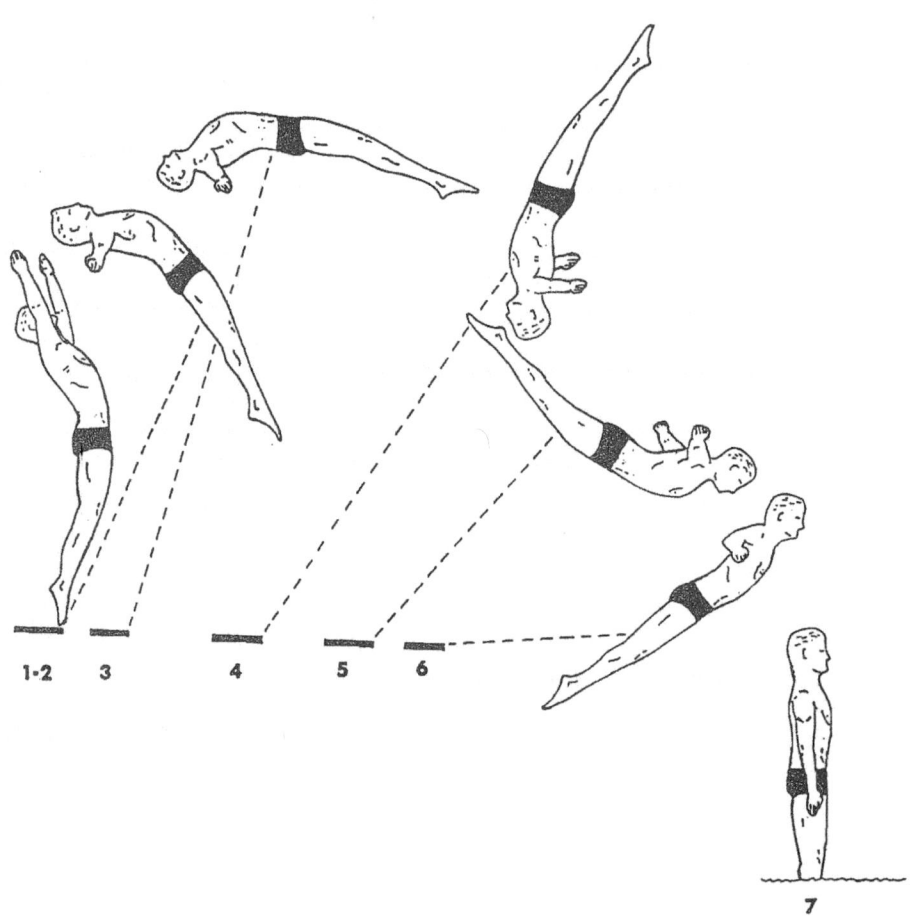

REVERSE SOMERSAULT - LAYOUT

(One Meter)

1. As the diver leaves the board, the arms are swept forward and upward past the vertical position. The head lifts as the arms pass overhead. The take-off is initiated by forceful extension of the legs, ankles and toes.

2. The head and chest move upward with great force as the diver leaves the board. The arms spread to a swan position at right angles to the body.

3-4. The hips and legs continue to move upward as the back is arched and the head is tilted back. The position of the arms remains fixed.

5. The water comes into view as the diver approaches three-quarters of a somersault. The body remains arched as the head drops slightly to an erect position.

6. As the body continues to rotate and near the completion of the somersault, the back begins to straighten by contraction of the stomach and thigh muscles. The arms then drop laterally to the sides in preparation for the entry.

7. The diver enters the water with the body straight and the head erect. The entry is slightly short of vertical.

REVERSE FLYING SOMERSAULT – TUCK

(One Meter)

REVERSE FLYING SOMERSAULT - TUCK

(One Meter)

1. As the body leaves the board, the arms rise directly over the head. The chest and hips also rise as the legs extend fully. The head tilts back slightly with the eyes looking in the direction of the hands.
2. The arms pull down laterally at right angles to the body as the legs and hips start to rise.
3. The diver continues to rotate in the layout position until the body is near the vertical position.
4. The body then changes from the layout to the tuck position by bending the legs and pulling the knees toward the chest. The water can be sighted from this position.
5. The hands grasp the knees and pull them close to the chest for a tight tuck. The head also pulls in close to the knees.
6. The hands release the legs at approximately three quarters of a somersault and the legs begin to rapidly extend.
7. The legs extend completely and pull down toward the water while the chest and head pull up to place the body in a straight and erect position.
8. With the body straight and the hands at the sides, the momentum of the somersault carries the body upright for a vertical entry.

REVERSE FLYING SOMERSAULT – PIKE

(One Meter) 312B

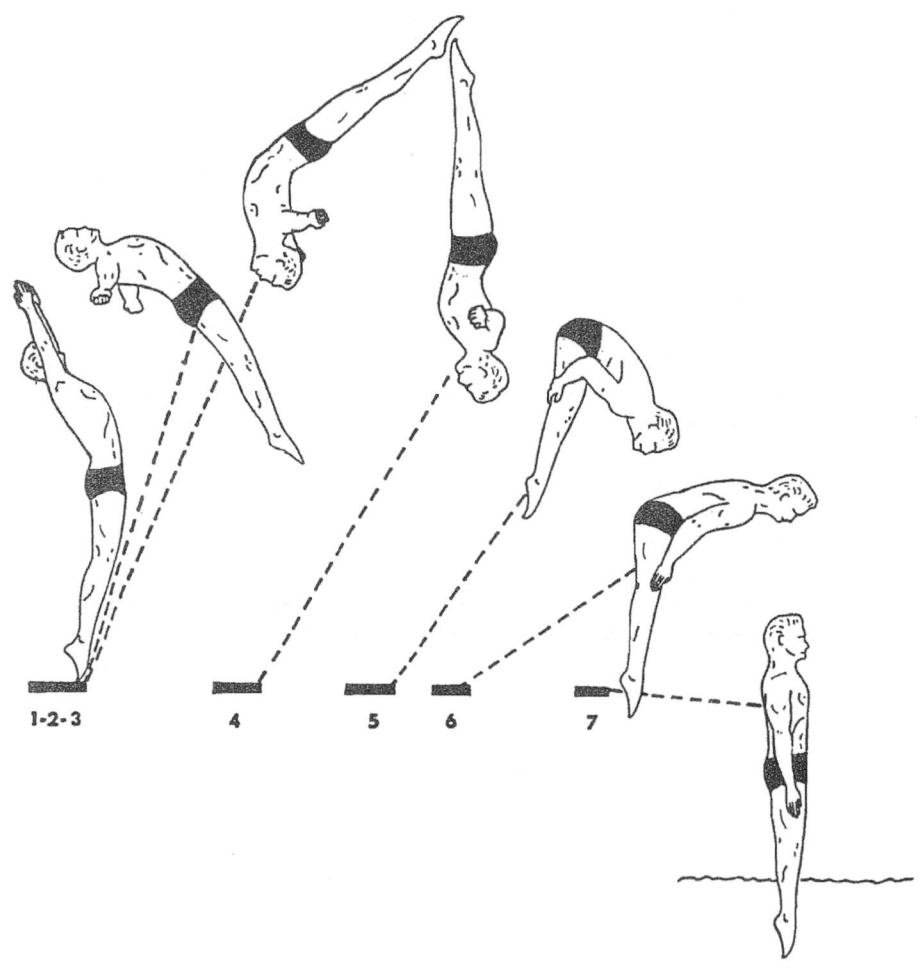

REVERSE FLYING SOMERSAULT - PIKE

(One Meter)

1. The take-off is made with the arms sweeping forward and upward over the head. The head and chest lift upward as the arms pass above shoulder level.

2. As the diver leaves the board, the arms pull down laterally to shoulder level. The back arches, and the body begins to rotate in the layout position.

3. When the diver approaches completion of the first half of the somersault, the water may be sighted.

4. The layout position begins to change to a pike position as the diver passes the vertical at the peak of the dive. The position is changed by contracting the abdomen and pulling the legs toward the chest. The chin is pulled in toward the chest, and the arms begin to move toward the legs.

5. The arms continue to move toward the legs as the body continues to pike. The hands then grasp behind the legs just above the knees and pull the legs toward the chest. The head is tilted up with the eyes sighting the water where the entry is to be made.

6. As the diver passes three-quarters of a somersault, the hands release the legs and the body begins to straighten for the entry. The arms move toward the sides of the body, and the head is placed in line with the body.

7. The entry is made slightly short of vertical, with the body erect, the head in line with the body, the eyes fixed on the other end of the pool, the arms at the sides, and the hands on the thighs.

8.

REVERSE 1 ½ SOMERSAULTS - TUCK

(Three Meter) 303C

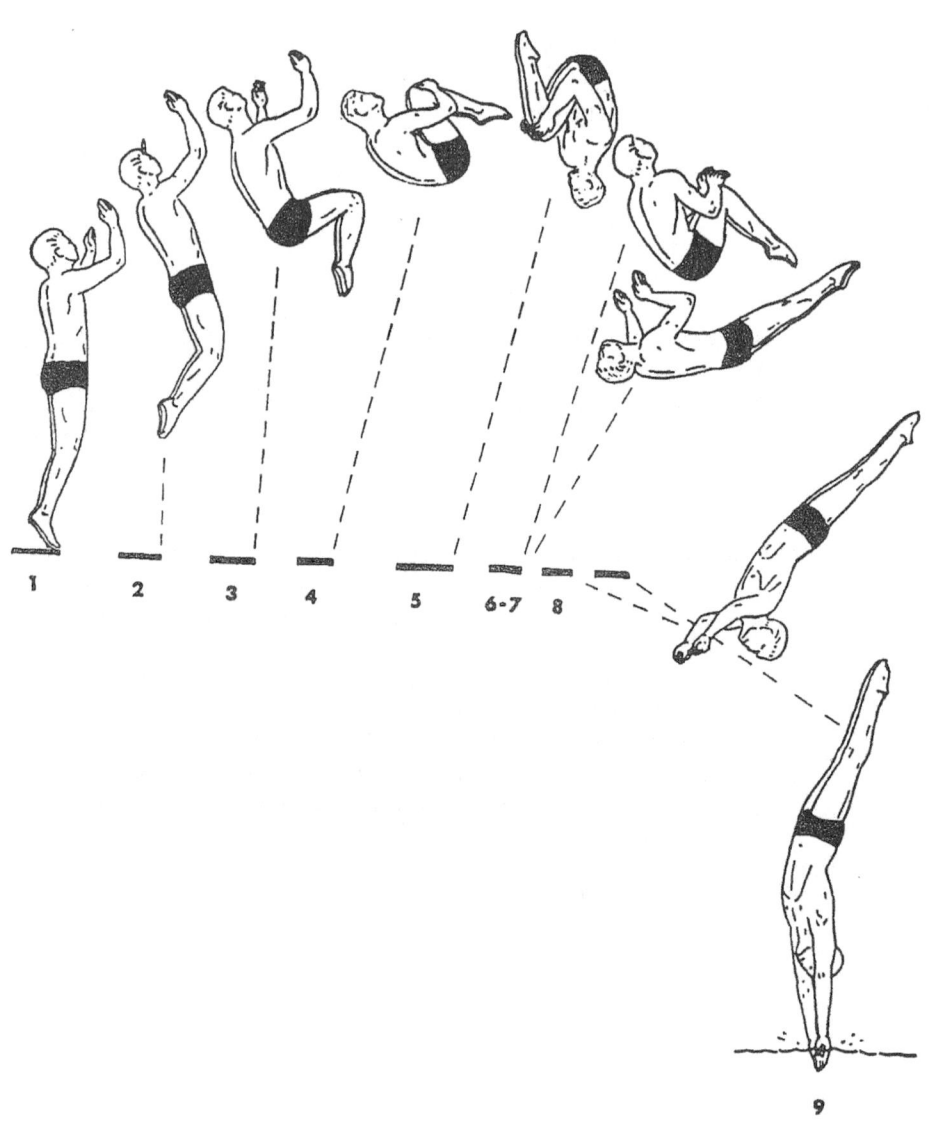

REVERSE 1 ½ SOMERSAULTS - TUCK

(Three Meter)

1. At the take-off from the board, the arms and head aim overhead at a point slightly in front of the body. The legs, ankles, and toes extend as the diver rises from the board.

2-3. As soon as the feet leave the board; the knees quickly draw up toward the hands. The arms and head remain in a fixed position during the lifting of the knees. *Caution:* The stomach and hips must not be thrust outward, to avoid hitting the board. The placement of the arms in the proper position at the take-off should provide enough room for the body to safely pass the board.

4. The hands grasp the knees and pull the legs into the chest with the head pulling inward toward the knees.

5-6. The speed of the somersault is increased by increasing the tightness of the tuck.

7-8. Just as the body passes the horizontal position after 1¼ somersaults, the hands release the knees and the legs sharply extend. The head drops back to sight the water as the arms start to reach overhead. For better safety, the diver may reach for the water with the arms moving in a lateral, semi-lateral or narrow and bent motion to avoid hitting the board.

9. When the water comes into view, the eyes spot the point of entry and the arms stretch over the head for the entry. A stretching of the body reduces the arch and allows for a straight vertical entry.

REVERSE 1½ SOMERSAULTS - PIKE

(Three Meter) 303B

REVERSE 1½ SOMERSAULTS - PIKE

(Three Meter)

1. The take-off is made by forcefully extending the legs, ankles, and toes and swinging the arms overhead. The head is raised as the arms reach overhead and the eyes look up at the hands.

2-3. As the feet leave the board, the pike is started with a sharp lift of the legs toward the arms, which remain in a fixed vertical position.

4. The legs continue to pull up toward the arms, which remain nearly vertical. When the legs reach the arms, the hands grasp behind, and just above, the knees and pull the legs toward the chest.

5. The head pulls in toward the body as the legs are pulled in tight and the elbows are kept close to the sides.

6-7. When the diver completes 1¼ somersaults, the water is sighted below the legs. At this point, the hands release the legs at a position just above horizontal.

8. The diver begins to straighten as the upper body pulls back and away from the legs. The head tilts back in search of the water.

9. The arms extend laterally, semi-laterally or narrow and bent over the head as the body straightens.

10. The diver stretches for a vertical entry with the arms extended completely over the head.

REVERSE 1 ½ SOMERSAULTS - LAYOUT
(Three Meter) 303A

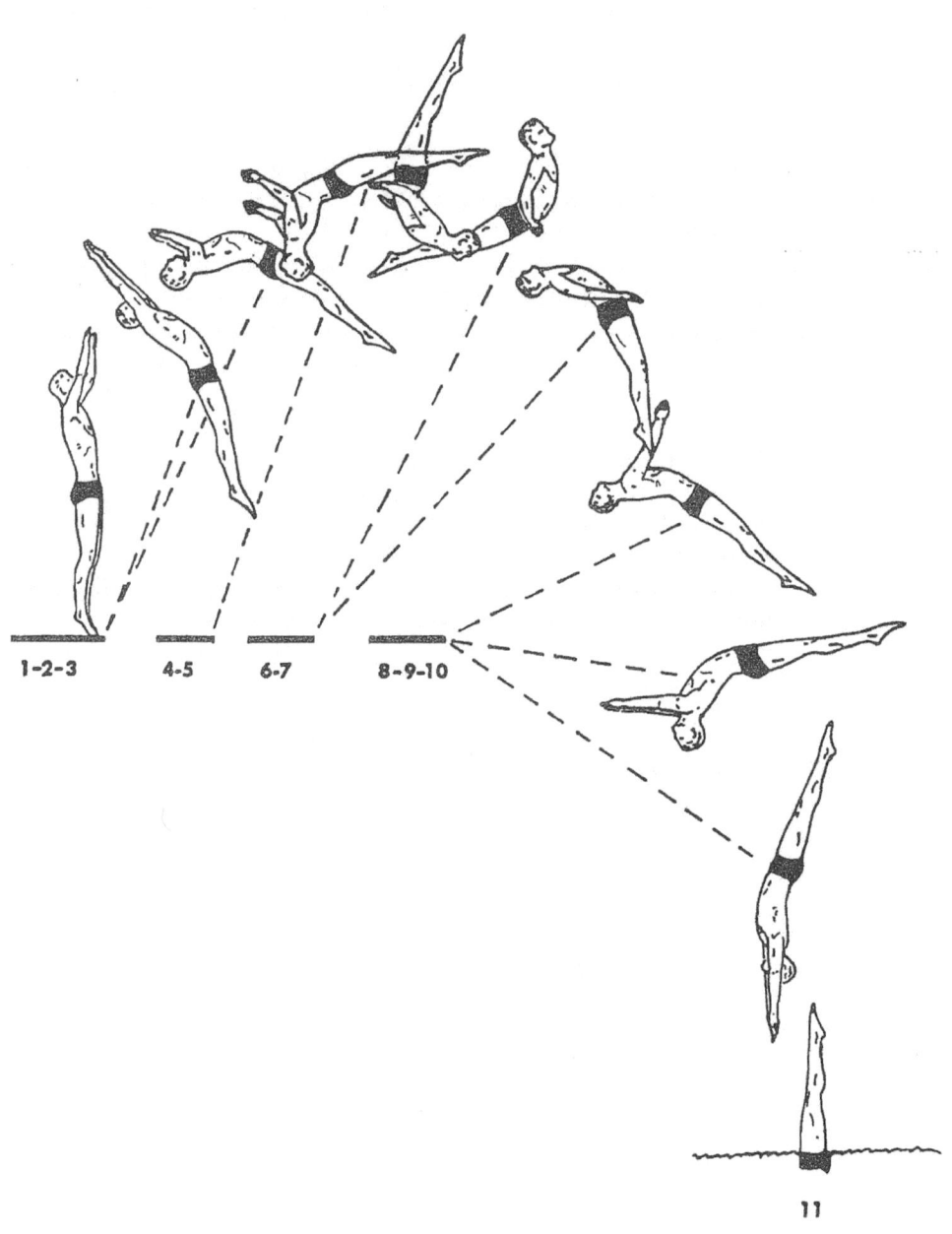

REVERSE 1 ½ SOMERSAULTS - LAYOUT

(Three Meter)

1. The diver begins the take-off with the knees flexed and the weight of the hips slightly behind the heels. With the head erect, the arms vigorously swing forward and upward over the head as the body rises nearly straight up.

2. The take-off is made by forcefully extending the legs, ankles, and toes while strongly lifting with the chest and pushing up with the hips. The head rises along with the arms as they reach overhead. As the diver leaves the board, the legs extend fully, and the hips move upward. The chest continues to rise, and the arms extend over the head to help create an arch in the back.

3-4-5. The legs and hips continue to move upward as the head and arms pull back behind the vertical paint. The arms then reverse their direction and push back toward the hips. The board can be sighted when the diver has completed a half somersault. The body continues to rotate backward with a deep arch in the back and with the head pulling back.

6-7. The hands clasp and press against the front of the hips as the body continues to somersault. The reverse action of the arms increases the speed of the somersault. As the first somersault nears completion, the diver increases her/his efforts to continue somersaulting by lifting harder with the chest and tightening the legs, keeping the head back.

8. The water comes into view at approximately 1¼ somersaults. The arms remain straight as they began to reach overhead, in a narrow position, for the entry.

9-10. As the arms extend over the head, the diver is in a position to adjust the body for the entry by increasing or decreasing the arch in the back.

11. The entry is made with the arms extending over the head and the hands clasped and the back slightly arched.

FLYING REVERSE 1 ½ SOMERSAULTS - TUCK

(Three Meter) 313C

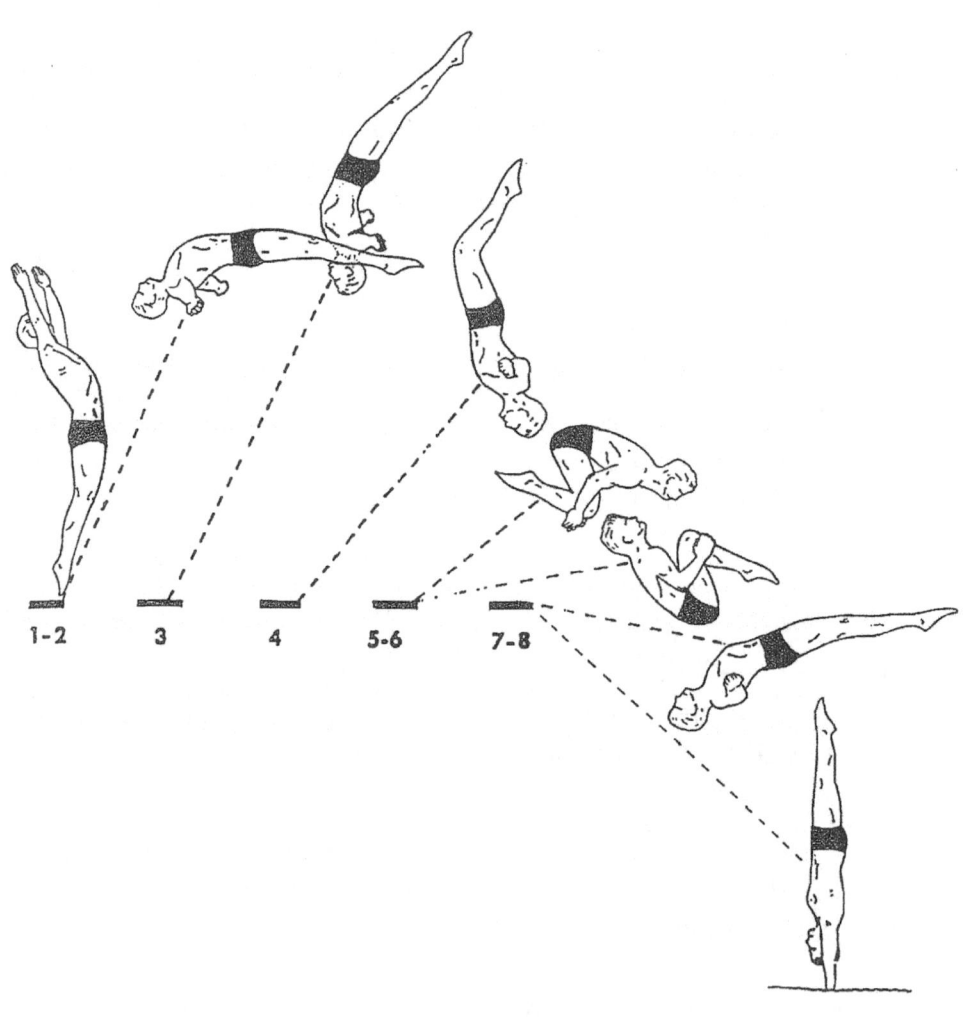

FLYING REVERSE 1 ½ SOMERSAULTS - TUCK

(Three Meter)

1. The diver begins the take-off from the board with a forceful lift of the arms forward and upward past the vertical position. The head rises with the arms as they reach overhead. The take-off is made by extending the legs, ankles, and toes while vigorously lifting the chest and hips.
2. As the diver leaves the board, the arms move laterally to shoulder level while the legs fully extend, and the hips move upward.
3. The back is arched, and the legs and hips continue to move upward as the diver reaches the peak of the dive. The head is tilted back slightly, and the water is sighted as the diver completes a half of a somersault.
4. As the diver passes the peak of the dive, the tuck position is started by drawing the knees toward the chest.

5-6. The tuck position is completed with the knees moving toward the chest and the hands clasping the legs just above the shins. The head is pulled in slightly to aid in the spin of the somersault.

7. When the body has completed a little more than three-quarters of a somersault, the diver straightens into a layout position. The arms move laterally, semi-laterally or narrow and bent over the head as the legs quickly extend. The head drops back to sight the water.
8. The vertical entry is made with the arms extended overhead and in line with the body.

REVERSE DOUBLE SOMERSAULT - TUCK

(Three Meter) 304C

REVERSE DOUBLE SOMERSAULT - TUCK

(Three Meter)

1. The diver leaves the board with the arms sweeping forward and upward slightly in front of the head. The head lifts as the arms reach overhead, and the eyes look at the hands. The toes press into the board as the legs fully extend.
2. As the feet leave the board, the legs bend, and the knees draw up toward the hands, with the arms and head remaining in a fixed position.
3. When the knees reach a near vertical position, the arms move forward a short distance to grasp the legs.
4. The hands grasp high on the shins, and the knees are drawn tightly against the chest. The head tilts in slightly to aid in the spin.

5-6. The hands continue to pull the tuck tight to increase the speed of the somersault. The diver may sight the water near the completion of the first somersault. The elbows are held close to the sides.

7-8-9. As the diver passes 1 ¾ somersaults, the water is sighted. The hands then release the legs, and the body begins to straighten.

10. As the body straightens for the feet-first entry, the head and shoulders are brought into an erect position. The arms are placed at the sides, with the hands placed slightly toward the front of the thighs. The entry is slightly short of vertical.

REVERSE DOUBLE SOMERSAULT - PIKE

(One Meter) 304B

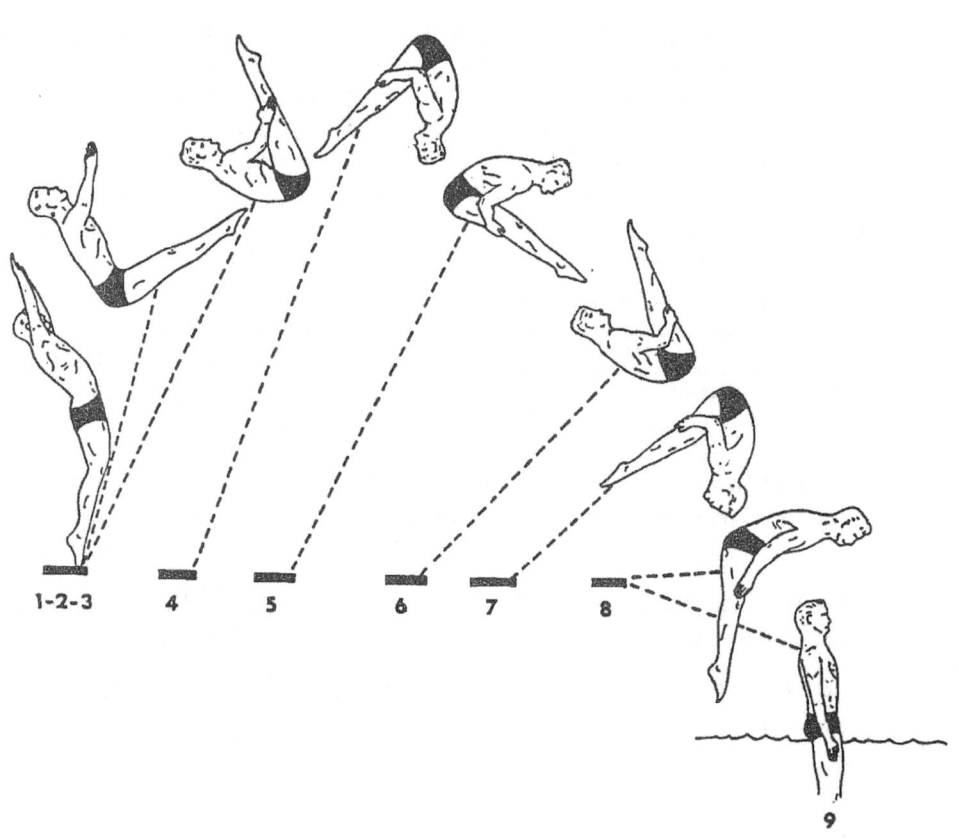

REVERSE DOUBLE SOMERSAULT - PIKE

(One Meter)

1. The take-off from the board is initiated by sweeping the arms forward and upward to a near vertical position. The head rises with the arms as they reach overhead.

2. As the toes leave the board, the legs are quickly lifted toward the arms by contraction of the stomach and thigh muscles. The quick lifting of the legs starts the rotation of the body. The arms and head remain in a fixed position.

3. As the legs rise to a near vertical position, the arms move forward slightly and clasp the legs behind, and slightly above, the knees. The head tilts in toward the body to aid in the spin of the somersault.

4-5-6. The speed of the somersault is increased by pulling the legs toward the chest as much as possible.

7. When approximately 1¾ somersaults have been completed, the water comes into view. The legs continue to be pulled toward the water.

8. As the legs are pulled down toward the water, the hands release them, and the body begins to straighten at the waist. Emphasis is placed on lifting with the shoulders.

9. The feet-first entry into the water is made after the body has straightened, with the head erect and the arms placed at the sides. The entry is slightly short of vertical.

REVERSE 2½ SOMERSAULTS – TUCK

(Three Meter) 305C

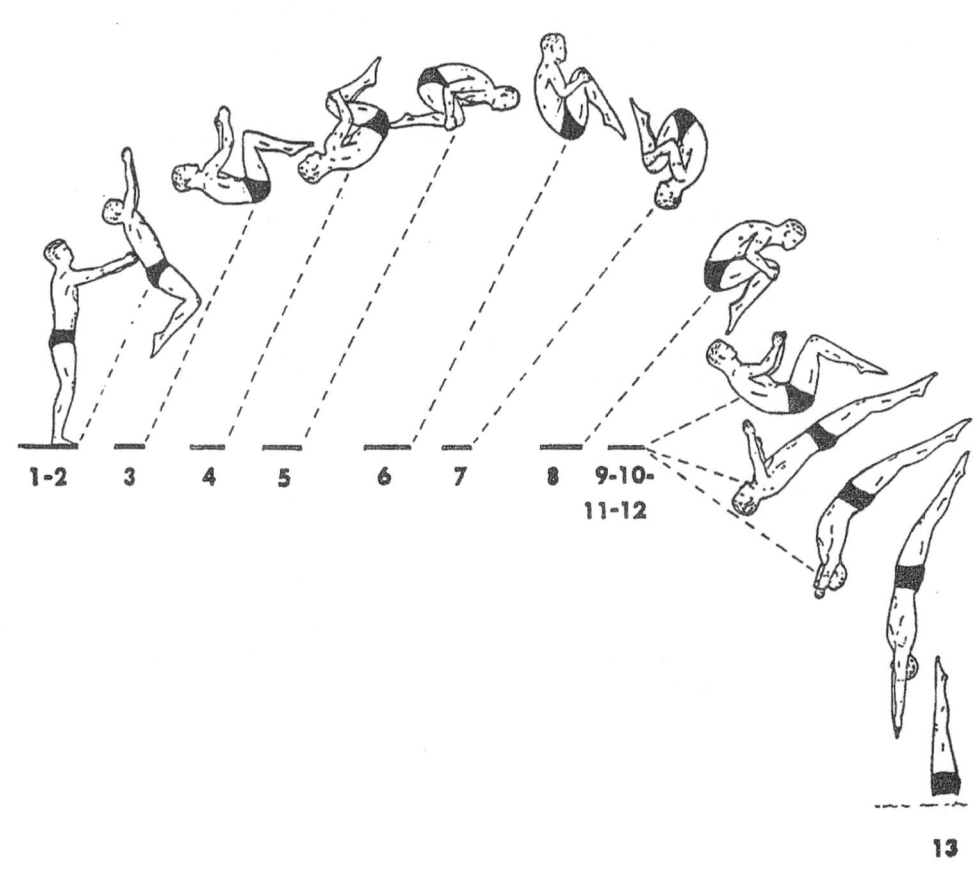

REVERSE 2½ SOMERSAULTS - TUCK

(Three Meter)

1. The diver initiates the takeoff with the arms swinging forward and upward overhead to a near vertical point. The legs, ankles and toes extend completely as the diver leaves the board.

2. The legs begin to bend, and the knees quickly draw up toward the hands when the toes leave the board. The arms and head remain in a fixed position as the knees begin to rise. *Caution:* The stomach and hips need not be thrust outward, to avoid hitting the board. The proper placement of the arms and head at the take-off should provide enough distance for the diver to pass the board safely.

3. The arms move forward a short distance to grasp the knees with the hands when the knees rise to a near vertical position. This reverse action increases the speed of the somersault. The head pulls in toward the knees during this action.

4-5
6-7-8. The knees are grasped just above the shins and pulled in tight with the elbows held close to the sides. An effort is made to pull the knees in tighter to the chest as the body somersaults. The water can be sighted at the completion of the first and second somersaults.

9-10-11. The hands release the knees and the legs extend with a snap when the diver reaches a "sitting" position slightly past the second somersault. The moment the knees are released, the upper part of the body pulls back toward the water. In this action, the head tilts back and the arms spread slightly as they straighten to reach overhead for the water.

12. An effort is made to look back and see the water as the arms extend over-head.

13. The diver enters the water in a vertical position with the body straight.

REVERSE 2½ SOMERSAULTS - PIKE

(Three Meter) 305B

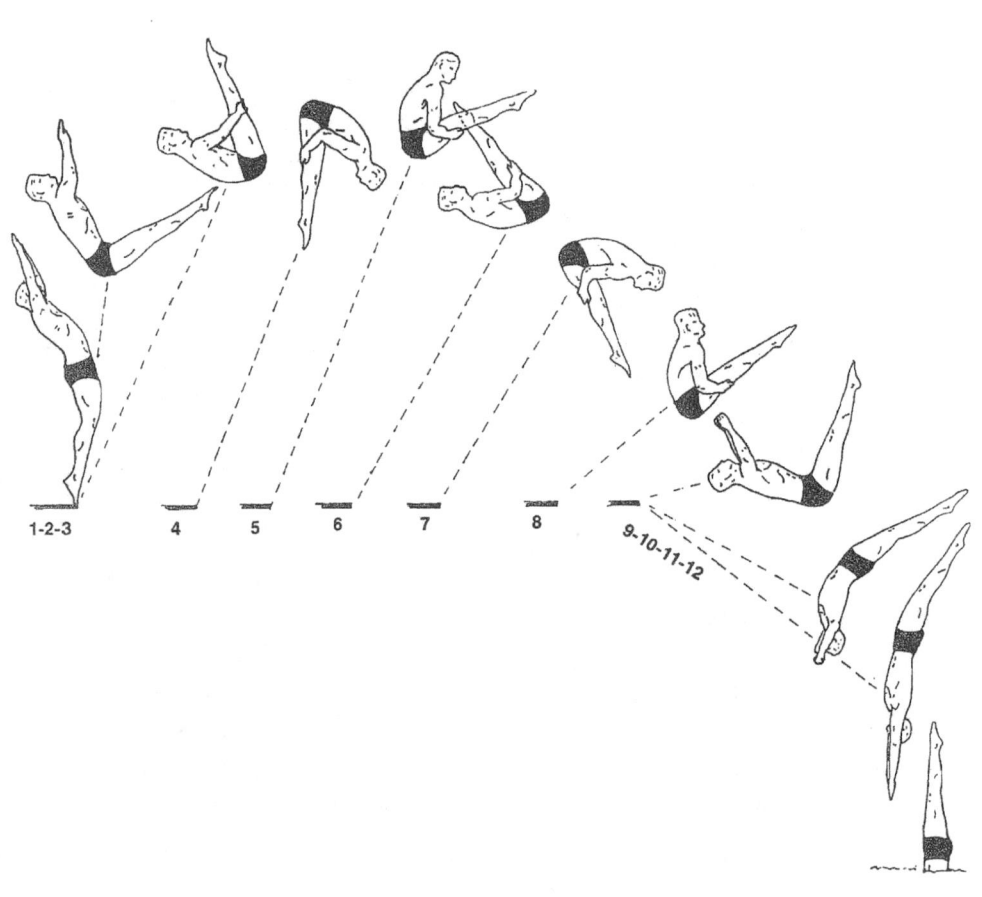

REVERSE 2½ SOMERSAULTS - PIKE

(Three Meter)

1. The diver leaves the board by swinging the arms forward and upward to a position near vertical. In the same motion, the legs, ankles and toes extend with the head looking upward toward the hands after the arms pass the level of the shoulders.
2. Once off the board, the body bends at the waist and the legs draw up toward the arms which are in a near fixed vertical position.
3. The arms move forward slightly to grasp the legs from behind at the knee level and pull them in toward the chest.

4-5

6-7-8. The head is pulled in toward the chest as the arms remain close to the sides. The legs are pulled in as tight as possible to create a faster rotation. The diver may sight the water near the completion of the first and second somersaults.

9. As the legs pass the 2¼ somersault line, the legs are released, and the upper body begins to pull back toward the water with the arms and head leading the motion. The arms remain straight and narrow during this movement to slow the rotation of the body
10. The arms continue to move narrowly over the head and the eyes look back to sight the water for the entry.
11. The diver sights the point of entry and reaches for that point with the arms. There is little arch in the back as the arms reach overhead for the entry.
12. The diver enters the water in a straight position slightly short of vertical.

REVERSE 3½ SOMERSAULTS – TUCK

(Three Meter) 307C

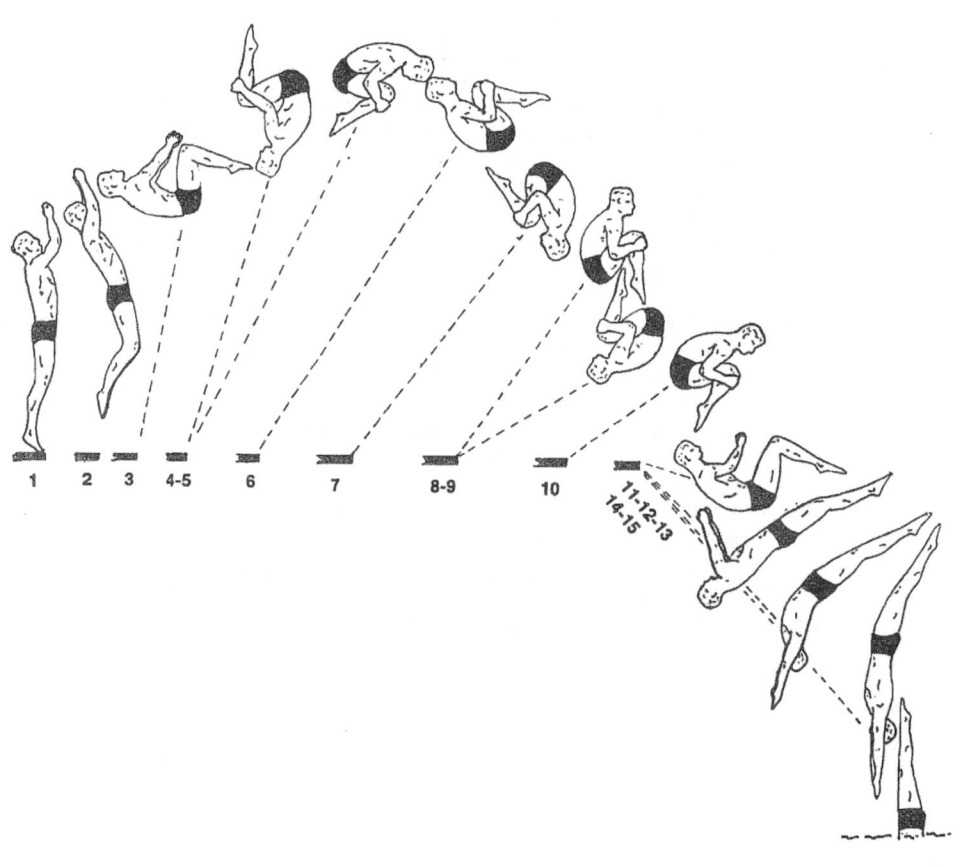

REVERSE 3½ SOMERSAULTS - TUCK

(Three Meter)

1. The arms swing forward and upward in a vertical direction as the legs, ankles and toes extend prior to the takeoff.

2-3. The arms reach a vertical point with the eyes sighting the hands, the legs bend, and the knees begin to draw upward toward the hands.

4-5-6-7
8-9-10. The arms reach forward slightly to grasp the legs above the shins. With the arms held close to the sides, the legs are drawn into a tight tuck position. The head tilts in toward the body to help create a tighter and closer tuck position. The diver can spot the water near the completion of the three somersaults.

11. As the diver passes 3¼ somersaults, the hands release the legs, which quickly extend, and the upper body begins to pull back toward the water.

12. The body straightens, and the arms begin to reach overhead in a narrow position with the head still held in slightly.

13. The head tilts back to sight the water just before the arms pass the level of the shoulders and extend overhead.

14-15. The arms line up with the body as they reach overhead and there is a slight arch in the back at this time. The entry is then made just a little short of vertical.

GROUP IV – INWARD DIVES

INWARD DIVE – TUCK

(One Meter) 401C

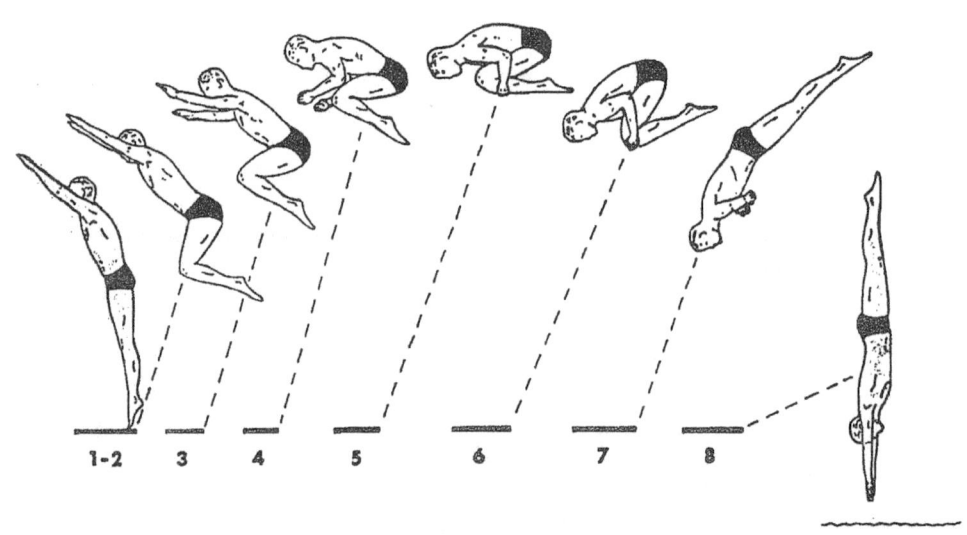

INWARD DIVE - TUCK

(One Meter)

1. Prior to the take-off, the legs flex as the arms swing forward and upward with the head erect. The diver takes off from the board by extending the legs, ankles, and toes and by continuing to reach over the head with the arms.

2. The knees quickly draw up toward the chest as the feet leave the board. The body bends forward at the waist, with the arms remaining extended over the head and the eyes spotting the water.

3-4-5. The arms move down in front of the face as the knees draw up to the chest. The hands then grasp the knees and draw them to the chest as the body reaches the peak of the dive. The head remains in line with the body and the eyes sight the water throughout the entire dive.

6-7. The hands release the knees as the body begins to descend. The legs rapidly extend toward a point slightly above horizontal. The balance of the dive is maintained by spreading the arms semi-laterally as they extend overhead for the entry.

8. The arms extend laterally over the head as the diver nears the water for the entry. The entry is vertical with the body straight.

INWARD DIVE – PIKE

(Three Meter) 401B

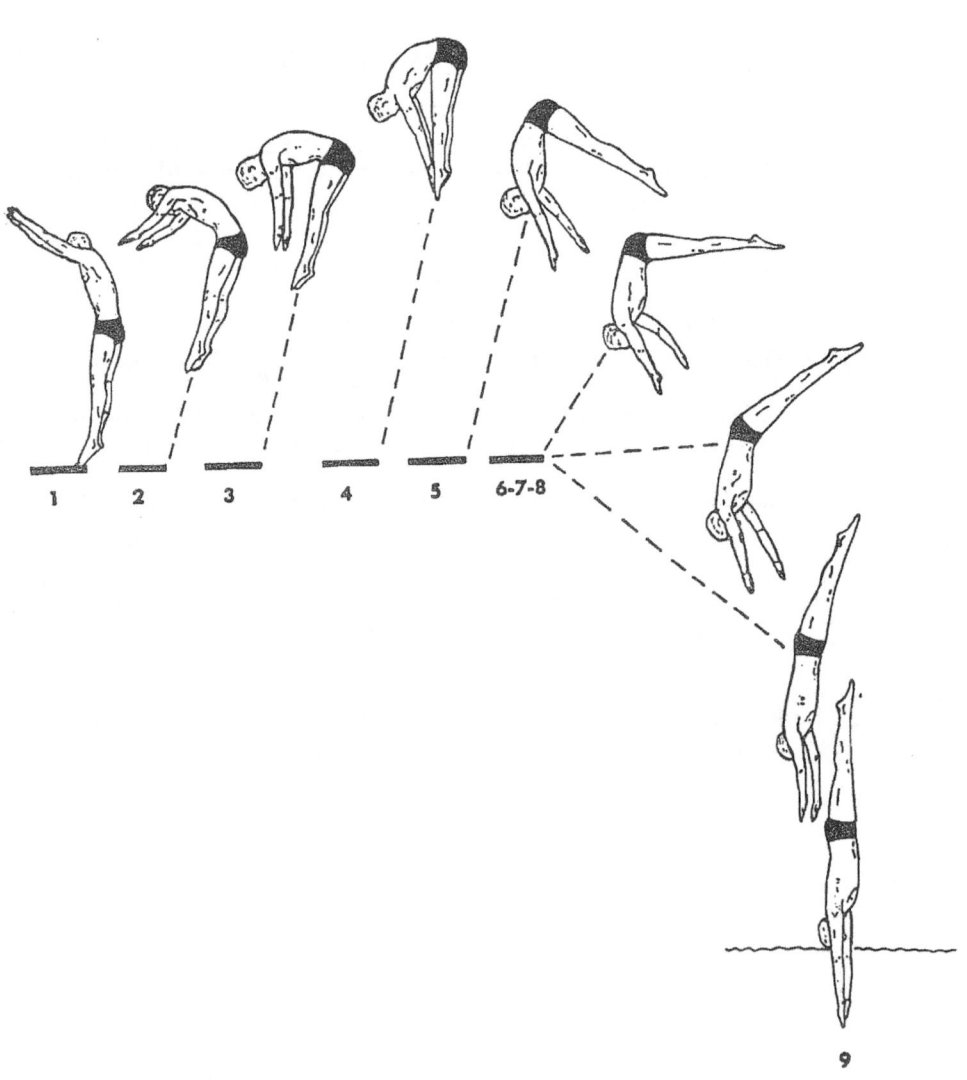

INWARD DIVE - PIKE

(Three Meter)

1. The legs extend with the weight directly above the balls of the feet as the diver leaves the board. The take-off is executed with the arms rising simultaneously over the head and in front of the face, with the head held erect.
2. The diver rises from the board by extending the legs, ankles, and toes and lifting upward with the hips. The body bends at the waist as the arms and shoulders move down toward the legs. Emphasis is placed on keeping the head and shoulders directly over the end of the board until the hips begin to rise.
3. While the hips rise, and the body continues to pike, the legs push back slightly to keep them in a vertical line. The water comes into view at this time.
4. The hands touch the toes, with the legs in a vertical position, at the very peak of the dive. The head faces the water, and the eyes are fixed on a point where the diver will enter the water.
5. Following the touch of the toes, the arms spread about shoulder width apart as they reach for the water. The legs begin to push upward while the eyes remain fixed on the point of entry.

6-7-8. The arms remain straight as they reach over the head toward the water. The legs continue to press upward, and the body begins to straighten for the entry.

9. The diver enters the water in a vertical position with the body straight.

INWARD DIVE - LAYOUT

(Three Meter) 401A

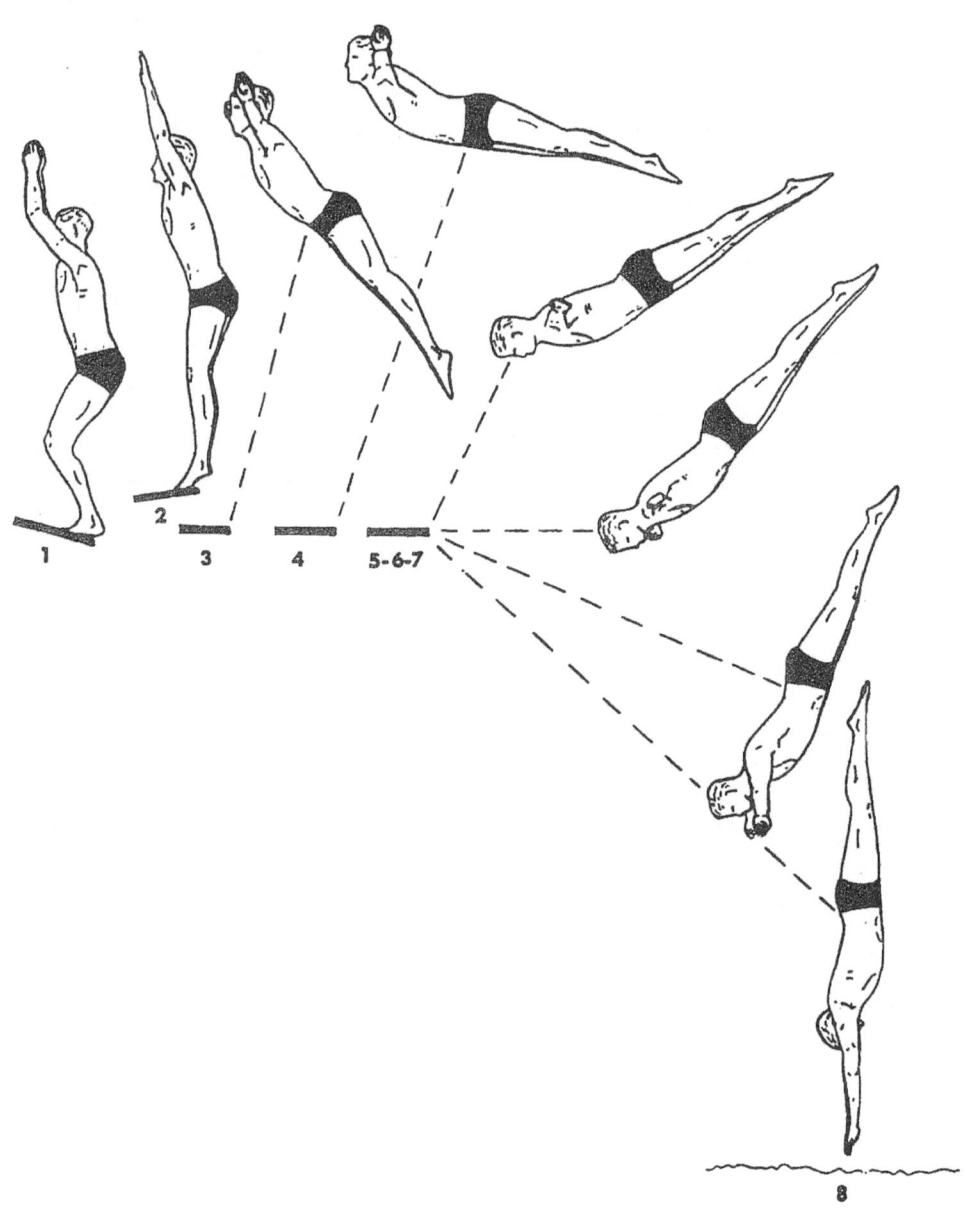

INWARD DIVE - LAYOUT

(Three Meter)

1-2. The diver begins the take-off with the arms over the head, the head erect, and the body leaning slightly forward. The arms pull down laterally to a position level with the shoulders and with the head erect *before the feet leave the board.*

3. The diver rises from the board by forcefully extending the legs, ankles, and toes. The legs drive up behind the body after the arms pull down laterally while still on the board.

4-5. The back arches slightly as the legs continue to move upward. The arms remain fixed in the swan position until the body has rotated to a near horizontal. position. At this point, the head tilts downward slightly to sight the water, then remains in a fixed position until the entry into the water.

6-7. As the diver approaches the water, head first, the arms extend laterally over the head and the hands clasp.

8. The entry is made with the body in a straight vertical position.

INWARD SOMERSAULT - TUCK

(One Meter) 402C

INWARD SOMERSAULT - TUCK

(One Meter)

1. Prior to the take-off, the arms are lifted over the head and in front of the face. The legs flex, with the hips located directly above the balls of the feet. The head is held erect.

2. The body rises from the board with the full extension of the legs, ankles, and toes. In the same motion, the hips thrust upward while the arms whip downward. Emphasis is placed on keeping the head and shoulders directly over the board until the hips start their upward motion.

3. As the body leaves the board, the hips continue to rise. The legs bend, and the knees pull in toward the chest while the arms, aided by the ducking of the head, whip downward and the hands grasp the legs at the shins.

4. The tuck is tightened, and the arms are kept close to the sides as the body somersaults.

5. The hands release the legs when the diver has nearly completed the somersault.

6. The legs then extend nearly straight down toward the water as the head is lifted to an erect position and the arms are placed at the sides. The body enters the water in an upright position.

INWARD SOMERSAULT – PIKE

(One Meter) 402B

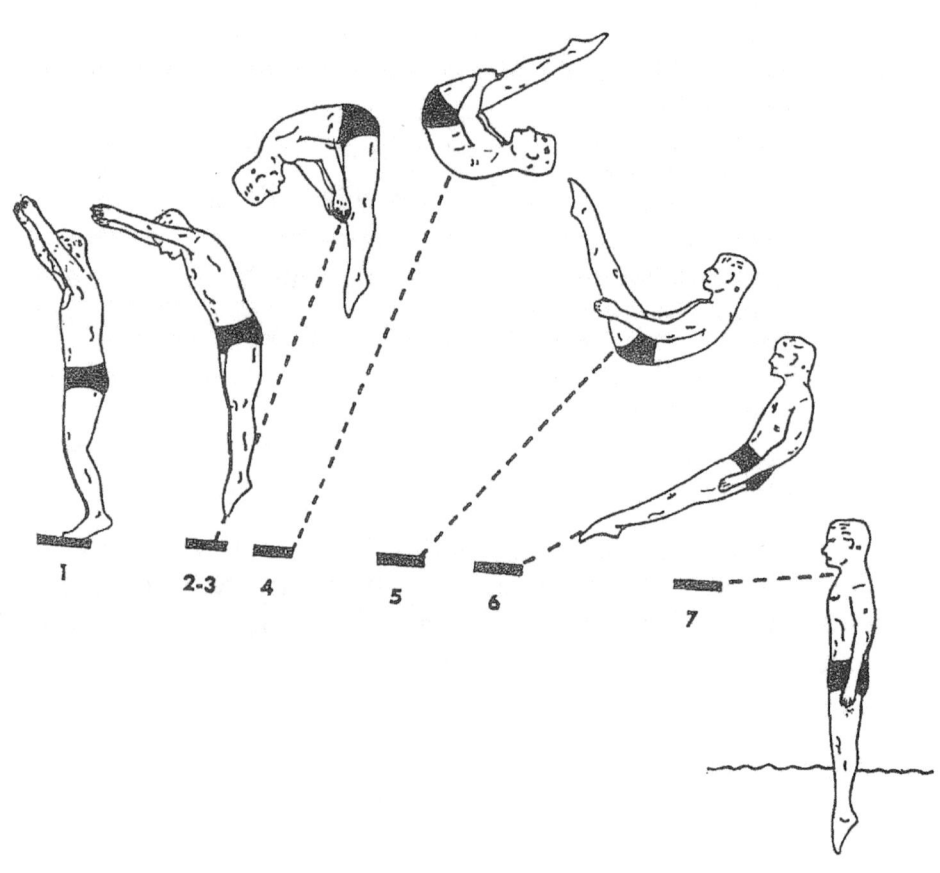

INWARD SOMERSAULT - PIKE

(One Meter)

1. The take-off is made with the arms lifted over the head and in front of the face. The head is held erect as the legs, ankles, and toes flex with the weight of the hips and shoulders directly above the feet.

2. The diver leaves the board, with the legs extending and the hips driving upward. The arms, shoulders, and head whip downward, and the body bends at the waist.

3. The body begins to rotate as the hips continue to move upward and the head, arms, and shoulders drive downward. The arms bend slightly to grasp the legs with the hands.

4. The hands clasp the legs behind, and a little above, the knees, with the elbows held close to the sides. The legs are then pulled as close to the chest as possible.

5-6. As the body rotates to a near "sitting" position, the legs are released and pushed down toward the water. The head and shoulders are lifted slightly in the straightening of the body for the feet-first entry.

7. The legs extend nearly straight down as the head remains erect and the arms are placed at the sides. The diver enters the water in an upright position.

INWARD FLYING SOMERSAULT - TUCK

(One Meter) 412C

INWARD FLYING SOMERSAULT - TUCK

(One Meter)

1. The take-off is made with the arms rising over the head. The weight of the body remains over the board, with the head erect.

2. From the overhead position, the arms pull down laterally toward the level of the shoulders before the feet leave the board. This action aids greatly in the legs' moving upward behind the body. The head is held up to allow the bony to maintain a layout position.

3. With the arms at shoulder level, the body continues to rotate in the layout position until it has reached a near vertical position. The diver can sight the water at this time.

4. As the peak of the dive is reached, the diver begins to change from a layout to a tuck position by drawing the knees toward the chest, pulling the arms forward, and dropping the chin toward the chest.

5-6. The tuck is completed with the hands grasping the legs high on the shins and pulling the legs to the chest. The heels move toward the buttocks.

7. As the diver passes three-quarters of a somersault, the hands release the legs and the body begins to straighten for the feet-first entry. The legs extend toward the water, the head rises to an erect position, and the arms slide to the sides of the body.

8. The entry is vertical with the diver in a position of attention. The hands are placed on the thighs to keep the body from arching.

INWARD FLYING SOMERSAULT - PIKE

(One Meter) 412B

INWARD FLYING SOMERSAULT - PIKE

(One Meter)

1. While standing on the board with the body erect and the arms overhead and the legs flexed, the diver pulls the arms down toward the level of the shoulders in a lateral direction. The head is erect and in a fixed position during this movement.
2. The legs are forced back and upward when the legs extend and leave the board and the body establishes a layout position with the head up.
3. When the diver reaches a near vertical position close to the peak of the dive, the head tilts back slightly and sights the water.
4. The diver then begins to pike at the waist by pulling the arms downward in a semi-lateral direction toward the knees.
5. The hands grasp the legs behind the knees and pull the legs close to the chest with the arms close to the sides and the head in.
6. The legs are released and push down toward the water as the diver passes three quarters of a somersault. The head and shoulders pull up to an erect position during this movement.

7-8. The legs continue to push down toward the water until the body is in an erect and vertical position with the arms at the sides.

INWARD 1½ SOMERSAULTS - TUCK

(One Meter) 403C

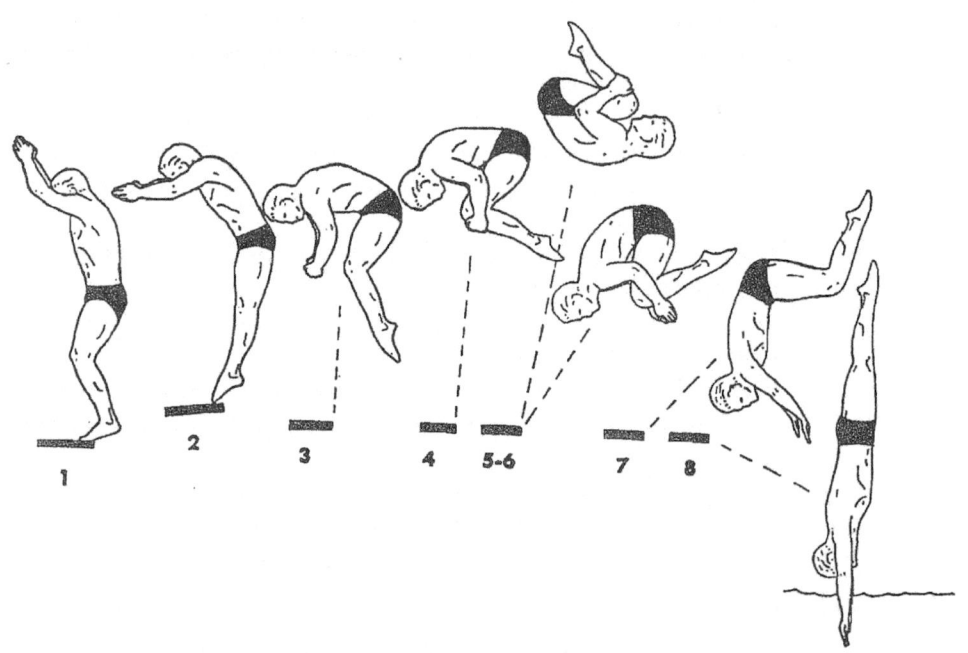

INWARD 1 ½ SOMERSAULTS - TUCK

(One Meter)

1. Prior to the take-off, the legs flex and push down on the board. This action is aided by a downward push of the hips, which are located directly above the balls of the feet. In the same motion, the arms rise over the head and in front of the face while the head is held erect.

2. The diver rises from the board with the extension of the legs, ankles, and toes. At the same time, the hips thrust upward, and the arms begin to whip down toward the legs. The head stays in line as the body bends at the waist. Emphasis is placed on keeping the head and shoulders directly over the end of the board until the hips begin to rise.

3. The knees begin to draw toward the chest, with the heels rising toward the buttocks as the hips continue to move upward. The arms, aided by the forward ducking of the head, continue to whip downward in chase of the legs.

4-5. When the hands meet the legs, they grasp them at the shins and pull the knees into the chest. The elbows are held close to the sides during the tuck.

6. As the diver completes approximately 1¼ somersaults, the water comes into view. The hands then release the shins, and the legs begin to extend.

7. With the eyes fixed on the water, the legs continue to extend toward the vertical line as the arms begin to extend in a semi-lateral direction over the head.

8. The body is made straight for the vertical entry into the water by a lifting of the legs to a vertical position and a stretching of the arms over the head.

INWARD 1 ½ SOMERSAULTS - PIKE

(One Meter) 403B

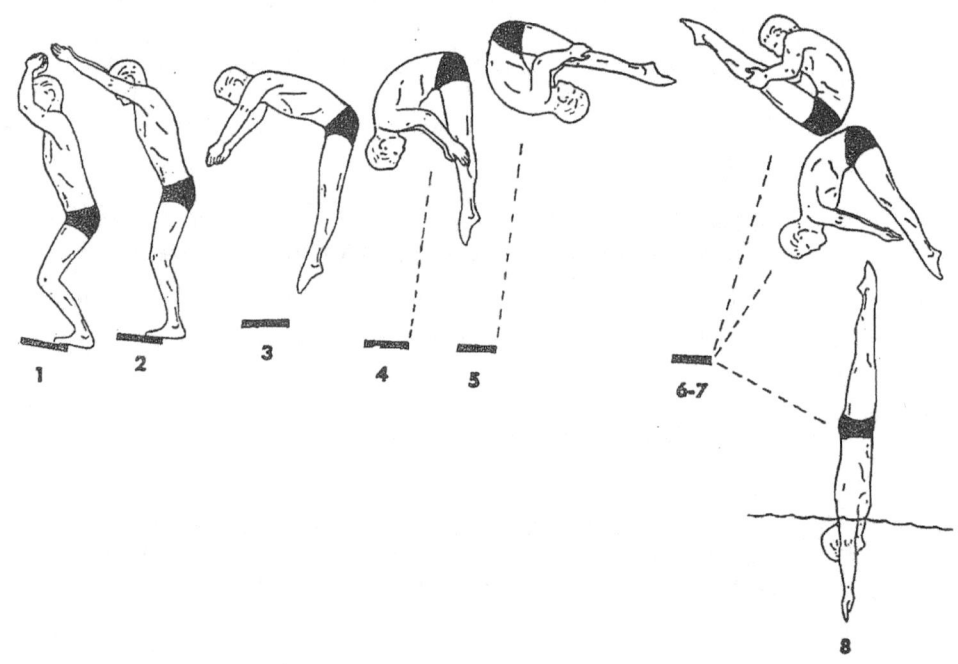

INWARD 1½ SOMERSAULTS - PIKE

(One Meter)

1. The legs flex and push down on the board prior to the take-off. This action is aided by the downward push of the hips, which are located directly above the balls of the feet. In the same motion, the arms lift over the head and in front of the face while the head is held erect.

2. The upward lift from the board is then initiated by extension of the knees, ankles, and toes. At the same time, the hips sharply thrust upward while the arms start to whip downward. Emphasis is placed on keeping the head and shoulders directly over the end of the board until the hips begin to rise.

3. As the body leaves the board, the hips continue to rise while the arms, aided by the ducking of the head, continue to whip downward. These movements cause the body to pike almost immediately after the diver leaves the board.

4. The arms continue to whip downward in chase of the legs. When the hands meet the legs, they grasp behind at the knee level.

5-6. The chest is then pulled down toward the legs with the head in and the arms

   close to the sides of the body.

7. The water is spotted at the end of one somersault. The legs are released and rise as the arms start to extend overhead in a semi-lateral direction. The eyes remain fixed on the point of entry as the body nears the water.

8. The legs continue to rise to a vertical position as the body straightens to make a vertical entry.

INWARD FLYING 1½ SOMERSAULTS - TUCK

(Three Meter) 413C

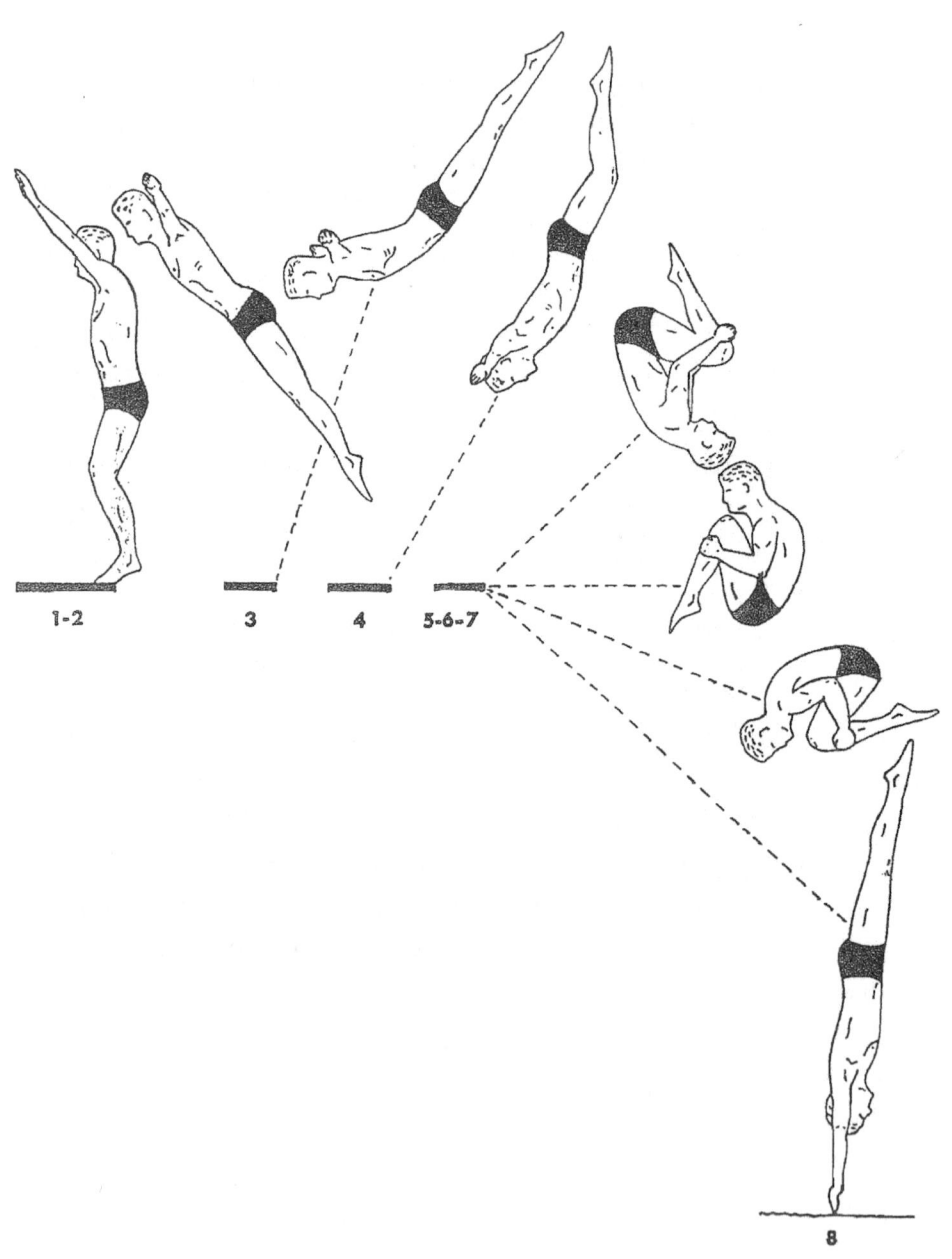

INWARD FLYING 1½ SOMERSAULTS - TUCK

(Three Meter)

1. As the diver prepares to leave the board, the arms are lifted overhead with the weight of the hips kept directly over the end of the board. The head remains upright, and the body does not lean.

2. The arms pull downward with a vigorous lateral movement. This permits the legs to move upward after they have been completely extended as the diver leaves the board. The head remains in line with the body to allow the back to arch. The arms become fixed when they reach the swan position.

3-4-5. The body begins to rotate in the layout position as the legs rise. It then begins to tuck as the diver reaches a near vertical position. The tuck is made by thrusting the arms forward and down toward the shins as the legs bend at the knees and the hips flex. As the knees draw toward the chest, the hands grasp high on the shins and pull the legs into a tight tuck position.

6-7-8. The body remains in a tight tuck until the diver nears 1½ somersaults. At this moment the water can be sighted. The legs are then released, and the body is straightened with a quick straightening of the legs and an extension of the arms overhead in a semi-lateral direction. The eyes continue to sight the water as the hands reach nearly straight down and the body completely straightens. The entry is made in a very nearly vertical position.

INWARD DOUBLE SOMERSAULT – TUCK

(One Meter) 404C

INWARD DOUBLE SOMERSAULT - TUCK

(One Meter)

1. In preparation for the take-off, the arms are lifted over the head. The legs flex with the hips and shoulders directly over the balls of the feet. The head is tilted downward slightly.

2. The body rises from the board with a forceful extension of the legs, ankles, and toes. In the same motion, the hips are driven upward as the arms, head, and shoulders thrust downward.

3. As the hips continue to rise, the knees are drawn toward the chest. The arms, aided by the ducking of the head, continue to whip downward in chase of the legs.

4-5-6. The hands grasp the legs at the shins and pull the knees tight against the chest. The head continues to duck, and the arms are held close to the sides during the tuck.

7. As the body reaches a "sitting" position, the hands release the legs, which snap down toward the water as the head and shoulders are lifted to help stop the spin. The body begins to straighten for the entry with the arms straight and at the sides.

8. The legs extend nearly straight down as the head remains erect. The diver enters the water slightly short of vertical.

INWARD DOUBLE SOMERSAULT - PIKE

(Three Meter) 404B

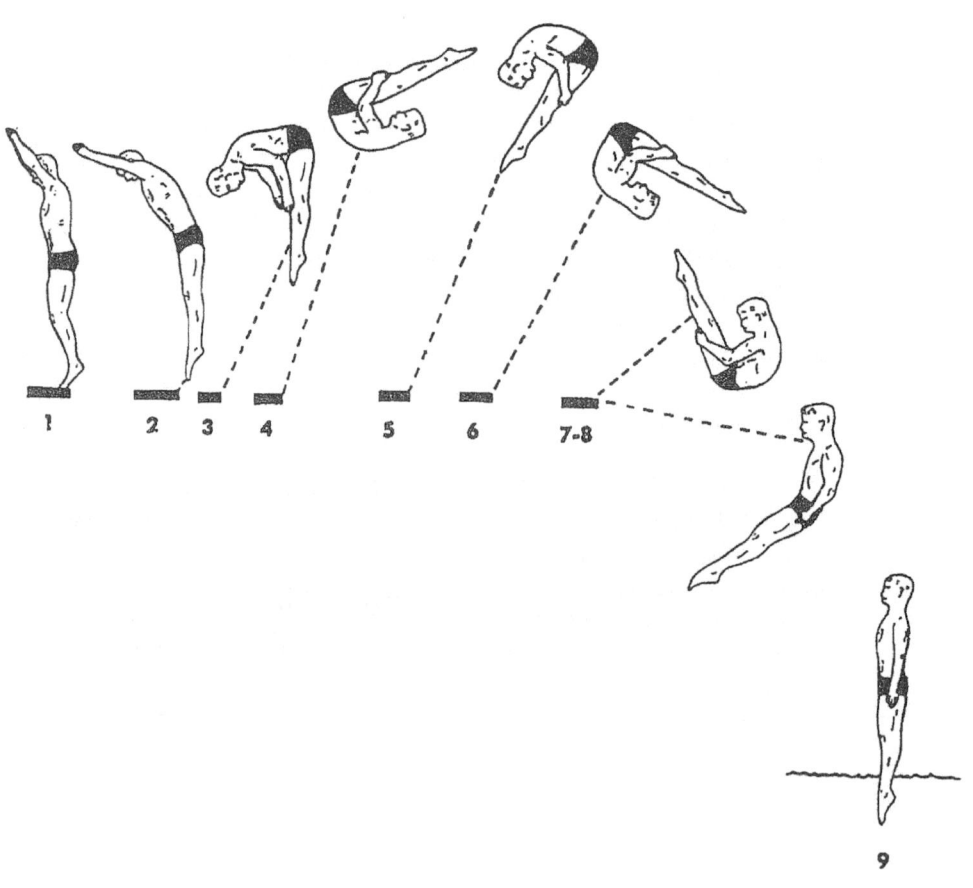

INWARD DOUBLE SOMERSAULT - PIKE

(Three Meter)

1. The take-off is made with the arms lifted over the head and in front of the face. The head is held erect as the legs, ankles, and toes flex with the weight of the hips and shoulders directly above the balls of the feet.

2. The diver leaves the board with the legs completely extending and the hips driving upward. In the same motion, the arms, shoulders, and head whip downward as the body bends at the waist.

3. The arms continue to whip downward in chase of the legs. The body begins to rotate with the head remaining ducked and the hips continuing to rise.

4-5-6. When the hands meet the legs, they clasp behind, and slightly above, the knees. The chest is then pulled close to the legs, with an effort to pull the face to the knees. The elbows are held close to the sides during the somersault.

7. As the body rotates to a near "sitting" position, the legs are released and pushed down toward the water. The head and shoulders are held erect to stop the spin of the somersault.

8. As the legs push toward the water and the head and shoulders remain erect, the body begins to straighten for the feet-first entry.

9. The legs extend nearly straight down with the arms placed at the sides as the diver enters the water slightly short of vertical.

INWARD 2½ SOMERSAULTS - TUCK

(Three Meter) 405C

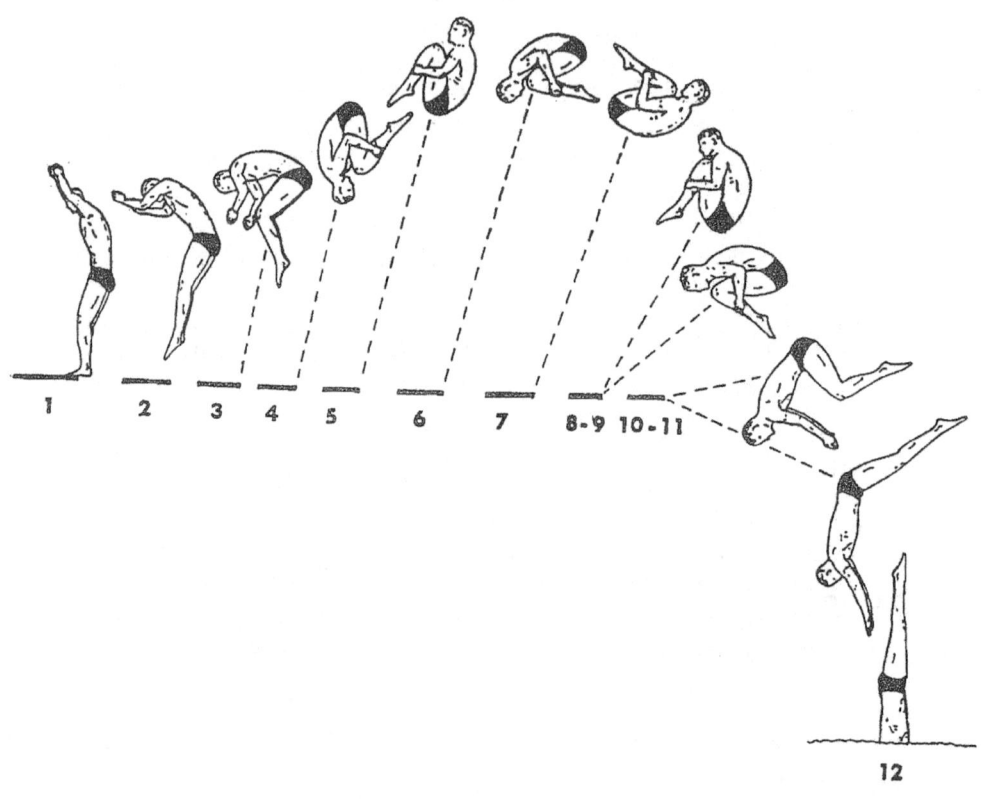

INWARD 2½ SOMERSAULTS - TUCK

(Three Meter)

1. Prior to the take-off, the legs flex and push down on the board. This action is aided by the downward push of the hips, which are located directly above the balls of the feet. In the same action, the arms rise over the head and in front of the face while the head is tilted down slightly.

2. The body rises from the board with a forceful extension of the legs, ankles, and toes. At the same time, the hips thrust sharply upward, and the arms begin to whip down toward the legs. The head stays erect as the body begins to bend at the waist. Emphasis is placed on keeping the head and shoulders directly over the end of the board until the hips begin to rise.

3. As the hips continue to rise, the knees are drawn toward the chest, with the heels rising toward the buttocks. The arms, aided by the ducking of the head, continue to whip downward in chase of the legs.

4-5

6-7-8. The hands grasp the legs at the shins and pull the knees tightly to the chest. The elbows are held close to the sides during the tuck.

9-10. As the diver completes approximately 2¼ somersaults, the water comes into view. The hands release the legs, which extend rapidly toward a vertical position as the arms quickly extend semi-laterally over the head.

11-12. With the eyes fixed on the water, the body is made straight for a vertical entry by raising the legs to a vertical position and stretching the arms over the head.

INWARD 2½ SOMERSAULTS - PIKE

(Three Meter) 405B

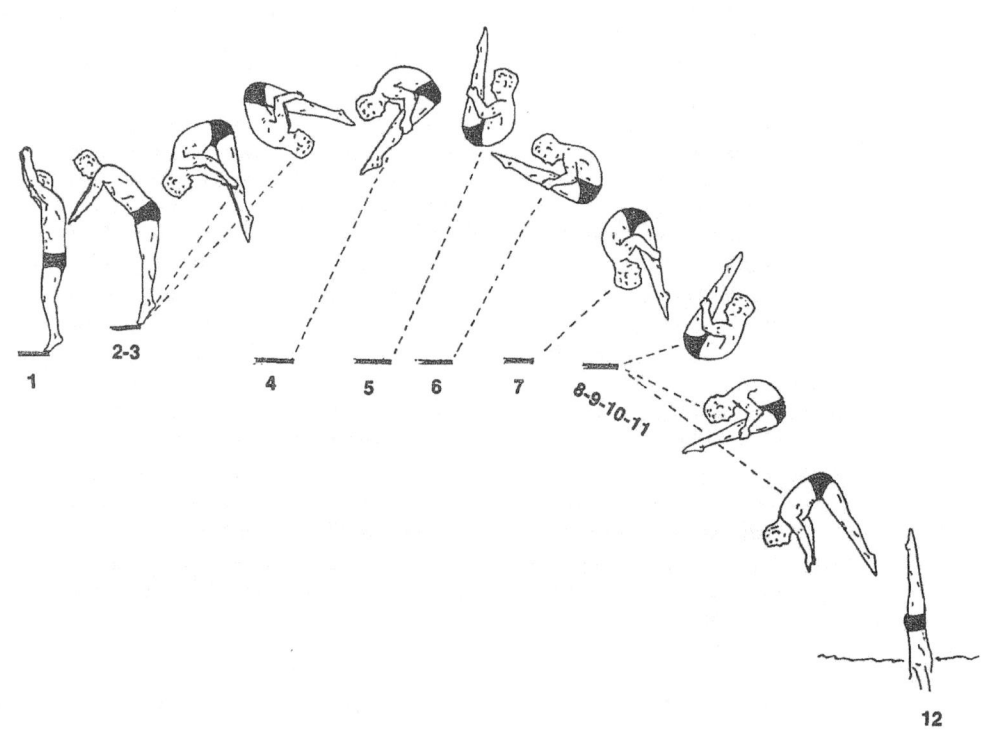

INWARD 2½ SOMERSAULTS - PIKE

(Three Meter)

1. The diver stands erect on the board with the arms swung overhead and with the head in an erect position.
2. The legs extend, and the hips push upward as the arms, head and shoulders drive downward toward the legs. These movements are all initiated before the feet leave the board.
3. The body continues to bend at the waist as the arms, head and shoulders move toward the legs.

4-5-6-7
8-9-10. The hands clasp the legs behind the knees and pull the legs in tight toward the chest. The face is held close to the knees and the arms are held close to the sides.

11. The legs are released as they pass the second somersault and the eyes sight the water while the arms begin to extend semi-laterally overhead for the entry.
12. The entry is made in a vertical position with the body straight.

INWARD 3½ SOMERSAULTS - TUCK

(Three Meter) 407C

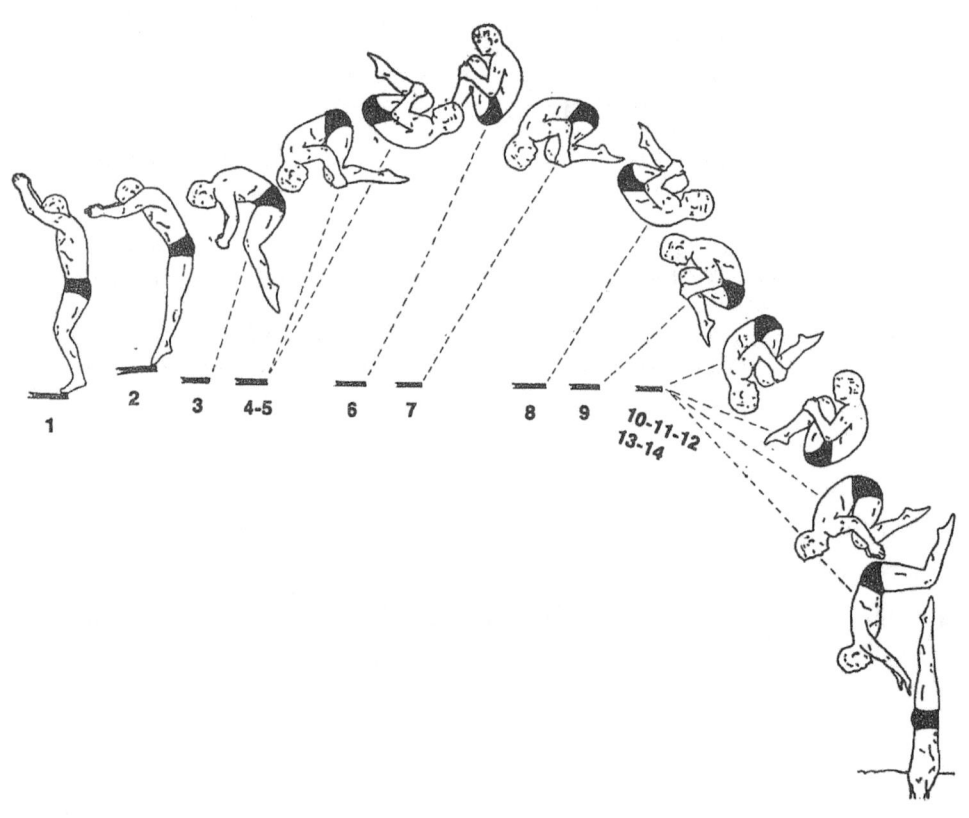

INWARD 3½ SOMERSAULTS - TUCK

(Three Meter)

1-2. The diver prepares to leave the board by swinging the arms overhead and with the eyes fixed on a spot at the far end of the board. The legs flex and the hips drive upward as the arms, head and shoulders push downward, bending at the hips.

3. The upper body continues to drive downward as the knees begin to draw in toward the chest.

4-5-6-7
8-9-10-11. The hands grasp the legs at the shins and pull the knees in tight to the chest with the arms close to the sides.

12. The hands release the legs slightly after the third somersault is completed and the eyes spot the water. They quickly straighten as the water is sighted and the arms begin to extend overhead.

13. The legs quickly straighten as the arms begin to extend overhead.

14. The arms continue to extend overhead as the body straightens to a near vertical position for the entry.

GROUP V – TWISTING DIVES

FORWARD DIVE, HALF - TWIST - PIKE

(One Meter) 5111B

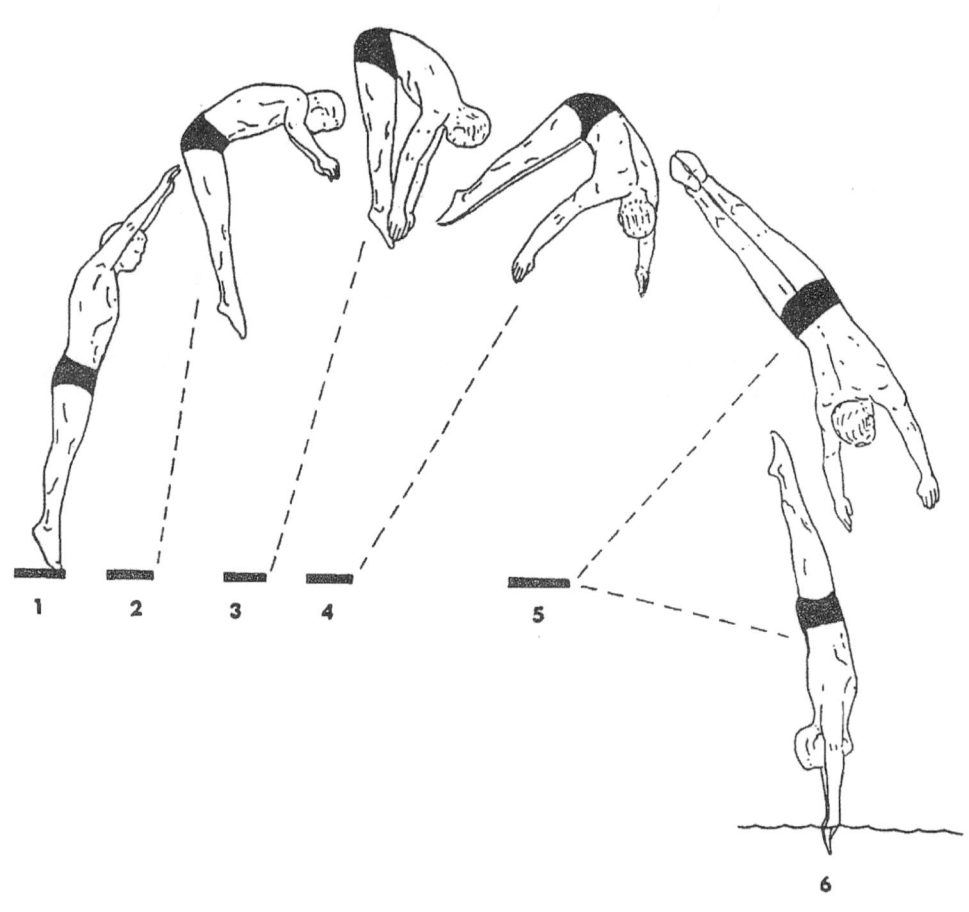

FORWARD DIVE, HALF - TWIST - PIKE

(One Meter)

1. Prior to the take-off, the arms swing forward and upward to a position above the head, which is held erect.

2. As soon as the diver leaves the board, the hips lift upward, and the legs extend while the arms, head and shoulders push downward with a bend at the hips.

3. The hands touch the toes at the peak of the dive where the legs are in a vertical line. The eyes sight the water where the entry will be made.

4. The hips and shoulders start the twist immediately following the touch. The extended arms, about shoulder width apart, are held overhead and slightly in front of the head to aid in balancing the body during the twist. The legs move upward as the twist progresses.

5. The body straightens as the half twist is completed. The eyes continue to spot the water.

6. The body then reaches for the water, with the entry slightly short of vertical.

FORWARD DIVE, HALF - TWIST - LAYOUT

(One Meter) 5111A

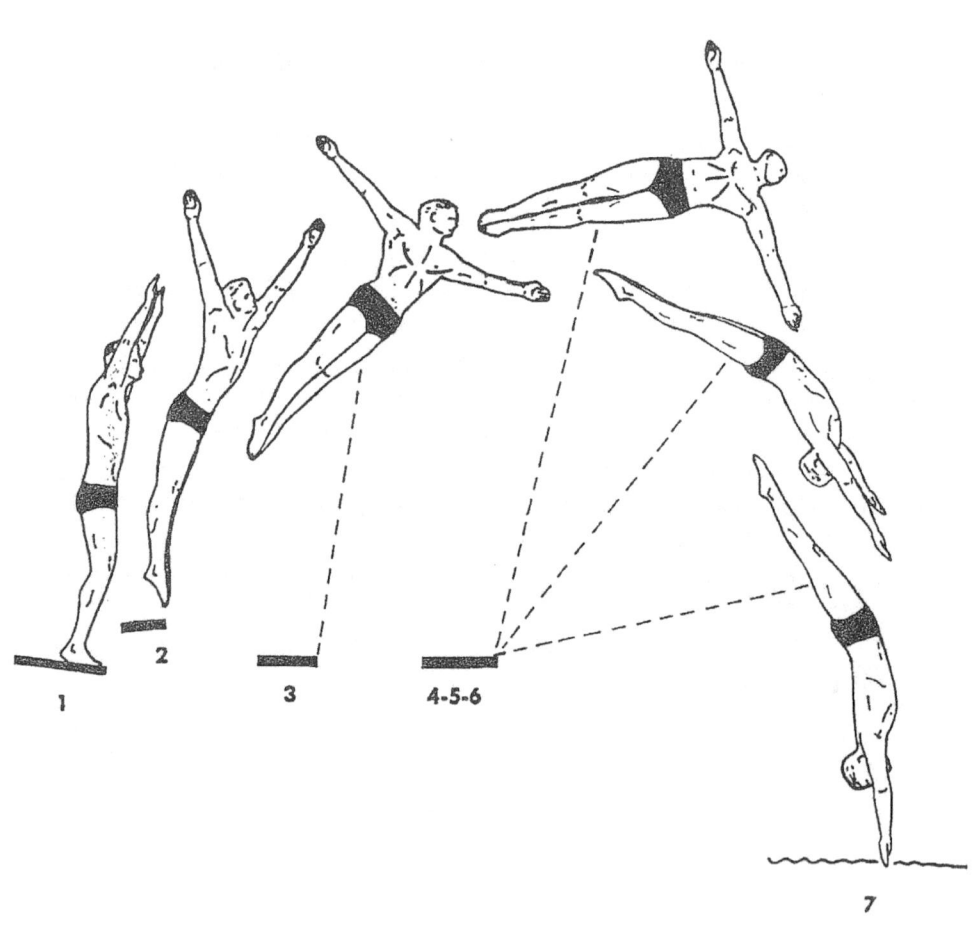

FORWARD DIVE, HALF - TWIST - LAYOUT

(One Meter)

1. The take-off is made with the diver leaning slightly forward as the arms rise in front of the head, which is held erect. The eyes sight the water in front of the board. The legs, ankles and toes extend to lift the diver from the board.
2. The arms begin to spread laterally toward a position level with the shoulders while the body begins to twist on its side. When the twist begins, the head is still held erect and straight with the eyes sighting the other end of the pool.
3. The legs continue to move upward and the shoulder tilts downward as the arms spread laterally to a position level with the shoulders near the peak of the dive.
4. When the body is nearly horizontal at the peak of the dive, one arm points at the water while the other points nearly straight up. At this moment, the head turns slightly sideward and downward and sights the water by LOOKING OVER the shoulder.
5. The eyes continue to spot the water as the body descends. The arms remain in a swan position until the entry into the water.
6. The upper arm extends laterally over the head to meet the lower arm just prior to the entry. The half-twist is completed by the time the arms are brought together over the head.
7. The entry is made with a slight arch in the back and slightly short of vertical.

FORWARD DIVE, ONE TWIST - PIKE

(Three Meter) 5112B

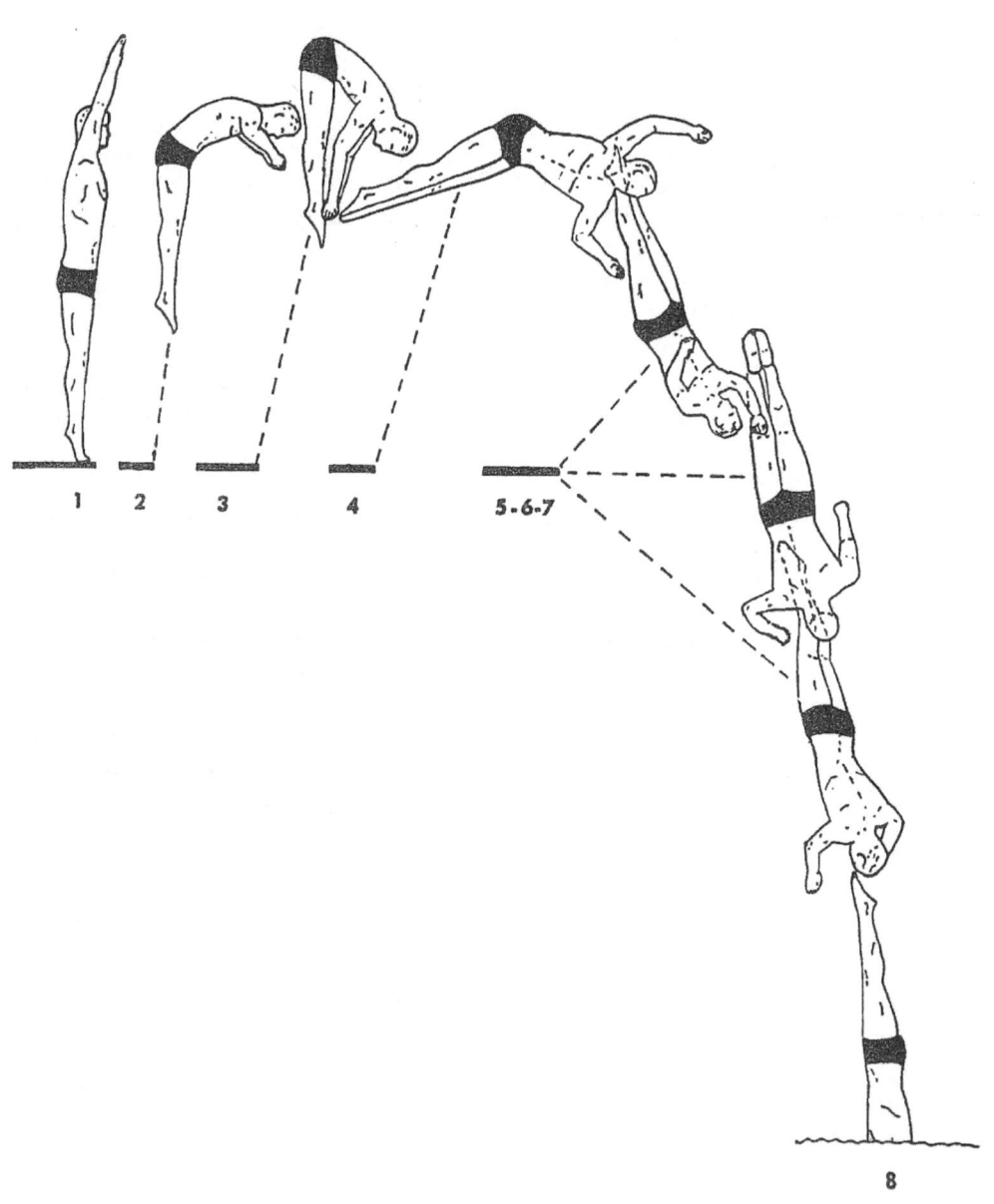

FORWARD DIVE, ONE TWIST - PIKE

(Three Meter)

1. At the take-off, the arms are raised above the head as the legs extend.

2. The hips move upward and the body bends at the waist as the legs extend and the arms, head and shoulders move downward.

3. The hands touch the toes near the peak of the dive with the legs vertical and the eyes sighting the approximate point of entry.

4. The twist is started as the diver passes the peak of the dive. As the body begins to straighten, one arm, bent at the elbow, crosses in front of the body at waist level while the other is raised above the head. The legs continue to move upward during the twisting action.

5-6. The twisting position is held until nearly one full twist is completed.

7. The arms are brought together at about shoulder level as the twist nears completion. The eyes then again sight the water where the entry is to be made.

8. When the water is sighted, the arms thrust overhead in line with the body and the entry is made slightly short of vertical.

FORWARD DIVE, ONE TWIST - LAYOUT

(One Meter) 5112A

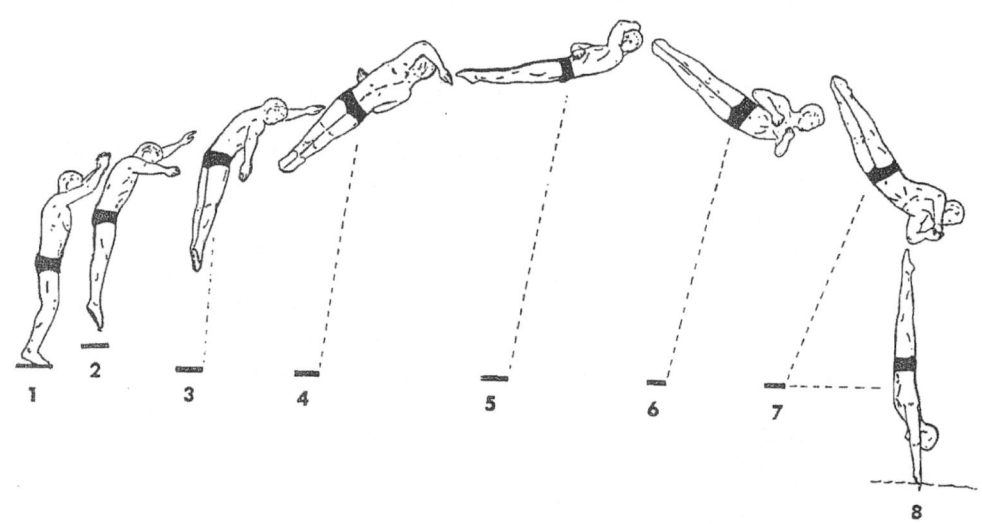

FORWARD DIVE, ONE TWIST - LAYOUT

(One Meter)

1. At the take-off, the arms are raised in front of the head. The head is erect with the eyes looking at the water about five feet in front of the board.

2. As the diver leaves the board, the arms begin to extend in a semi-lateral direction. The arms remain level while the eyes still spot the water.

3-4. The legs then push upward with little or no bend in the waist. During this action, one arm, bent at the elbow, is extended over the head while the other, also bent at the elbow, drops down and crosses in front of the stomach. As soon as the arms are placed in position, the head begins to turn in the direction of the arm that is overhead.

5. As the body completes half of a twist, at which time the body is nearly horizontal, the upper arm begins to pull down toward the body and in front of the head. The head continues to turn and looks over the shoulder for the water.

6. When the water comes into view, the upper arm continues to drop down as the lower arm is being raised in front of the chest.

7. With the head in line with the body and the eyes focused on the point of entry, the hands are brought together at chin level, ready to be extended for the entry.

8. The arms quickly extend over the head, and the body stretches for an entry slightly short of vertical.

FORWARD SOMERSAULT, HALF – TWIST - PIKE

(One Meter) 5121B

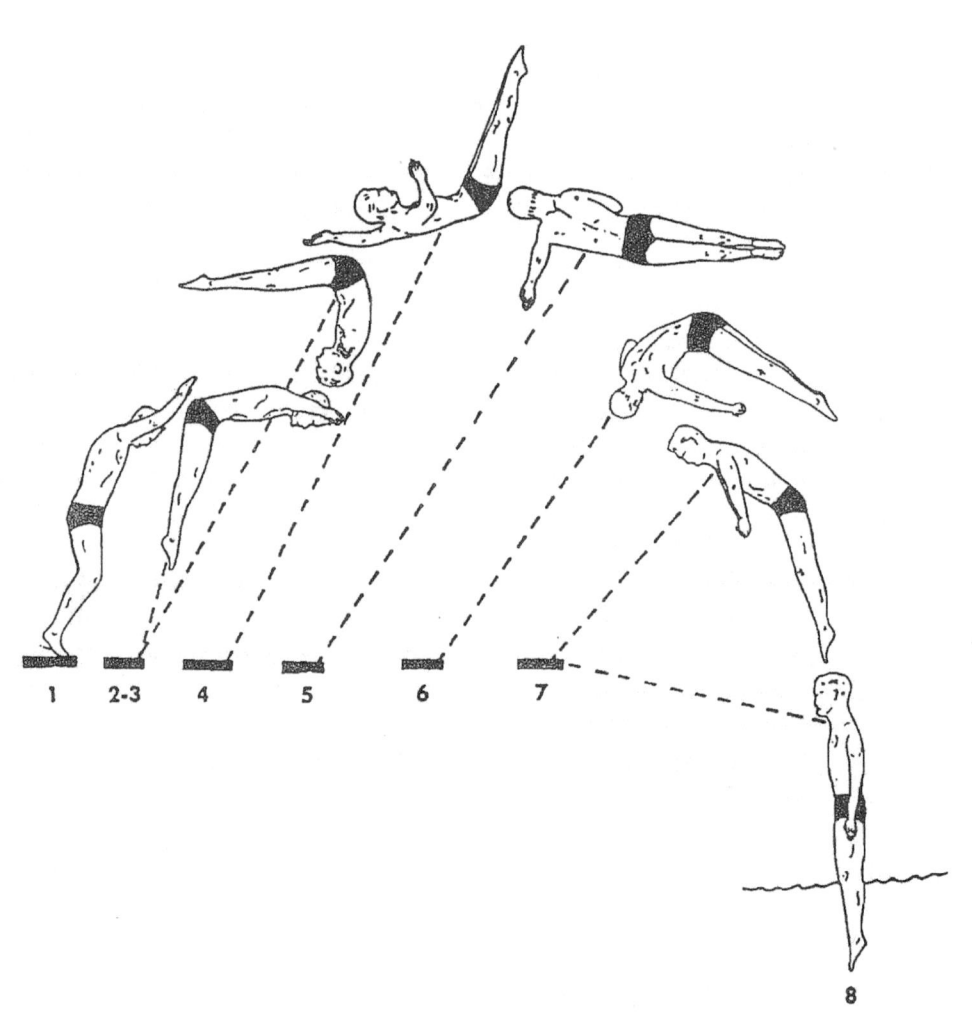

FORWARD SOMERSAULT, HALF – TWIST - PIKE

(One Meter)

1. At the take-off, the arms are lifted upward in front of the head. The head tilts down slightly with the eyes sighting the water in front of the board. The legs begin to extend with the hips moving upward behind the body.

2. The diver begins to form an open pike position by bending at the waist as the hips move upward behind the body and the arms move laterally toward the level of the shoulders. The head is kept in line with the body, and the eyes remain focused on the water.

3. The open pike position is formed when the body is bent at right angles at the waist and the arms are at shoulder level. The head is tilted toward the chest with the eyes sighting the knees.

4-5. As the diver nears the peak of the dive, one arm, bent at the elbow, moves across the body in front of the chest while the other arm, also bent at the; elbow, moves above the head. The head turns in the direction of the upper. arm. This action starts the twisting of the body.

6. The diver sights the water as the twisting action is performed. When the water is sighted, and the half-twist nears completion, the arm that crossed the body is pulled back to the side to help stop the twisting action and to balance the dive.

7. With the twist completed, the diver begins to straighten the body for the entry into the water by dropping the arms to the sides and pulling the legs down toward the water. The eyes continue to sight the water so the proper adjustment for the entry can be made.

8. The entry is slightly short of vertical, with the body straight, the head erect, the arms at the sides, and the hands on the thighs.

FORWARD SOMERSAULT, HALF – TWIST - LAYOUT

(One Meter) 5121A

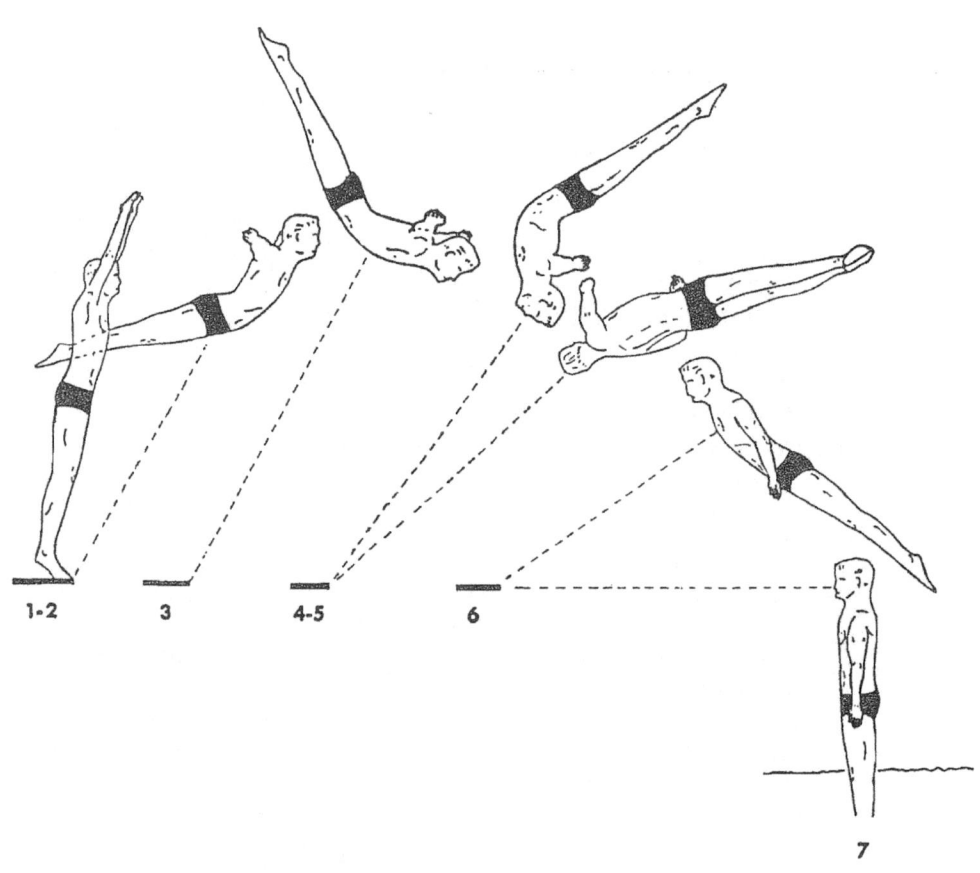

FORWARD SOMERSAULT, HALF – TWIST - LAYOUT

(One Meter)

1. The take-off is made with the head held erect, the arms lifted above the head, and the body leaning slightly forward. The diver should concentrate on pressing the toes into the board on the take-off as the arms pull down laterally from overhead toward shoulder level.

2. As the diver leaves the board, the head remains up, the back arches, and the legs begin to rise behind the body. The upward action of the legs is aided by a forceful lateral movement of the arms from above the head to a position level with the shoulders.

3-4. The layout position with the arms extended at shoulder level continues until the diver passes the peak of the dive. To maintain the layout position, the head must remain up.

5. Soon after the diver passes the peak of the dive, one arm crosses in front of the chest and the other bends at the elbow and is pulled in toward the side of the body. The head moves in the direction of the arm that crosses the body.

6. Near the completion of the twist, the water is sighted, and the arms move toward the sides of the body to stop the twist and maintain balance in the dive. The head remains up so that the body can stay in a layout position.

7. The entry is made slightly short of vertical with the arms at the sides and the hands on the thighs. The head is erect and in line with the body.

FORWARD SOMERSAULT, ONE TWIST-FREE POSITION (One Meter) 5122D

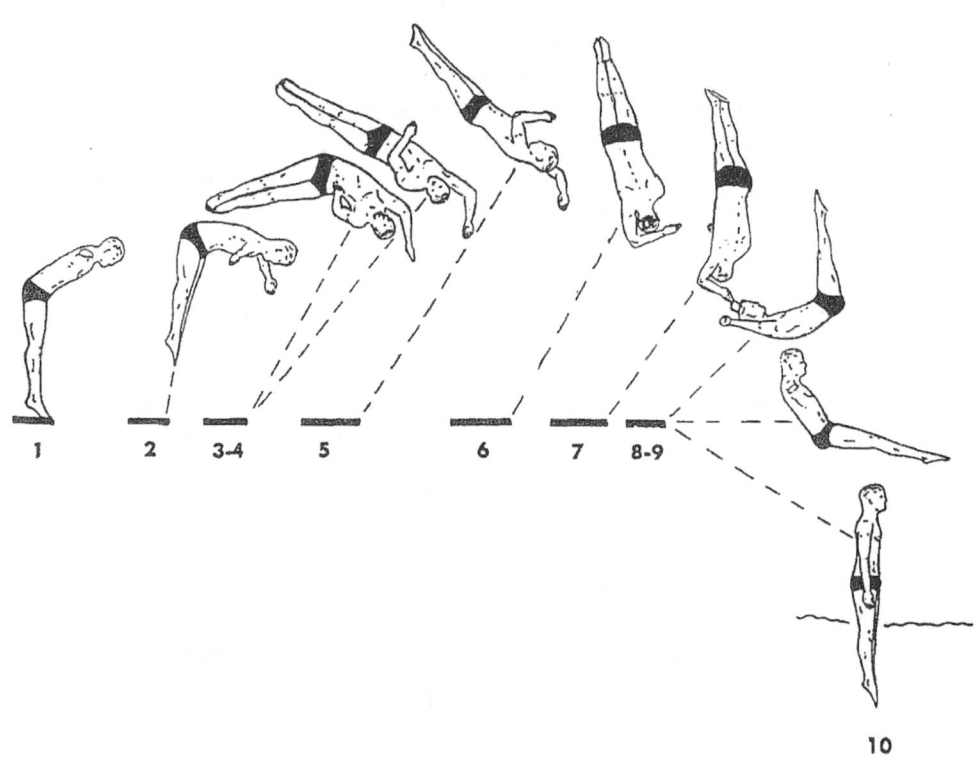

FORWARD SOMERSAULT, ONE TWIST- FREE POSITION (One Meter)

1. The legs extend, and the hips move upward behind the body as the diver is set to leave the board. In the same movement, the body bends at the waist and the arms pull down laterally toward the level of the shoulders. This action aids in the rotation of the body. The head remains in line with the body, with the eyes sighting the water.

2-3-4
5-6-7. With the continued upward movement of the hips, the arms move into the twisting position. Bending at the elbow, one arm crosses in front of the chest while the other arm lifts above the head and pulls back at the elbow. The arm positions permit the body to straighten for the twist movement. The head moves in the direction of the upper arm.

8-9. At the completion of one twist, the twisting action is stopped by extending the arms to a position at right angles to the body and at shoulder level. Great emphasis is placed on the top arm pulling down to shoulder level from above the head. In the same motion, the diver bends at the waist by pulling the head and chest in the direction of the legs. This puts the diver in the open pike position.

10. The entry is made by forcing the legs down toward the water, with the head remaining upright and the eyes fixed on the other end of the pool. This permits the body to straighten from the pike position. The arms are placed at the sides, and the entry is made in a vertical position.

FORWARD SOMERSAULT, DOUBLE TWIST-FREE POSITION (One Meter) 5124D

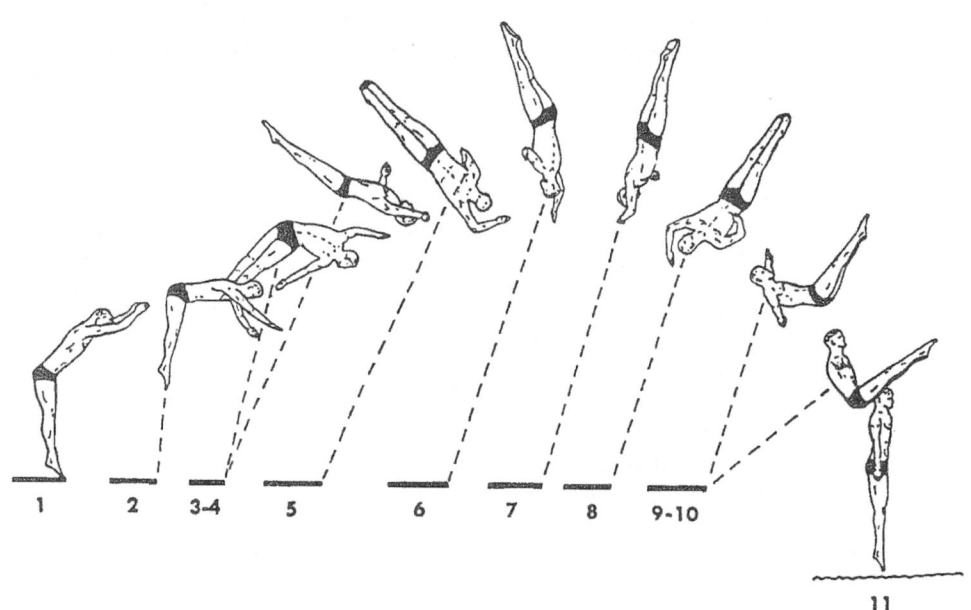

FORWARD SOMERSAULT, DOUBLE TWIST- FREE POSITION (One Meter)

1. At the take-off, the body leans slightly forward with the arms extended above, and in front of, the head. The head is in line with the body, with the eyes fixed on the water in front of the board.
2. As the diver leaves the board, the legs fully extend, and the hips are thrust upward behind the body while the arms drop laterally to shoulder level with force to place the body in the open pike position. The eyes remain focused on the water.

3-4-5
6-7-8. With the legs and hips continuing to move upward, the twist is initiated by bending both arms at the elbow with one crossing in front of the chest while the other lifts over the head and pulls back at the elbow. The arm above the head is usually bent at the elbow, with the force pulling backward at the elbow. The head turns in the direction of the arm that is lifted above it. The action of the arms and the forceful lifting of the legs permit the body to lay out, which allows for a quick twisting action.

9. The two twists are completed before the arms begin to pull to the sides away from the body. The twist stops when the top arm is pulled forward and laterally down toward the side while the other is pulled back from across the body. This action also permits the body to again pike by pulling the chest toward the legs.

10-11. While the arms are moving to the sides of the body for the entry, the legs are forced down toward the water, changing the pike position to a straight position. The dive is controlled during this action by keeping the head erect. The entry is made slightly short of vertical with the arms at the side and the hands on the thighs.

FORWARD 1 ½ SOMERSAULTS, HALF – TWIST - TUCK

(One Meter) 5131C

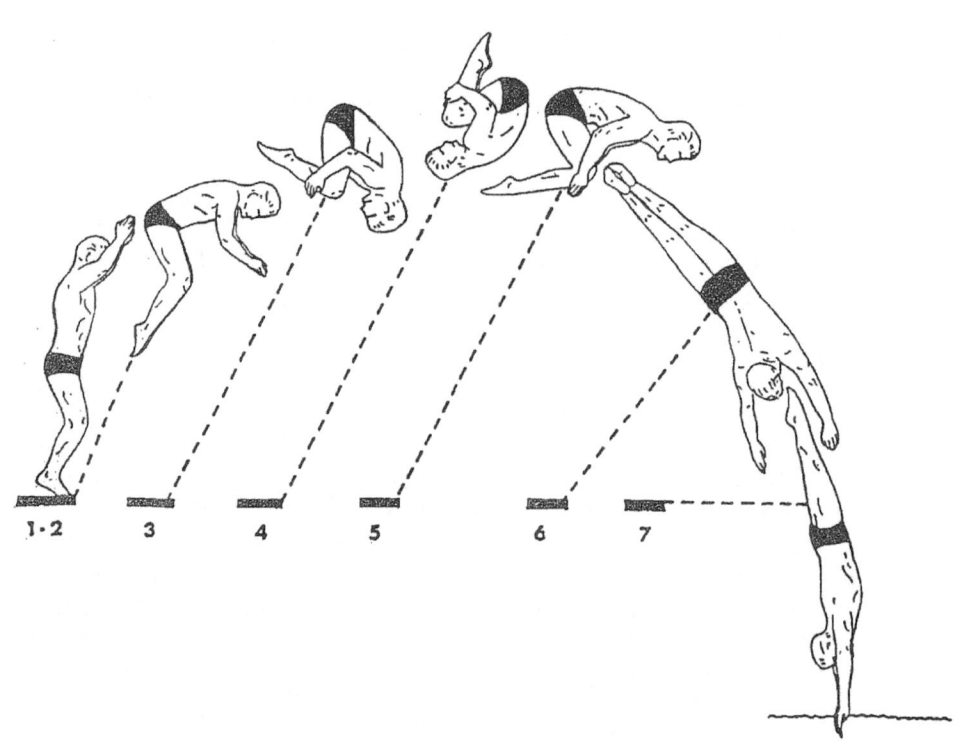

FORWARD 1½ SOMERSAULTS, HALF – TWIST-TUCK (One Meter)

1. At the take-off, the arms are lifted above, and in front of, the head, which is kept in line, with the eyes on the water in front of the board.
2. As the diver leaves the board, the legs extend, and the hips push upward behind the body while the arms and head go downward in chase of the legs. At the same time, the knees bend, and the feet move in the direction of the buttocks.
3-4. The arms continue to move toward the legs until the hands grasp the shins and pull the knees to the chest. The heels pull in close to the buttocks, and the head is pulled down with the chin close to the chest.
5. When the body completes approximately 1¼ somersaults, the hands release the legs, the head lifts slightly with the eyes sighting the water,

    and the diver straightens the body by extending the legs and then reaching overhead with the arms.
6. When the arms extend over the head, one shoulder drops down while the other lifts up. This causes the body to twist, and the twist can be controlled by the movement of the arms. The eyes sight the water where the entry is to be made.
7. When the half-twist is completed, the arms close over the head and the hands clasp for the entry, which is slightly short of vertical.

FORWARD 1 ½ SOMERSAULTS, HALF-TWIST-PIKE

(One Meter) 5131B

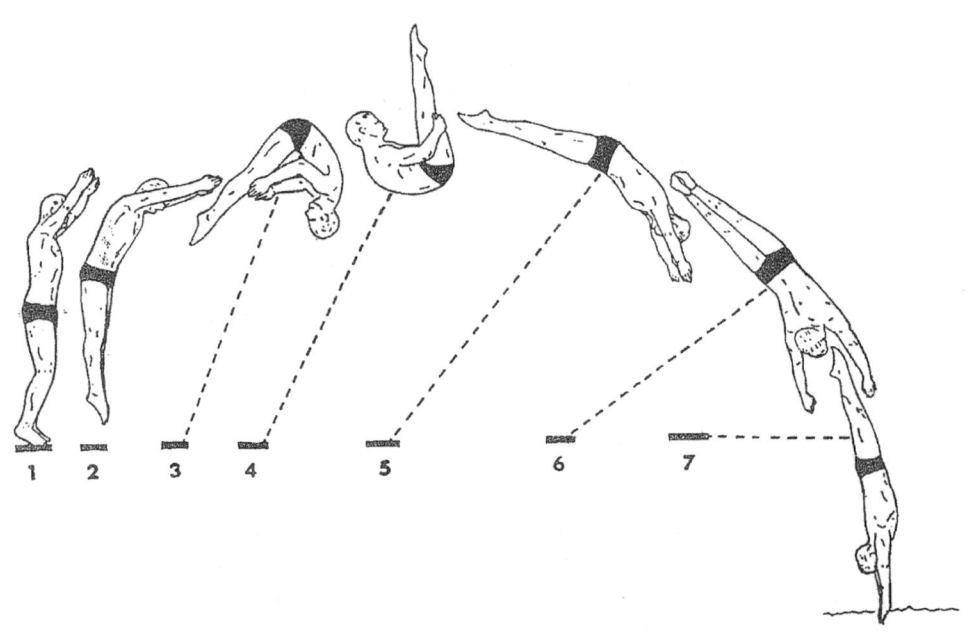

FORWARD 1 ½ SOMERSAULTS, HALF – TWIST - PIKE

(One Meter)

1. At the take-off, the arms are lifted above, and in front of, the head. The diver leans slightly forward; the head is in line with the body; and the eyes are fixed on the water in front of the board.

2. As the diver leaves the board, the legs extend, pushing the hips upward behind the body. The arms and head simultaneously move down toward the legs to form an open pike position.

3-4. The arms and head continue to move in chase of the legs while the hips continue to move upward. The rotation of the body is furthered when the hands grasp the legs behind the knees and pull the legs toward the chest and head.

5. When 1¼ somersaults are completed, the hands release the legs and the diver begins to straighten by extending the arms over the head while the legs continue to move upward. During this action, the eyes sight the water at the approximate point of entry.

6. As the arms extend over the head, one shoulder drops slightly while the other lifts. This starts a twisting action that is controlled by movement of the arms and the firmness of the hips and legs.

7. At the completion of the half-twist, the hands clasp overhead for the entry, which is slightly short of vertical.

FORWARD 1½ SOMERSAULTS, ONE TWIST-FREE POSITION (One Meter) 5132D

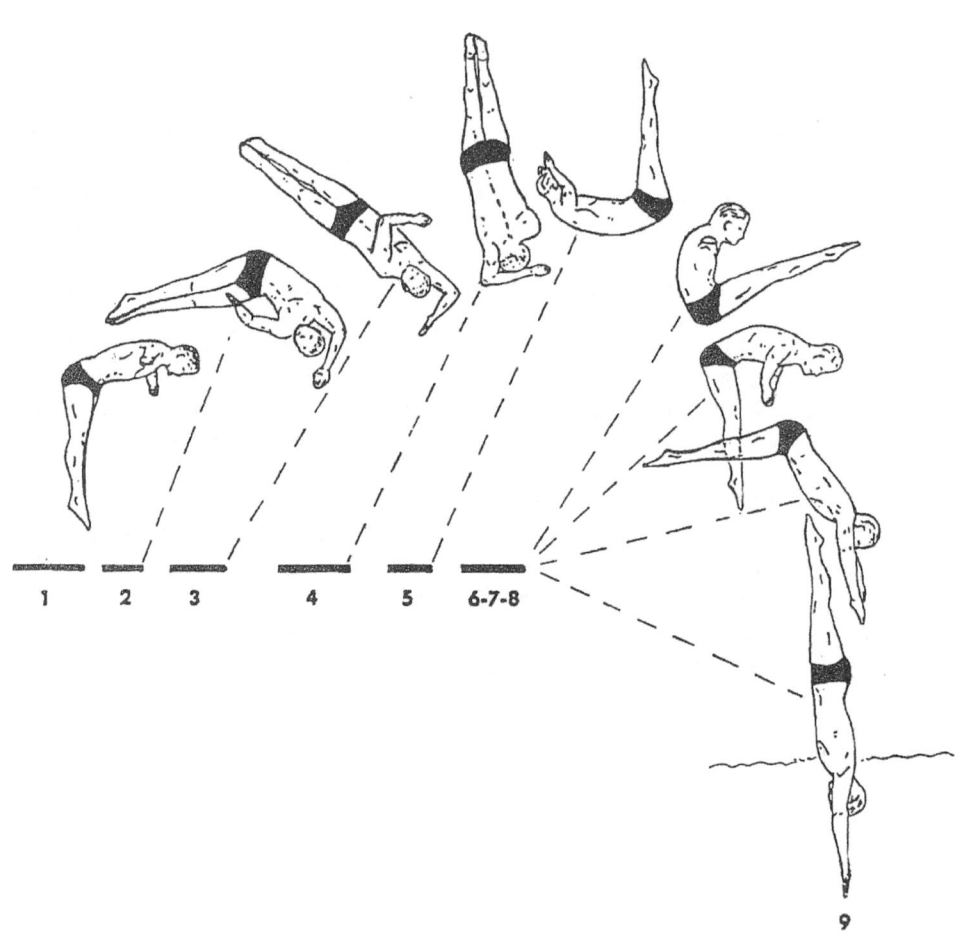

FORWARD 1½ SOMERSAULTS, ONE TWIST- FREE POSITION (One Meter)

1. The diver establishes an open pike position on leaving the board by extending the legs, pushing upward with the hips, bending at the waist and pulling the arms downward laterally to the shoulder level while sighting the water.

2-3-4. The twist is started with the arms bending at the elbow and placed with one arm across the chest level and the other arm above the head and pulling back at the elbow. The high position of the arms permits the body to straighten and allows for a fast twisting action.

5-6-7. At the completion of one twist, the top arm forcefully pulls downward from overhead and the lower arm pulls away from the chest and both arms are placed at shoulder level. Pulling the top arm downward permits the body to gain an open pike position.

8. The water comes into view as the body passes 1¼ somersaults. At this point, the legs press down past the vertical and then up behind the body while the arms reach down toward the water.

9. The eyes spot the point of entry as the arms extend over the head and the legs rise to straighten the body for a vertical entry.

FORWARD 1½ SOMERSAULTS, DOUBLE TWIST- FREE POSITION (Three Meter) 5134D

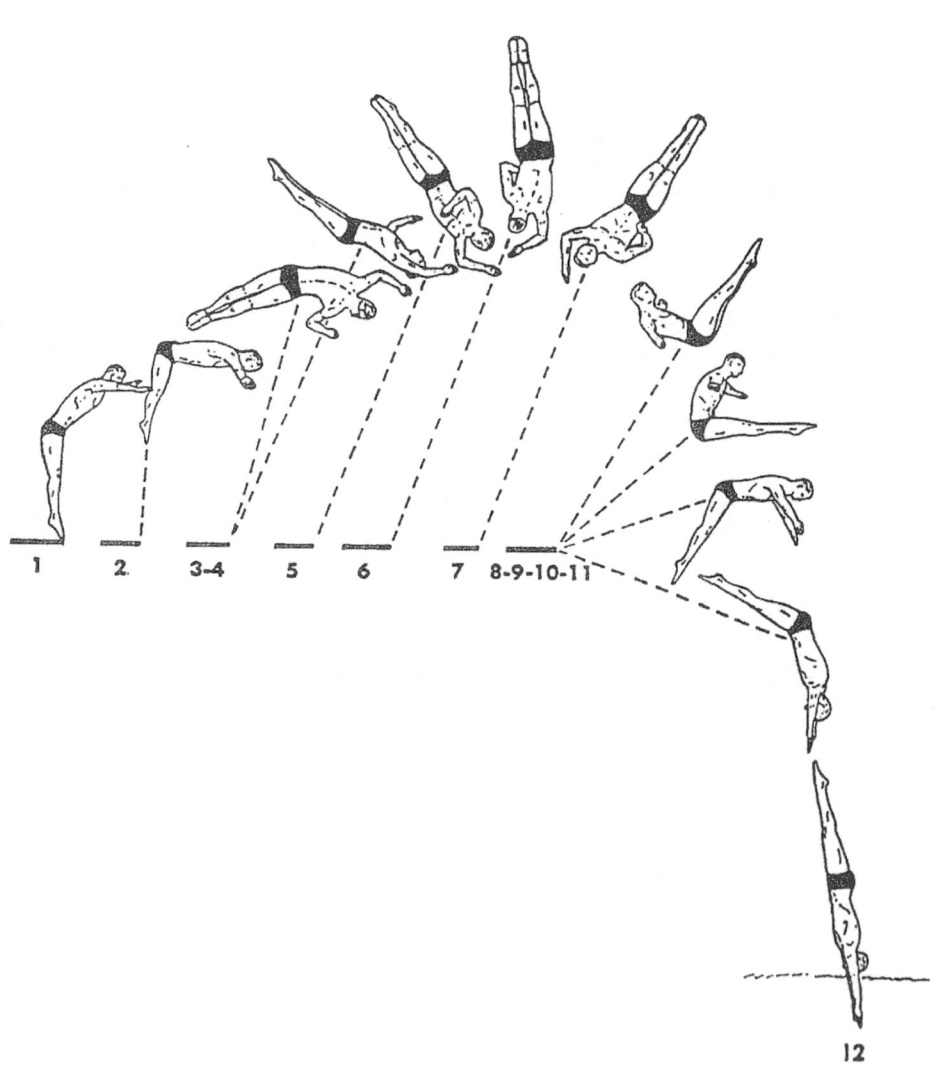

FORWARD 1½ SOMERSAULTS, DOUBLE TWIST-FREE POSITION (Three Meter)

1. At the take-off, the body leans slightly forward with the arms extended over the head. The head is kept in line with the body, and the eyes are fixed on the water in front of the board.

2. The legs, ankles, and toes completely extend as the diver leaves the board. The hips rise, and the body bends at the waist to assume a pike position. The arms pull down to a lateral position at right angles to the body, and the head remains in line with the body.

3-4

5-6-7. The twist is then initiated by a continued upward thrust of the hips. In the same motion, the arms help start the twist, with one arm extending across the body and pressing close to the chest. The other arm extends overhead and pulls back. Both arms bend at the elbow during the twisting action. The continued upward thrust of the legs places the body in a layout position permitting for a quick twisting action while the diver is nearly upside down.

8-9. The twisting action is stopped near the completion of the double twist, by lateral extension of the arms. In the same motion, the body bends at the waist, with the chest pressing toward the legs to form an open pike position. The head ducks as the body pikes.

10-11. The water comes into view as the diver passes 1¼ somersaults. The legs push down at this point, move past the vertical, and then press up behind the body as the arms reach down toward the water.

12. With the eyes spotting the water, the legs rise, and the arms extend over the head to straighten the body. The entry into the water is slightly short of vertical.

FORWARD 1½ SOMERSAULTS, TRIPLE TWIST-FREE POSITION (Three Meter) 5136D

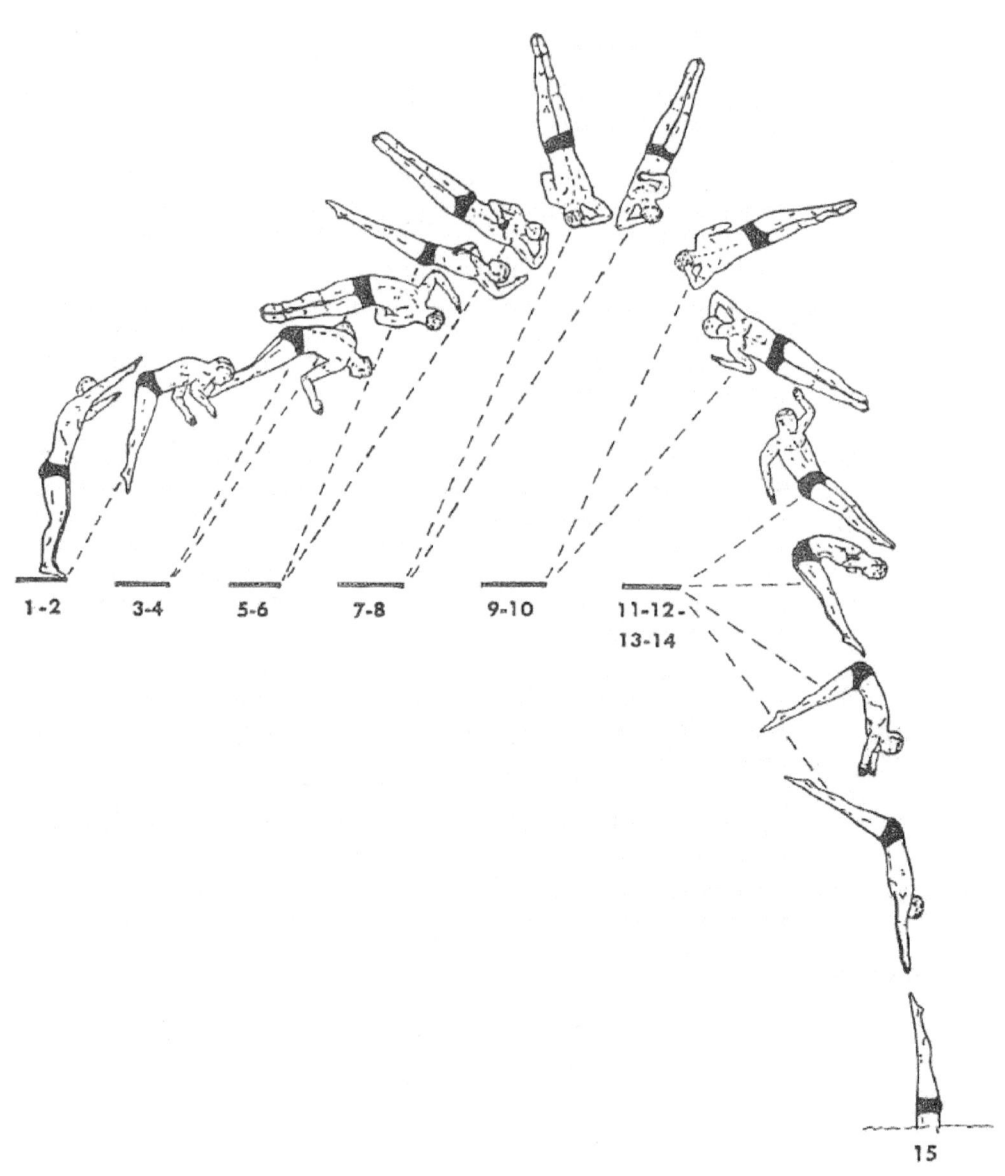

FORWARD 1½ SOMERSAULTS, TRIPLE TWIST-
FREE POSITION (Three Meter)

1. The body leans slightly forward with the arms overhead during the take-off. The eyes sight the water in front of the board.

2. As the diver leaves the board, the legs, feet, and toes extend completely, with the shoulders remaining on an even level. The hips rise, an<l the body begins to pike at the waist while the arms pull down laterally from overhead to a position level with the shoulders.

3-4-5. The twist is started with one arm crossing in front of the chest while the other is lifted above the head. Both arms bend at the elbow during these simultaneous movements. The diver pulls back with the elbow of the upper arm while pushing the lower arm farther across the chest. The hips continue to rise during the twisting action. Once the twisting action is started, the body straightens to permit a faster twisting motion. The position of the arms causes the body to straighten while twisting. Care should be taken to try not to twist too soon, or the somersault action will become extremely difficult to complete.

6-7

8-9-10. The diver continues to work the arms in the described twisting positions until three twists are completed. The legs must remain straight and together if control of the twists is to be maintained.

11-12. The arms pull outward and extend laterally at shoulder level at the completion of three twists. This stops the twisting and permits the diver to bend at the waist and assume a pike position. The water can be sighted during the somersaults, which permits the diver to adjust the somersault action in anticipation of the entry into the water. The sighting of the water usually occurs at about 1¼ somersaults.

13-14. Once the water is sighted and the diver regains the pike position, he reaches for the water while pushing the legs overhead to straighten the body for a near vertical entry.

15. The entry is made with the arms extended overhead and in line with the body. The body straightens completely, and the eyes continue to sight the water until the head passes through the surface.

FORWARD 2½ SOMERSAULTS, ONE TWIST - PIKE
(Free Position) (Three Meter) 5152D

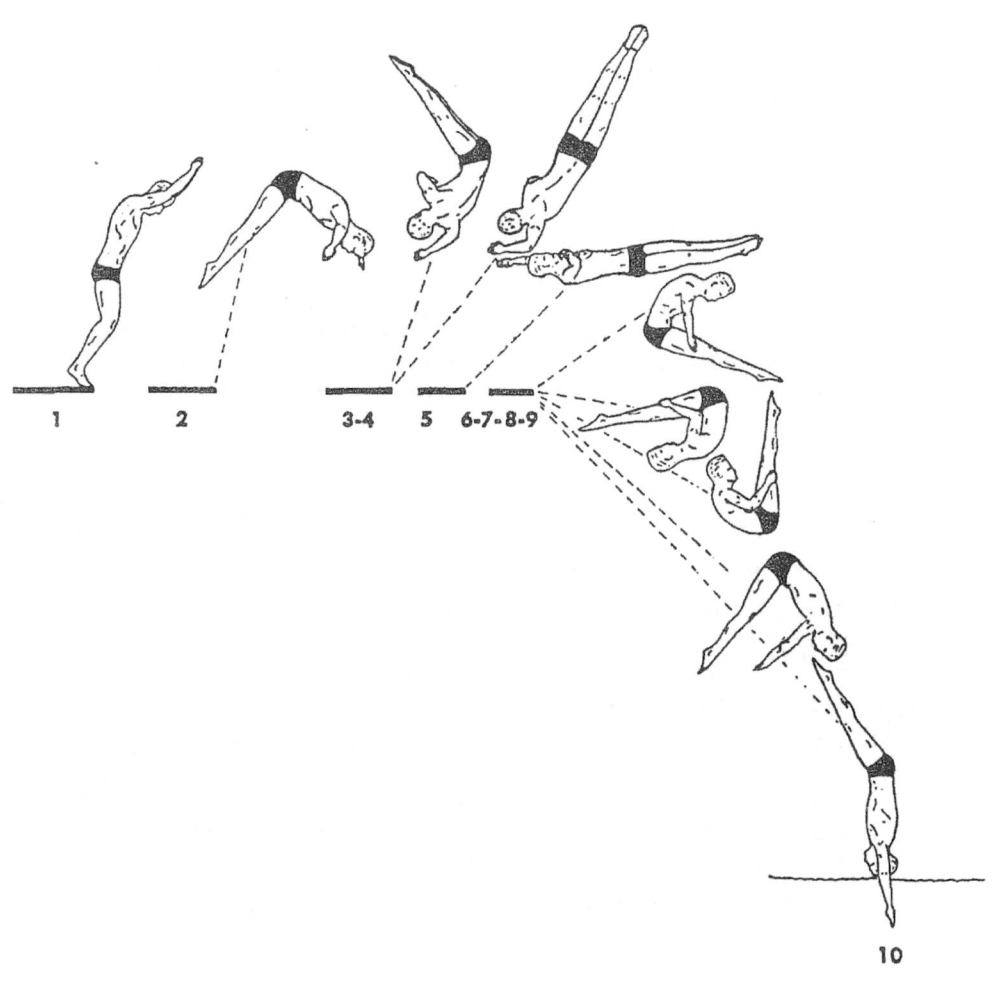

FORWARD 2½ SOMERSAULTS, ONE TWIST - PIKE

(Free Position) (Three Meter)

1. As the diver readies for the take-off, he leans slightly forward with the arms extended overhead. The head remains in line with the body, and the eyes sight the water in front of the board.

2. As the diver leaves the board, the legs, feet, and toes extend with force while the hips thrust upward. The body bends at the waist in the same motion with the arms, head and shoulders pushing downward. Emphasis is placed
on setting up a strong somersault action.

3-4-5. The twisting action is started as soon as the hips begin to rise by bending both arms at the elbow and placing one across the chest and the other above the head, pulling back at the elbow. During this twisting action, the legs rise, and the body momentarily assumes a layout position.

6-7-8. At the completion of one twist, the arms pull down toward the legs and

the body assumes a deep pike position. This is done by grasping behind the knees with the hands and drawing the head down as close to the knees as possible. This causes the diver to increase the speed of the somersault.

9. The hands release the legs as the diver completes 2¼ somersaults. The diver then sights the water and reaches for the point of entry as the legs are pushed overhead to help straighten the body.

10. As the diver approaches the water, the body completely straightens with the arms extended overhead and in line with the body. The entry is slightly short of vertical.

FORWARD 2½ SOMERSAULTS, DOUBLE TWIST-PIKE (Free Position) (Three Meter) 5154D

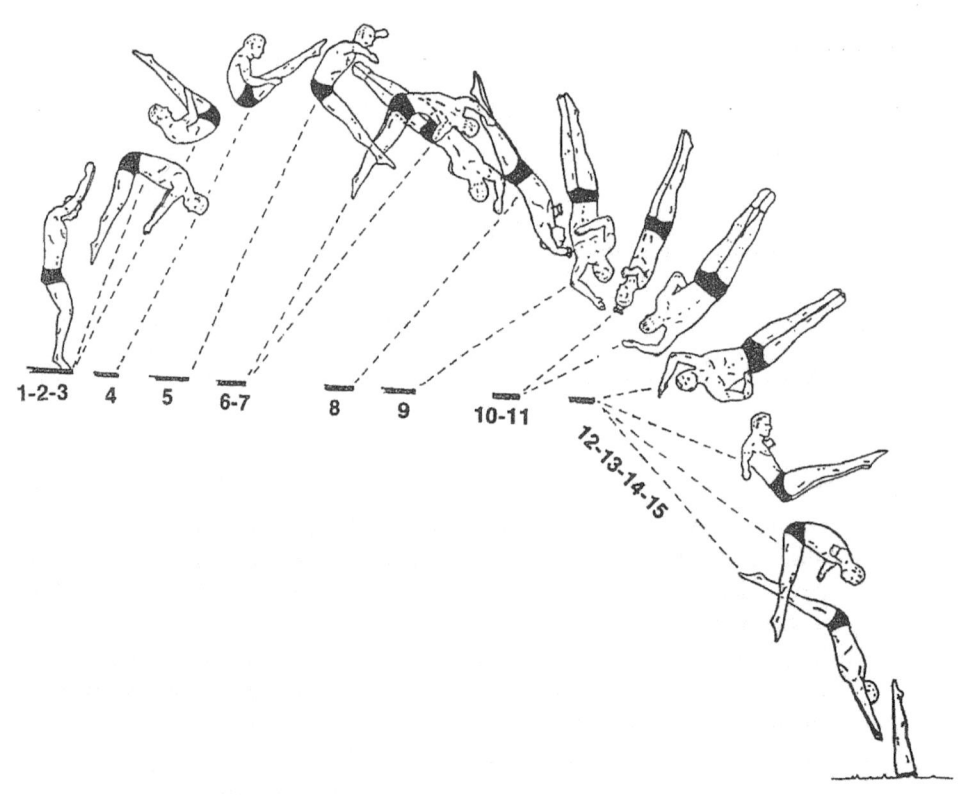

FORWARD 2½ SOMERSAULTS, DOUBLE TWIST-PIKE (Free Position) (Three Meter)

1. Before leaving the board, the legs began to extend with the arms extended overhead.
2. On leaving the board, the legs completely extend, the diver bends at the waist, and the arms, head and shoulders quickly push downward toward the legs.
3. The hands grasp the legs behind the knees and pull them toward the chest, keeping the head in and the arms close to the body.

4-5-6. The diver remains in the pike position until three quarters of a somersault has been completed, at which time the legs are released and the arms lift to a twisting position. Bent at the elbow, one arm crosses in front of the body at chest level while the other arm lifts above the head and pulls back at the elbow.

7-8-9

10-11. The high position of the arms aids in the body straightening while performing the twist action.

12-13. As the diver nears the completion of two twists, the arms begin to extend and move to a position at shoulder level. Pulling the top arm down to shoulder level permits the diver to bend over into the pike position. The water can be sighted at this point.

14-15. The arms extend overhead and reach for the point of entry slightly short of vertical as the body straightens.

BACK DIVE, HALF – TWIST – PIKE

(One Meter) 5211B

BACK DIVE, HALF - TWIST - PIKE

(One Meter)

1. Before the take-off, the arms swing forward and upward to a position overhead while the legs extend, and the body is erect.

2. As the diver leaves the board, the legs extend and rise toward the hands, which remain stationary. The legs are lifted by contracting the abdominal and thigh muscles.

3-4. The legs continue to rise toward the hands until the legs reach a near vertical position, at which time the hands move forward slightly and touch the insteps. The head remains in an erect position and the eyes sight the feet as the hands make the touch at the peak of the dive.

5-6-7. As the diver drops from the peak of the dive, the upper part of the body drops away from the legs, which remain vertical. During this action, one arm, bent at the elbow, rises above the head while the other crosses in front of the body at chest level to create a twisting movement. As the twist nears completion, the upper arm pulls down to meet the lower arm to stop the twisting movement. The water is sighted during this action. It is noted that this action also causes the legs to drop slightly so that the diver may line his body up for the entry.

8. When the water is sighted, and the twist is completed, the arms are extended over the head for the entry, which is slightly short of vertical.

BACK DIVE, HALF - TWIST - LAYOUT
(Three Meter) 5211A

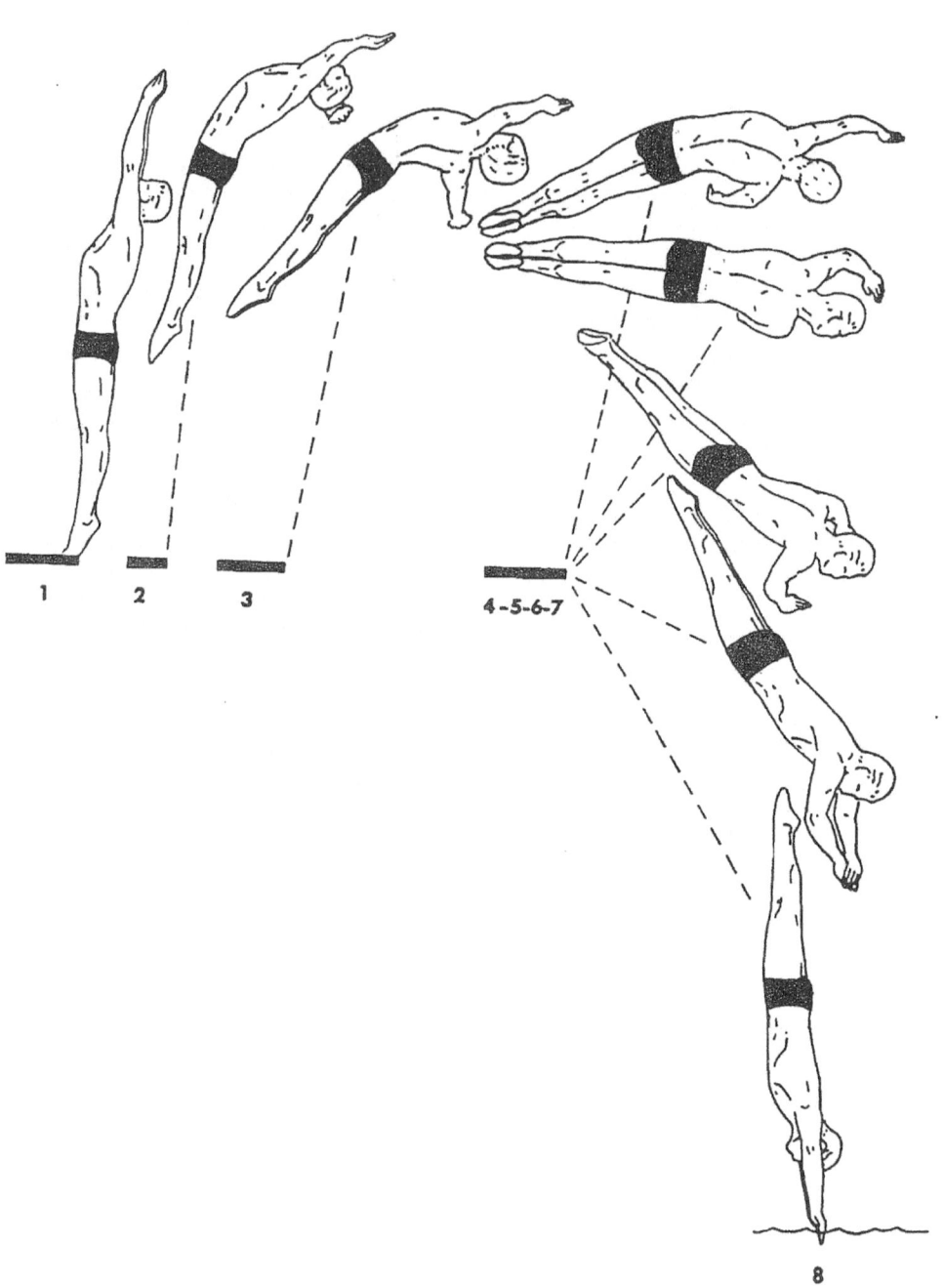

BACK DIVE, HALF - TWIST - LAYOUT

(Three Meter)

1. The diver rises from the board by extending the legs and pushing off with the toes. Simultaneously, the arms and head rise straight up.

2. Before leaving the board, the arm pull downward in a lateral motion toward the level of the shoulders and the head remains in line with the body.

3. At the peak of the dive, the head tilts back with a slight arch in the back.

4-5. The twist begins when the body assumes a near horizontal position at the peak of the dive. One arm bends at the elbow and is drawn across the chest while the other is lifted slightly over the head and pulled across the top of the body. The head is turned toward the lower arm to aid in the twist.

6. When the body completes one twist, the lower arm is moved forward and laterally as the upper arm is pulled backward to shoulder level. The head is placed in line with the body, with the eyes spotting the water.

7. The hands clasp in front of the face and extend over the head for the entry into the water. The eyes continue to spot the water.

8. The entry is made slightly short of vertical and with the body straight.

BACK DIVE, ONE TWIST - LAYOUT
(Three Meter) 5212A

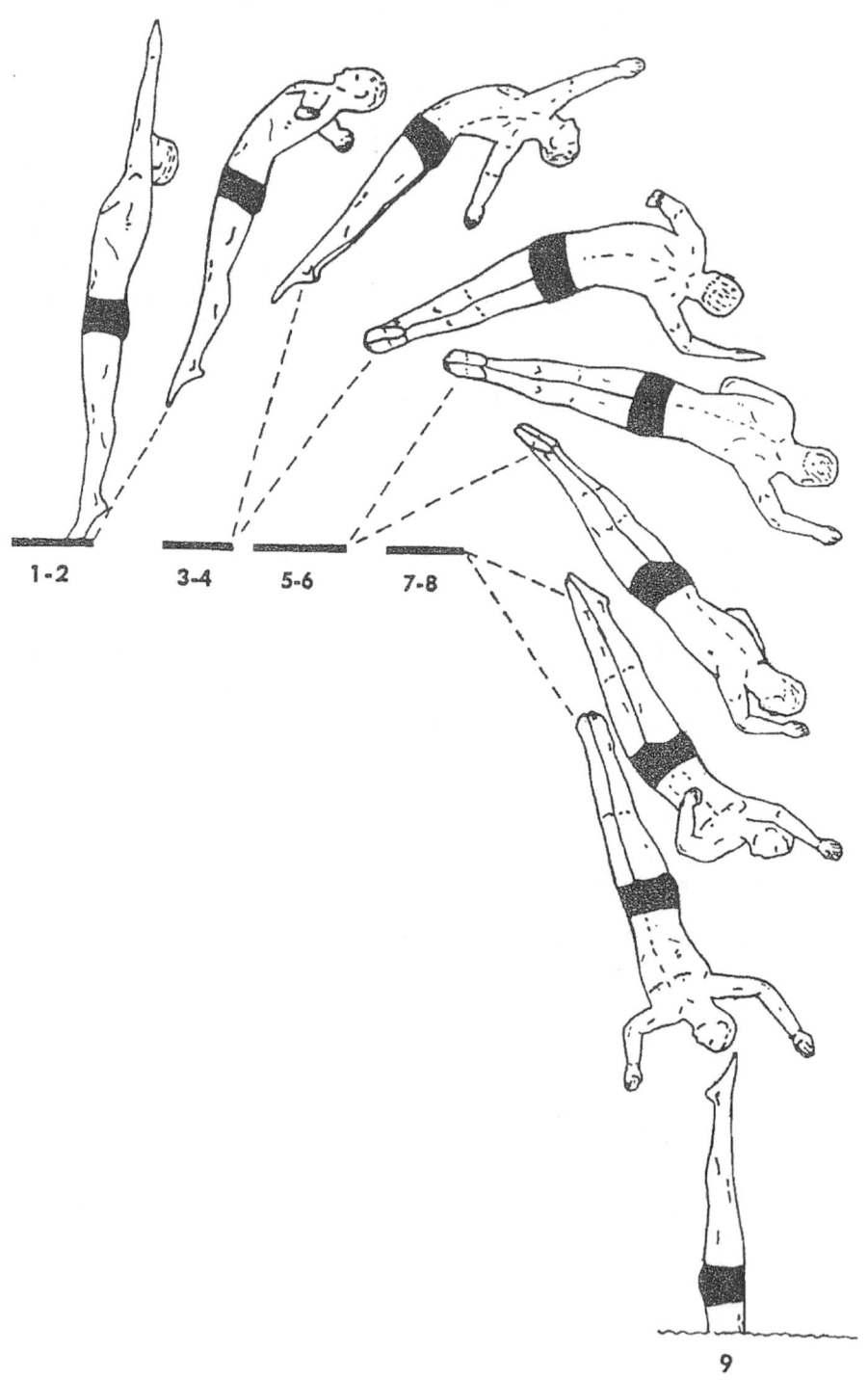

BACK DIVE, ONE TWIST - LAYOUT

(Three Meter)

1. As the diver is about to leave the board, the arms rise in front of the head, which is tilted upward slightly. The legs extend, and the body is straight.

2. The arms pull down laterally toward the level of the shoulders as the diver leaves the board. The back begins to arch, and the head remains in line with the body.

3-4. The twist is started just before the peak of the dive is reached. The full twist is executed by bending the elbows of both arms. One arm will cross in front of the chest, while the other arm reaches overhead and the head and body move in the direction of the upper arm.

5-6-7. At the completion of one half-twist, it is possible for some divers to spot the water. Other divers sight the water as the full twist nears completion.

8-9. As the full twist is completed, the arms extend over the head to prepare for the entry into the water. The entry is made slightly short of vertical.

BACK SOMERSAULT, HALF - TWIST - PIKE
(Free Position) (One Meter) 5221D

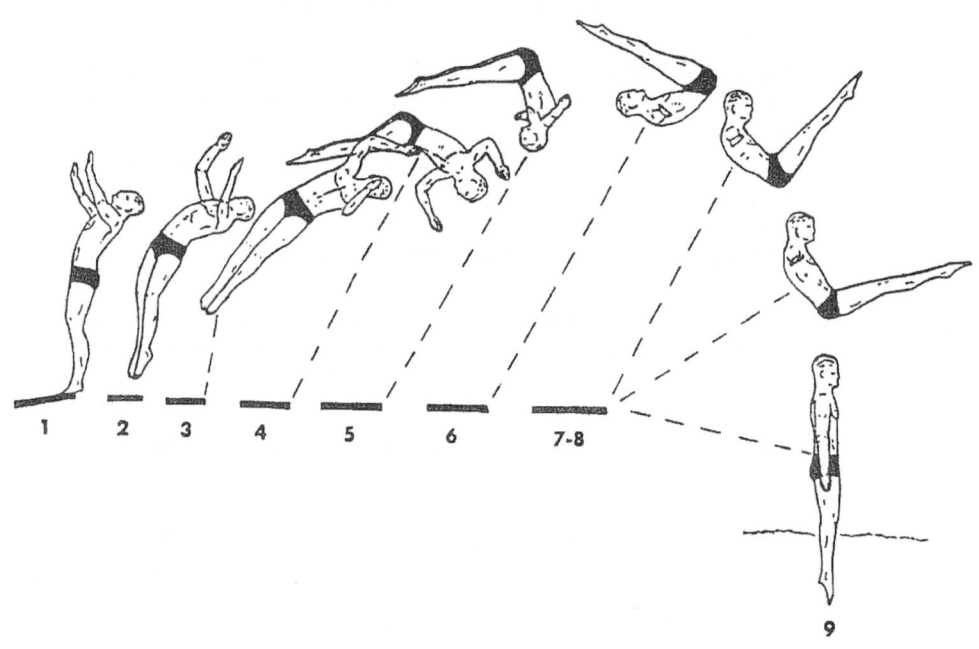

BACK SOMERSAULT, HALF - TWIST - PIKE
(Free Position) (One Meter)

1. The take-off is made with the arms moving straight overhead. The head is tilted back with the eyes sighting the hands. The legs extend with force, and the chest rises, creating a high arch in the back.

2-3. The legs begin to rise as the diver leaves the board. The twist is started by pushing downward with the arm and shoulder on one side while raising the arm and shoulder of the other side. The head pulls back and turns toward the arm that is pulling downward. The diver can sight the water at this point.

4. The arms start a lateral movement toward the shoulder level as the body twists. This is done to control the twist and place the diver in the position to start a pike action.

5. The diver stops at one half twist and continues to pike by pulling the arms away from the body to a near swan position.

6-7-8. The diver remains in the open pike position until three quarters of a somersault have been completed, at which time the body begins to straighten by forcing the legs down toward the water with the head held erect.

9. The body straightens with the head held upright and the eyes looking straight ahead. The diver enters the water slightly short of vertical with the arms at the sides.

BACK SOMERSAULT, HALF - TWIST - LAYOUT
(Free Position) (Three Meter) 5221D

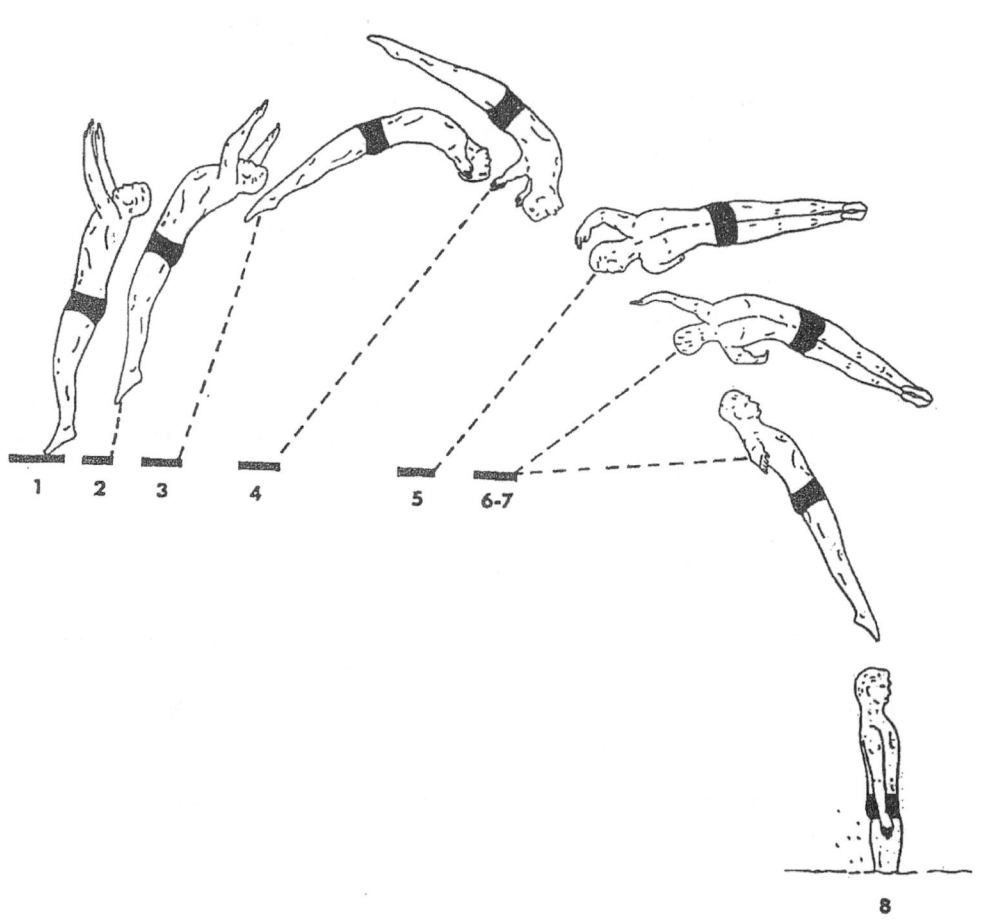

BACK SOMERSAULT, HALF - TWIST - LAYOUT
(Free Position) (Three Meter)

1. The take-off is made with the arms sweeping over the head, the head tilting back, and the chest rising.
2. As the diver leaves the board, the arms continue to pull upward and back. The rising of the chest creates a high arch in the back, and the legs begin to move upward to start the body somersaulting.
3-4. As the legs continue to move upward, the head keeps pulling back and the arms pull laterally to a swan position, which is held until the diver completes a little more than a half-somersault. It may be noted that the water can be sighted as the diver reaches the upside-down position.
5. With the arms bending at the elbow, one arm pulls across the chest while the other arm lifts above the head. The head turns in the direction of the upper arm. These movements are made when the diver starts into the second half of the somersault.
6. When the half-twist nears completion, the high arm begins to pull down laterally to shoulder level while the lower arm straightens and also moves to shoulder level.
7. There is a slight arch in the back as the arms reach shoulder level and the head is held erect.
8. The entry is made by dropping the arms to the sides of the body just before the feet touch the water. The entry is slightly short of vertical.

BACK SOMERSAULT, ONE TWIST - PIKE
(Free Position) (One Meter) 5222D

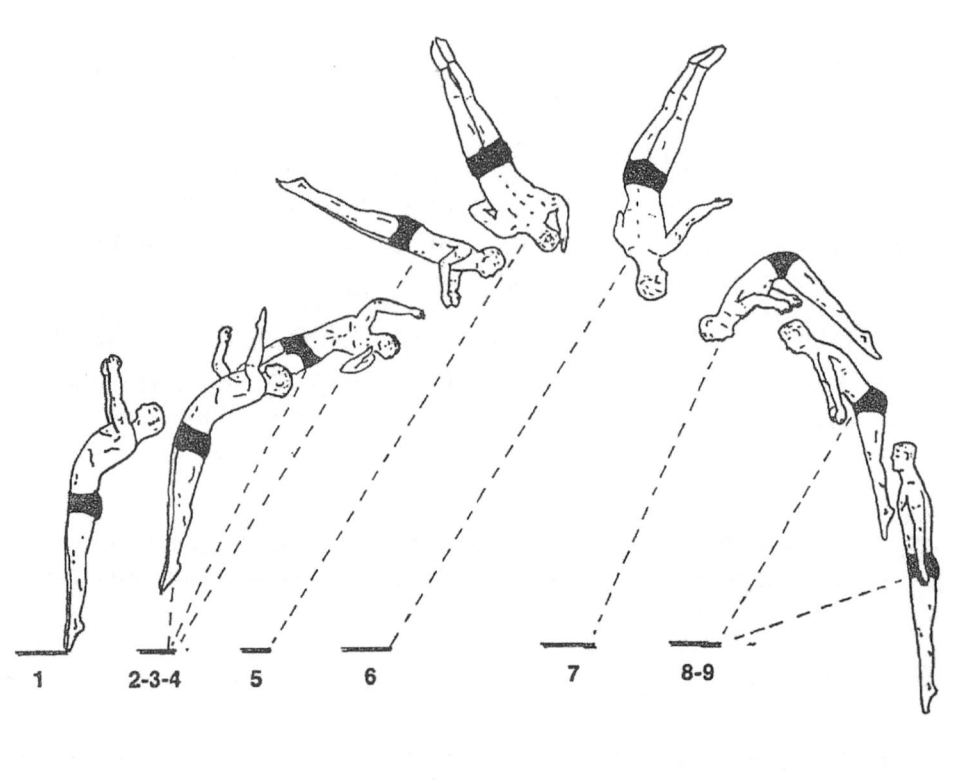

BACK SOMERSAULT, ONE TWIST - PIKE
(Free Position) (One Meter)

1. The take-off from the board is made with the arms sweeping overhead and the chest rising. The head tilts back slightly during this action. The rise of the chest creates a high arch in the back.

2-3
4-5. The twist is started immediately after the feet leave the board by bending the arms at the elbow, with one arm dropping below the shoulder and pulling back while the other arm lifts slightly above the head and moves forward. The arms, still bent, then change position, with the top arm dropping down and across the chest while the lower arm lifts up above the head.

6-7. The twist is nearly completed as the diver approaches three-quarters of a somersault. The water is also sighted when the diver has completed this much of the dive. As the twist is completed, the upper arm begins to straighten and move down laterally toward the sides while the other arm begins to extend and pull back toward the side of the body. In the same motion, the body begins to pike by contraction of the muscles in the thighs and abdomen.

8-9. The diver straightens the body for the entry by raising the chest as the arms move down toward the sides of the body. The entry is made slightly short of vertical with the head erect and the body straight.

BACK SOMERSAULT, ONE TWIST - LAYOUT
(Free Position) (One Meter) 5222D

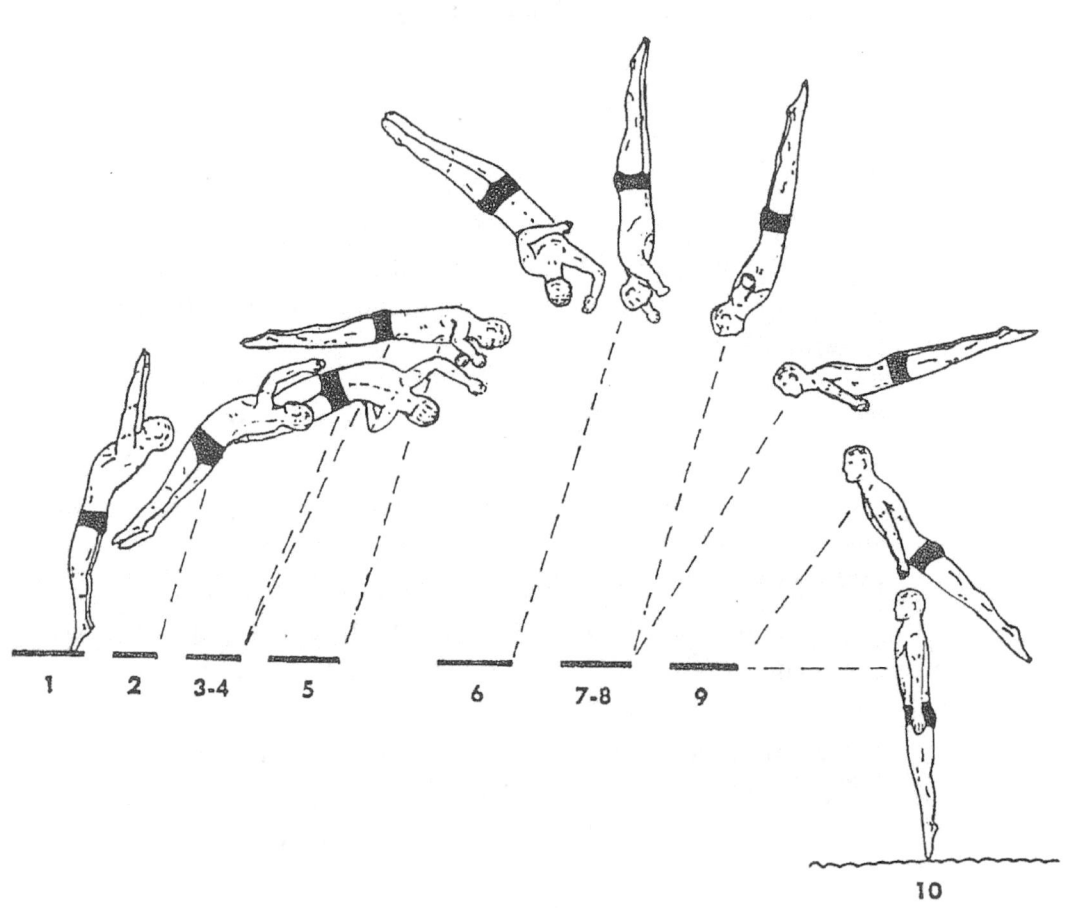

BACK SOMERSAULT, ONE TWIST - LAYOUT
(Free Position) (One Meter)

1. The take-off from the board is made with the arms rising overhead. The head tilts back and the chest rises with the arms.

2-3. The twist is started as the feet leave the board and the legs start an up - ward movement. The twist starts with both arms bending at the elbow and one arm dropping below the shoulder and pulling back while the other arm lifts above the head and moves forward.

4-5. The arms then change position with the lower arm lifting above the head and pulling back at the elbow while the upper arm drops down and across the chest.

6-7. The twist is completed near the peak of the dive at one half somersault. The diver can sight the water at this time. The diver stops the twist at this time by extending the arms to a position level with the shoulders, making sure that the head remains tilted up so that the body will remain in a layout position.

8-9. The body continues to somersault in the layout position and the arms begin to drop laterally to the sides with the head held erect as the diver nears the surface of the water.

10. The entry is made slightly short of vertical with the arms at the sides.

BACK SOMERSAULT, 1 ½ TWISTS - PIKE
(Free Position) (One Meter) 5223D

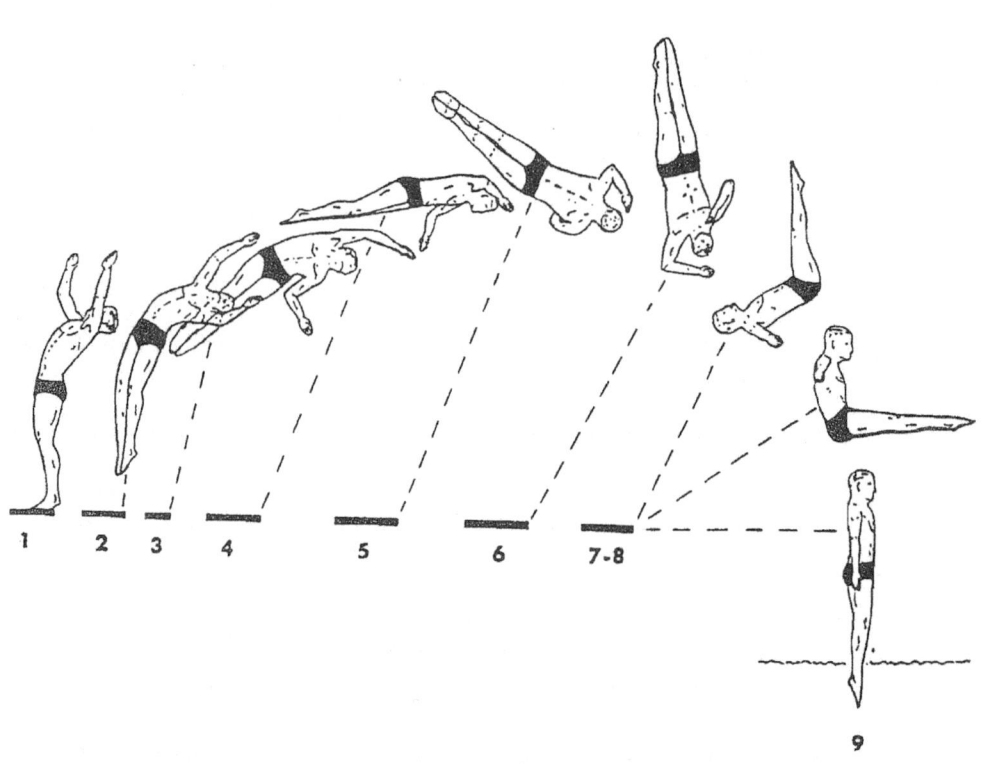

BACK SOMERSAULT, 1 ½ TWISTS - PIKE
(Free Position) (One Meter)

1. The take-off is made with the arms rising over the head while the head and chest rise to form a high arch in the back.

2-3. The twist is started immediately as the **legs** move upward on the take-off. As the arms begin to bend at the elbow, one arm and shoulder pulls back and downward while the other arm begins a movement in the direction of the chest.

4-5-6. The arms then begin to change position with the lower arm lifting upward in a lateral direction to a position above the head and the upper arm continuing to move downward and across the chest. The head turns toward the arm that is finally placed overhead.

7-8. At the completion of 1½ twists, the tw1stmg action is stopped with the extension of the arms in a lateral position at right angles to the body. Simultaneously, the body bends at the waist, with the chest pulling down toward the legs to form an open pike position. The head is held erect directly in line with the body.

9. The entry is made by forcing the legs down toward the water while lifting slightly with the chest. This causes the body to change from a pike to a straight position. The arms move laterally as they drop to the sides for the vertical entry.

BACK SOMERSAULT, 1½ TWISTS - LAYOUT
(Free Position) (One Meter) 5223D

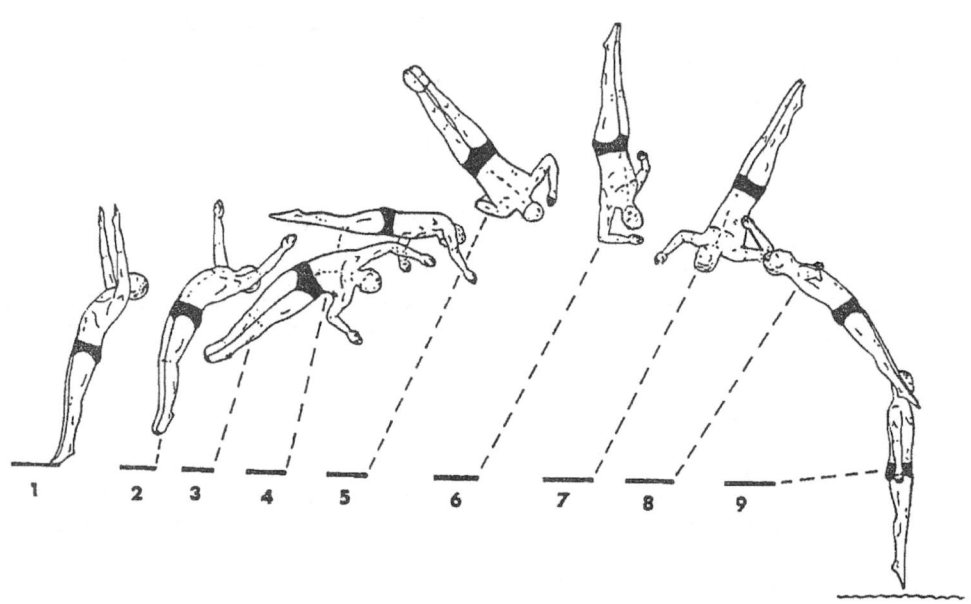

BACK SOMERSAULT, 1 ½ TWISTS - LAYOUT
(Free Position) (One Meter)

1. The take-off is made with the arms rising over the head as the head and chest rise to form a high arch in the back.

2-3
4-5-6. The back somersault starts immediately after the diver's feet leave the board and the legs begin moving upward. A reverse action of the arms is used as the twist is made. With one arm pulling down while bent at the elbow and held close to the side of the body, the other arm remains overhead. In simultaneous movements, the lower arm rises above the shoulder and pulls back while the other arm moves down across the body at around the level of the chest. The head turns in the direction of the arm that is lifted overhead. This position is held until nearly 1½ twists have been completed.

7-8. As the diver nears the completion of 1 ½ twists, the twisting action is stopped by moving both arms to an extended position at right angles to the sides of the body at shoulder level. A slight arch remains in the back as this position is assumed.

9. The arms drop to the sides as the diver approaches the water for an entry slightly short of vertical. The body enters the water in a straight position with the head erect and in line with the body.

BACK 1 ½ SOMERSAULTS, HALF – TWIST - TUCK
(Free Position) (Three Meter) 5231D

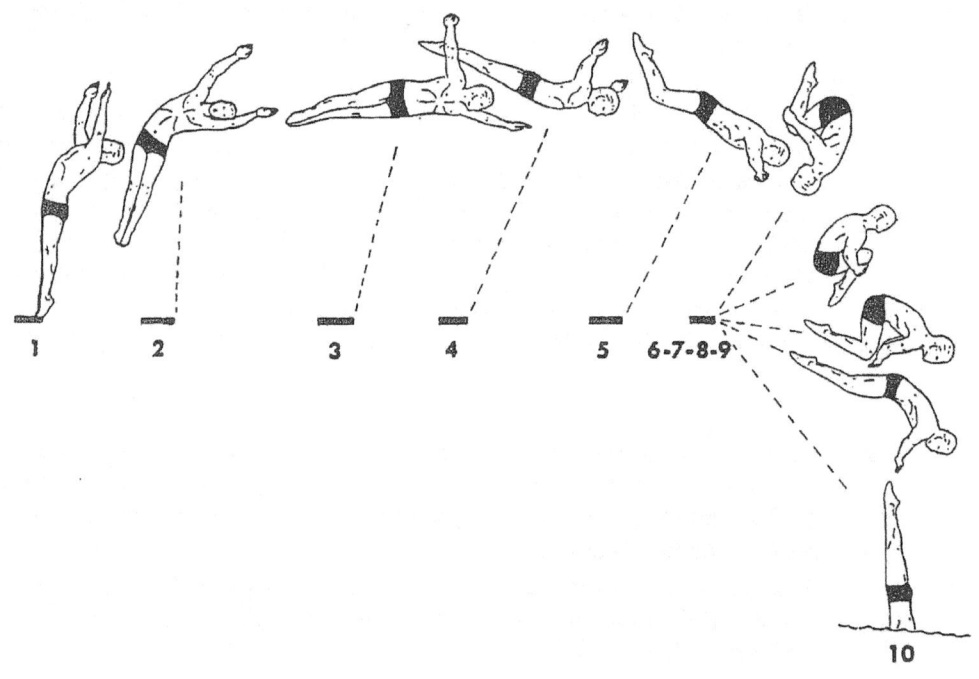

BACK 1 ½ SOMERSAULTS, HALF - TWIST - TUCK
(Free Position) (Three Meter)

1. The diver jumps from the end of the board by reaching straight overhead with the arms. The head tilts back with the eyes looking upward in the direction of the hands. The legs extend with force, and the chest rises, creating a high arch in the back.

2. The twist starts as soon as the legs and hips begin to rise from the board. The twist is made by pushing downward with the arm and shoulder of one side while lifting with the arm and shoulder of the other side. The head pulls back and turns toward the arm that is pushing downward.

3. The diver stops at one half-twist by pulling the arms to a swan position. The eyes then spot the water in front of the board as the legs continue to move upward to a horizontal position.

4. The legs continue to move upward with the body in a layout position and with the arms extended laterally.

5. When the legs near the vertical position, the diver starts to move into a tuck by pulling the arms toward the legs. The knees begin to bend with the feet drawn in toward the buttocks.

6. The head is ducked as the hands chase the legs. When the knees are brought close to the chest, the hands grasp the shins and pull the knees still closer to the chest to tighten the tuck. The head continues to duck during this movement.

7. The water comes into view just after completion of a somersault.

8-9. With the eyes spotting the water, the hands release the knees and then the legs begin to extend while the hands begin to reach overhead for the water.

10. The entry is made slightly short of vertical with the arms fully extended over the head and with the legs straight.

BACK 1 ½ SOMERSAULTS, HALF - TWIST - PIKE
(Free Position) (Three Meter) 5231D

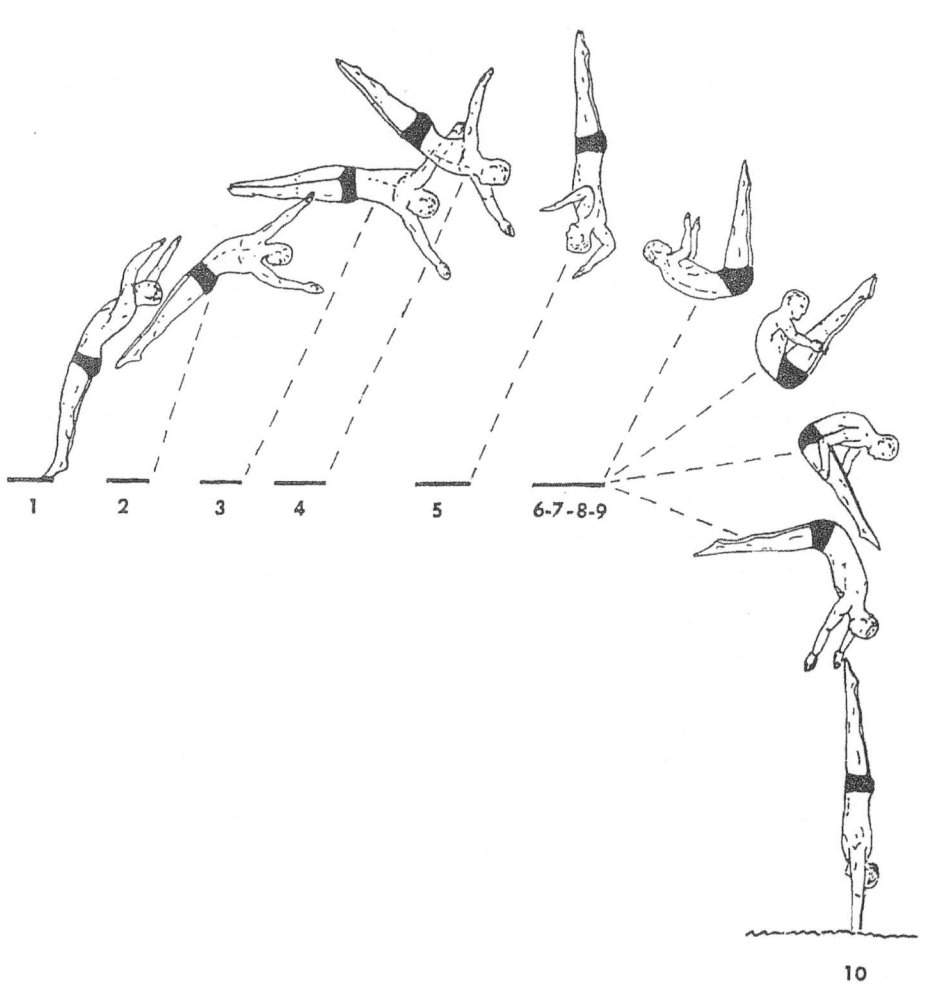

BACK 1½ SOMERSAULTS, HALF - TWIST - PIKE
(Free Position) (Three Meter)

1. The diver lifts himself from the end of the board by reaching straight overhead with the arms. The head tilts back with the eyes looking upward in the direction of the hands. The legs extend with force, and the chest rises, creating a high arch in the back.

2. The twist starts as soon as the legs and hips begin to rise. It is made by pushing downward with the arm and shoulder of one side while lifting the arm and shoulder of the other. The head pulls back and turns toward the arm that is pulling downward.

3-4. The diver stops at one half-twist by pulling the arms backward to a lateral position. As the legs continue to move up-ward to a horizontal position, the eyes spot the water in front of the board.

5. The legs continue to move upward with the body in a layout position, and the arms begin to bend at the elbows and start moving toward the legs.

6. The body bends at the waist when the legs near a vertical position. The arms then move toward the legs, and the head is ducked.

7. The arms continue to chase the legs until the hands clasp the legs behind the knees with the arms held close to the sides. The chest is then drawn toward the legs to tighten the pike.

8-9. The water comes into view as the body completes one somersault. The hands then release the legs, and the eyes spot the water at approximately where the entry will be made. The legs rise toward the vertical as the arms begin to reach over the head for the entry.

10. The eyes continue to spot the water as the legs rise and the arms extend over the head. The entry is made slightly short of vertical.

BACK 1½ SOMERSAULTS, 1½ TWISTS - PIKE
(Free Position) (Three Meter) 5233D

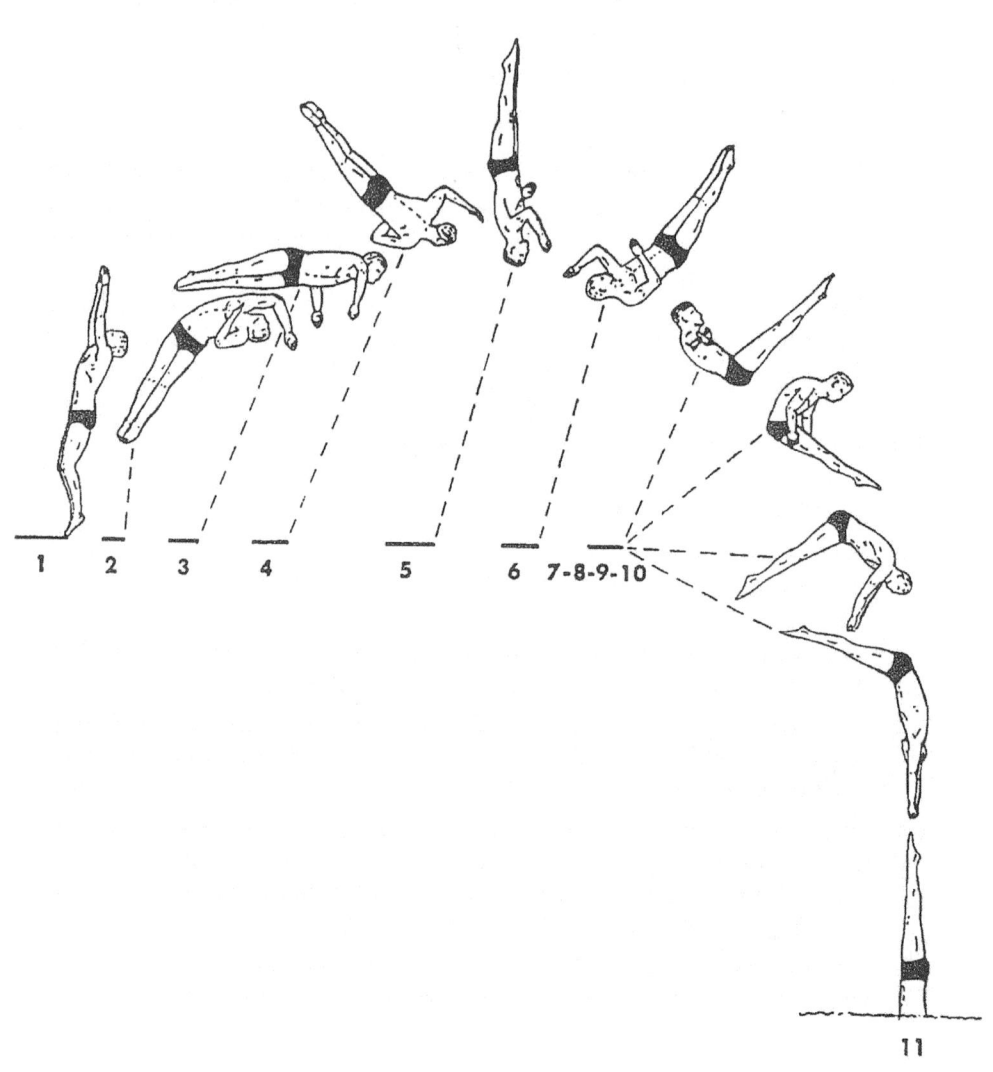

BACK 1½ SOMERSAULTS 1½ TWISTS - PIKE
(Free Position) (Three Meter)

1. The take-off is initiated with the arms rising over the head. The head and chest rise to form a high arch in the back. At the same time, the legs, ankles, and toes extend forcefully.

2-3

4-5. The twist commences as soon as the body leaves the board. The twist starts with both arms over the head and moving simultaneously. With both arms bending at the elbow, one arm pulls back and downward around the level of the chest while the other arm pushes forward slightly over the head. The arms then start to change position with the lower arm lifting laterally overhead as the upper arm moves in a direction across the chest. The head moves in the direction of the established upper arm.

6-7. Near the completion of 1½ twists, the twisting action is stopped by ex- tending the arms and placing them in a lateral position at right angles to the body. Simultaneously, the body bends at the waist, with the chest pressing toward the legs to form an open pike position. The head pulls down as the body pikes.

8-9. The water comes into view as the body passes 1¼ somersaults. At this point, the legs press down hard past the vertical and then up behind the body while the arms begin to move in an overhead direction with the eyes sighting the water.

10-11. The arms extend over the head with the eyes spotting the water. The legs rise toward a vertical position as the body straightens and makes a near vertical entry into the water.

BACK 1 ½ SOMERSAULTS, 2½ TWISTS - PIKE
(Free Position) (Three Meter) 5235D

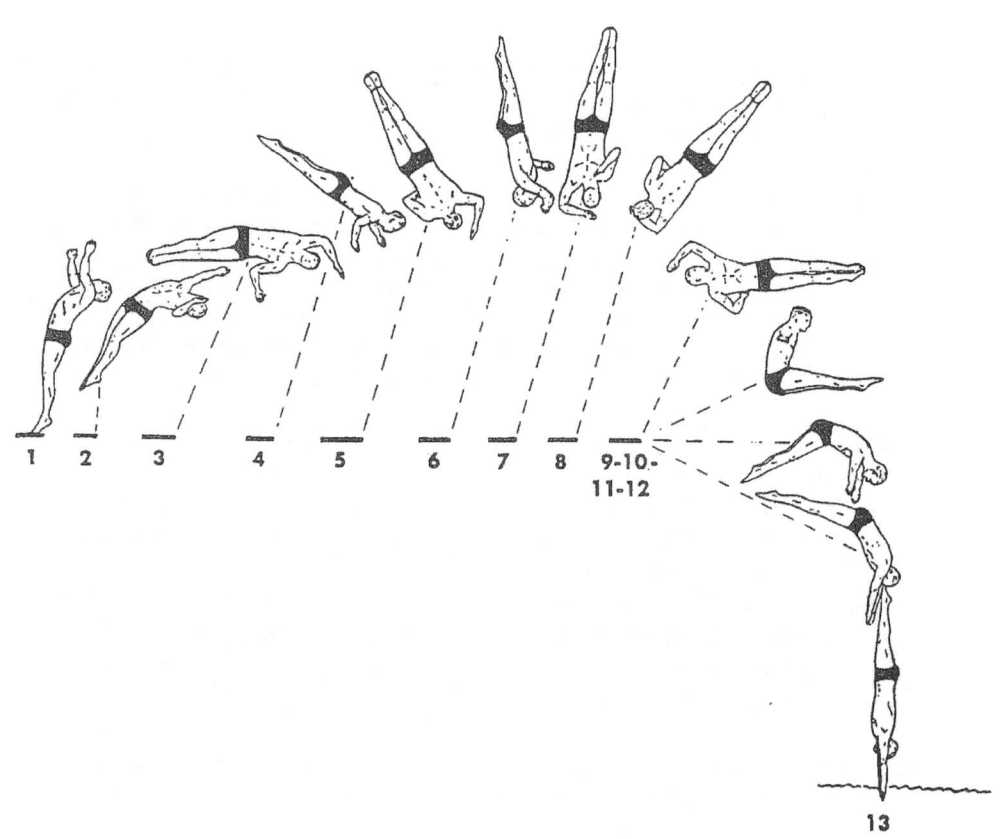

BACK 1½ SOMERSAULTS, 2½ TWISTS - PIKE
(Free Position) (Three Meter)

1. The take-off is initiated by the diver leaning slightly back with the knees flexed and the weight of the hips over the heels. The arms then rise forward and overhead as the head and chest rise to form a high arch in the back. Simultaneously, the legs, ankles, and toes forcefully extend.

2-3

4-5

6-7-8. The twist commences as soon as the diver leaves the board. The twist starts with both arms over the head and moving simultaneously. One arm bends slightly at the elbow and pulls back to a position below the shoulder. The other arm also bends slightly at the elbow as it passes in front of the head and then lowers to press across the chest. The head turns toward the arm that pulls back. While one arm lowers to press across the chest, the arm that was originally pulled back is raised overhead and bent at the elbow.

9-10. The twisting action is stopped near the completion of 2½ twists. This is accomplished by pulling the arms away from the body and extending them in a lateral position. Simultaneously, the body bends at the waist, with the chest pressing down toward the legs to form an open pike position. The head ducks as the body pikes.

11-12. The water comes into view as the body passes 1¼ somersaults. At this point, the legs move down past the vertical and then upward behind the body while the arms reach down toward the water.

13. The arms extend over the head with the eyes spotting the water, and the head and legs move into a vertical position as the body straightens for a near vertical entry into the water.

BACK 1½ SOMERSAULTS, 3½ TWISTS - PIKE
(Free Position) (Three Meter) 5237D

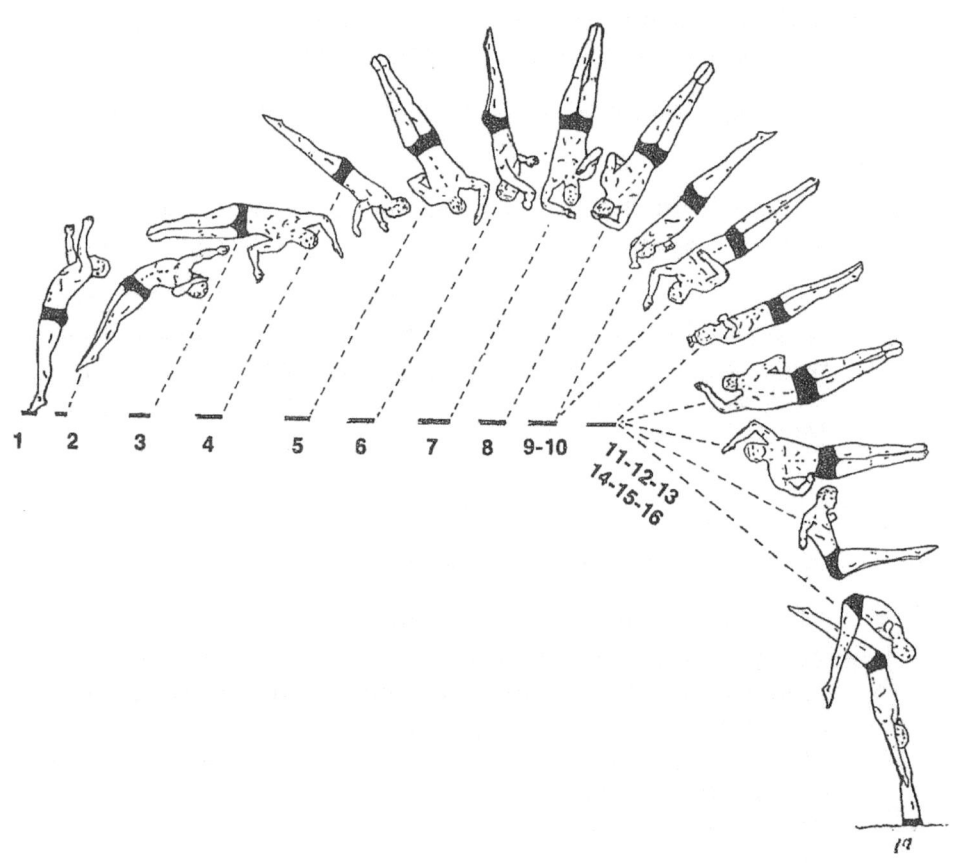

BACK 1½ SOMERSAULTS, 3½ TWISTS - PIKE
(Free Position) (Three Meter)

1. The take-off commences with the diver leaning back slightly with the weight of the hips over the heels. The arms swing forward and upward to a position overhead while the head and chest lift upward to form a high arch in the back. During this motion, the legs, ankles and toes extend.

2-3. The twist begins as soon as the diver leaves the board with both arms overhead and moving simultaneously. With both arms beginning to bend at the elbow, one arm and shoulder pulls back and downward while the other arm pushes forward and downward toward the area of the chest.

4-5. The arms then start to change position with the lower arm lifting laterally overhead while the upper arm continues to move across the body at chest level. The head moves in the direction of the established upper arm.

7-8-9
10-11-12. The body remains in the twisting position until 3½ twists are nearly completed.

13-14. The diver stops the twisting action at 3½ twists by pulling the arms away from the body to a position at right angles to the body at shoulder level, with emphasis on the top arm pulling downward. This motion permits the diver to bend at the waist and form an open pike position. The diver can sight the water at this time.

15-16-17. Spotting the point of entry, the diver extends the arms overhead as the legs move upward to straighten the body. The entry is made slightly short of vertical.

REVERSE DIVE, HALF - TWIST - PIKE
(One Meter) 5311B

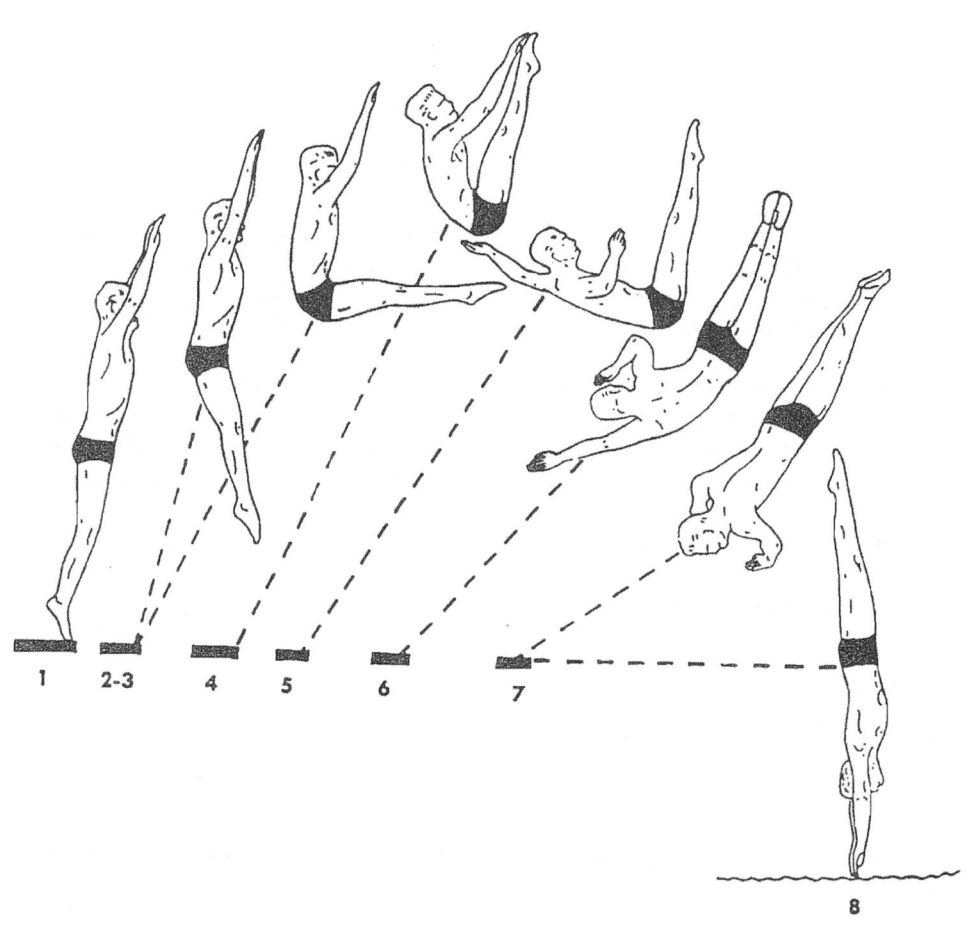

REVERSE DIVE, HALF - TWIST - PIKE
(One Meter)

1. The arms are extended overhead slightly in front of the face on the take-off. The legs extend, and the diver leaves the board from the tips of the toes.

2. As the diver leaves the board, the legs rise in front of the body by contraction of the muscles in the abdomen and thighs. The arms remain stationary as the body pikes.

3-4. The legs continue to move upward toward the hands, which remain overhead. The hands touch the insteps, with the legs approaching a vertical position. The head is held in a position that allows the eyes to sight the hands as they touch the feet. The touch is made near the peak of the dive.

5-6. As the diver begins to drop from the peak of the dive, the upper part of the body pulls away from the legs, which remain vertical. During this action, one arm remains extended over the head while the other arm bends at the elbow and crosses in front of the body at chest level. The shoulder of the crossing arm also moves forward, all of which creates the twist. The head moves in the direction of the upper arm.

7. As the twist nears completion, the upper arm pulls down to meet the lower arm around shoulder level to stop the twisting action. At this moment, the diver can sight the water at the point of entry.

8. With the water sighted and the twist completed, the arms extend overhead, and the diver enters the water, in a vertical position.

REVERSE DIVE, HALF - TWIST - LAYOUT
(Three Meter) 5311A

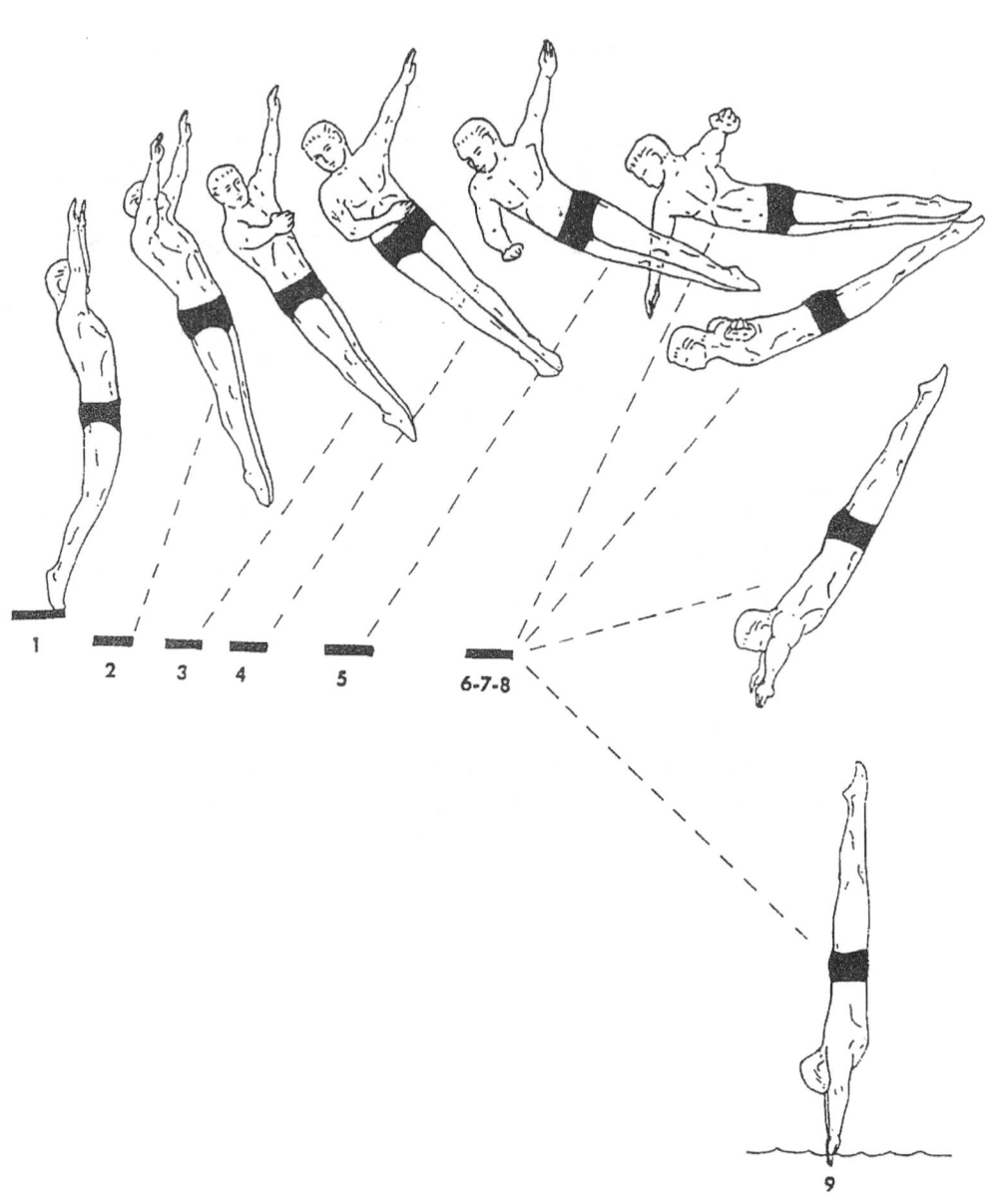

REVERSE DIVE, HALF - TWIST - LAYOUT
(Three Meter)

1. The diver jumps from the board by extending the legs, ankles, and toes. Simultaneously, the chest and head rise, and the arms reach straight overhead, then begin to pull down laterally toward the level of the shoulders.
2. The arms continue to move laterally, as the legs move upward.
3-4. The twist is started as the body moves toward the peak of the dive. The twist is made by bending one arm and pressing it across the chest while keeping the other straight and pushing it forward. The head turns and looks over the shoulder of the arm that is across the chest.
5-6-7. The water and diving board come into view as the half-twist is completed. The arms then straighten and are placed in a lateral position at right angles to the body.
8. The arms remain straight as they extend laterally over the head for the entry into the water, which the eyes continue to spot as the body descends.
9. The entry is made slightly short of vertical and with the body straight.

REVERSE DIVE, ONE TWIST - LAYOUT
(One Meter) 5312A

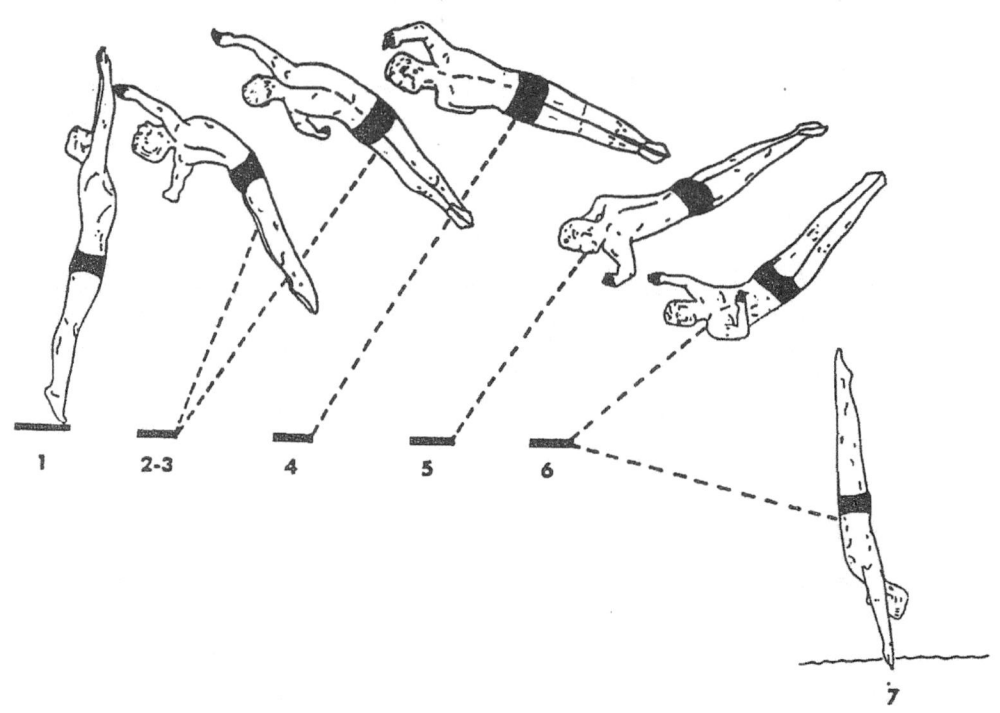

REVERSE DIVE, ONE TWIST - LAYOUT
(One Meter)

1. As the diver takes off from the board, the legs extend, and the arms rise overhead. The head is tilted upward slightly.

2. Once the diver is off the board, the arms move laterally to a position slightly above the shoulders. The back arches as the shoulders pull back and the legs move upward.

3-4. As the diver nears the peak of the dive, one arm bends at the elbow and pulls down toward the chest while the other arm pushes forward near the head level. This action creates the twist.

5-6. The twist continues by keeping the arms in place and putting emphasis on the pushing and pulling of the shoulders. The head should remain tilted back slightly so that the water can be sighted at the completion of the full twist. Some divers can spot the water momentarily at the completion of the first half-twist.

7. When the full twist is completed, the arms are thrust overhead to help stop the twist and reach for the water so that the body can enter in a vertical position.

REVERSE SOMERSAULT, HALF - TWIST - TUCK
(Free Position) (One Meter) 5321D

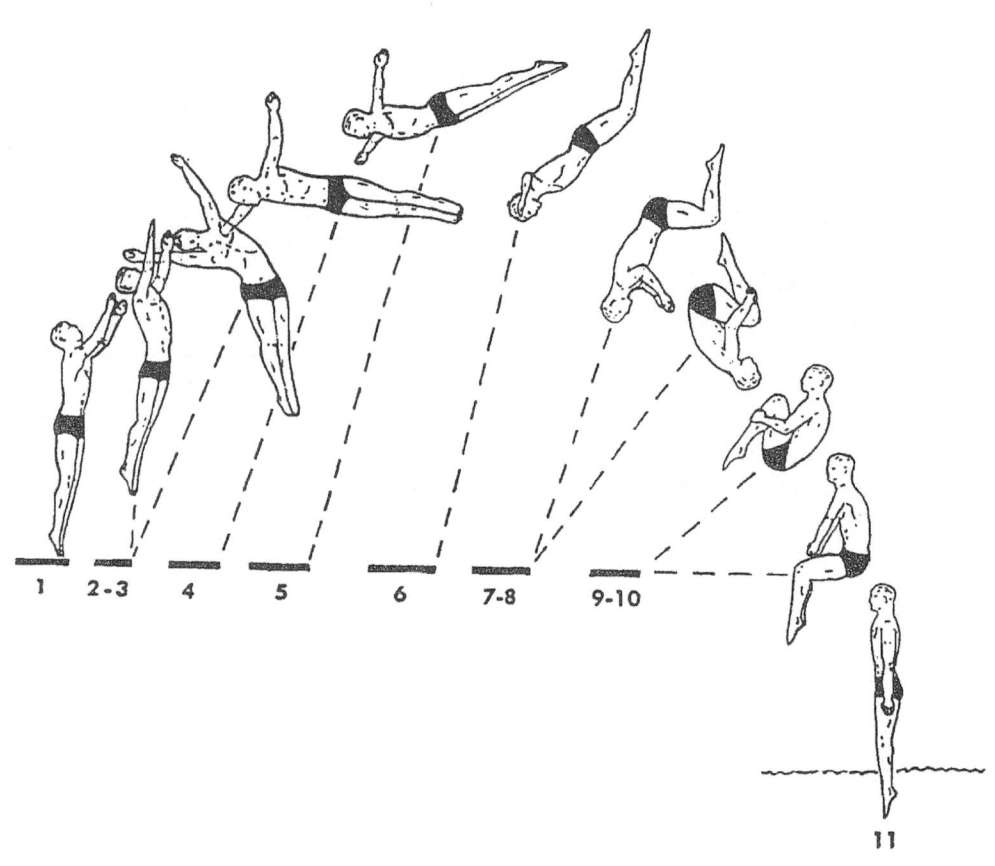

REVERSE SOMERSAULT, HALF - TWIST - TUCK
(Free Position) (One Meter)

1. The take-off from the board is made with the arms rising overhead. The head tilts upward with the eyes looking in the direction of the hands. The chest also rises, creating a high arch in the back.
2. The legs extend and begin moving upward in front of the body as the diver leaves the board. The arms continue to pull upward and back.
3-4. As the somersault starts, the half-twist is executed by pulling down and back with one arm while pushing the other arm toward the front of the body. The head turns toward the arm that pulls down and back. The legs continue to move upward during this action.
5. The water may be sighted as the half-twist nears completion. The twisting is stopped by moving the arms to a lateral position.
6-7. As the diver reaches the peak of the dive facing the diving board, the tuck position begins by thrusting the arms, head and shoulders downward as the body bends at the waist and the legs bend at the knees. The arms continue their movement toward the legs and the feet move in close to the buttocks.
8-9-10. The hands then release the legs as the diver completes three-quarters of a somersault. The legs extend as the chest and head rise slightly to stop the motion of the somersault.
11. The legs are then pushed downward in the direction of the water, and the arms are placed at the sides as the body enters the water in a vertical position with the head erect.

REVERSE SOMERSAULT, HALF-TWIST-PIKE
(Free Position) (One Meter) 5321D

REVERSE SOMERSAULT, HALF - TWIST - PIKE
(Free Position) (One Meter)

1. At the take-off, the arms rise overhead and the head tilts upward. The chest also rises, to create a high arch in the back.
2. The legs extend and start to move upward in front of the body as the diver leaves the board. The arms also continue to pull upward and back.
3. As the legs continue to move upward, the diver starts the twist by pulling back with one arm while the other arm pushes toward the front of the body. The head turns toward the arm that pulls back.
4. The water may be sighted as the half-twist is well started. The half-twist is stopped by placing the arms in a lateral position level with the shoulders.
5. The diver executes the somersault as he reaches the peak of the dive, by thrusting the arms, head, and shoulders downward and bending the body at the waist. The arms continue to move toward the legs.

6-7-8. The hands grasp the legs behind the knees and the chest is pulled toward the legs. As the diver passes three-quarters of a somersault, the hands release the legs. The diver then begins to straighten by forcing the legs down toward the water and slightly lifting the chest and head. The arms move toward the sides of the body as it straightens for the entry.

9. The body straightens completely as it approaches the water for a vertical entry.

REVERSE SOMERSAULT, ONE TWIST - TUCK
(Free Position) (One Meter) 5322D

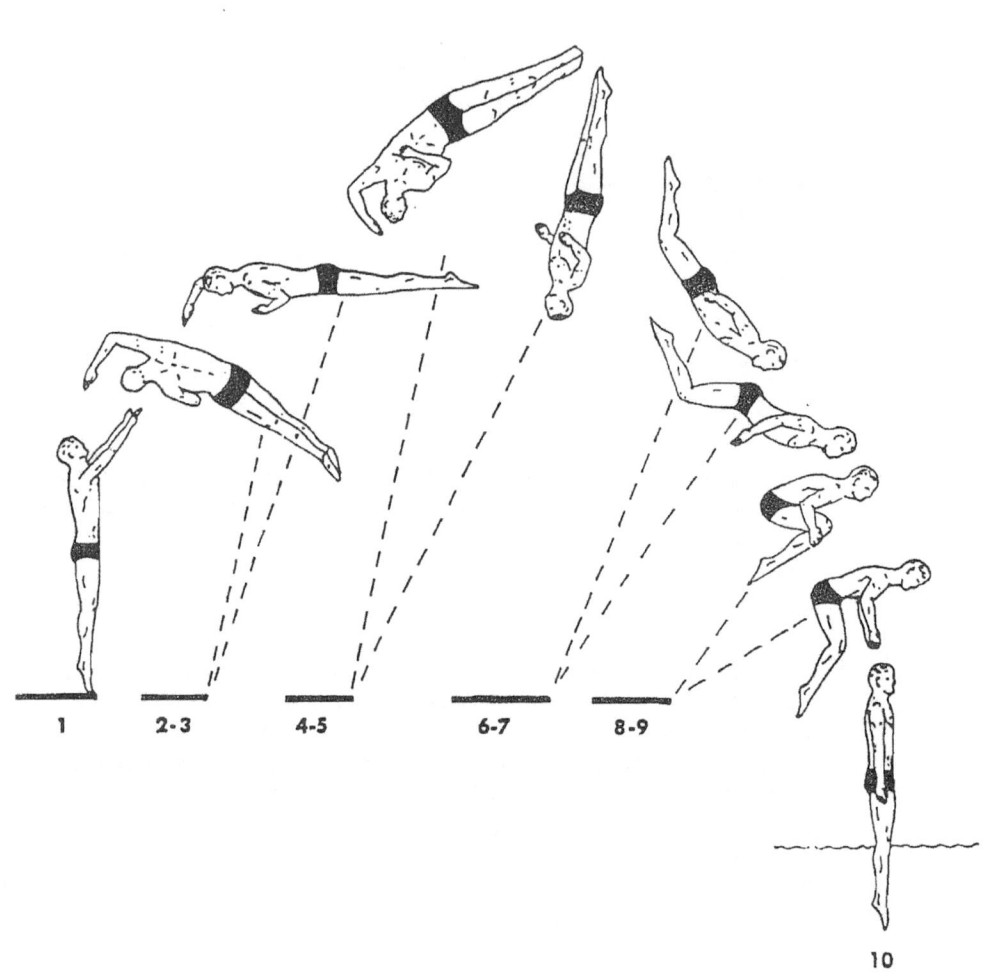

REVERSE SOMERSAULT, ONE TWIST - TUCK
(Free Position) (One Meter)

1. The take-off is made with the arms rising overhead, the head tilting upward, and the eyes looking in the direction of the hands. In the same motion, the chest rises to form a high arch in the back.

2-3-4. The body begins to rotate in a layout position as the feet leave the board and the legs begin to move forward and upward. The twist is started as the legs near a horizontal position in the somersault. The twist starts by bending the arms at the elbow and pulling one arm down and back while the other arm pushes forward and across the face. The arms then change position with the lower arm lifting laterally overhead while the top arm drops down and across the chest level. The head and body turn toward the arm that is pulled back.

5. The arms begin to pull downward as the diver completes the twist while passing over the peak of the dive.

6. The knees begin to pull in toward the chest as the twist is completed at approximately three-quarters of a somersault. The heels move toward the buttocks as the legs begin to tuck, and the head is in a position that permits the water to be sighted.

7-8. As the knees pull in toward the chest, the arms drop down and grasp the legs high on the shins and pull the knees still closer to the chest. The eyes continue to sight the water during this action. The tuck position must be held only for a very short time if the somersault is to be controlled.

9-10. The hands release the legs as the body passes three-quarters of a somersault, and the legs begin to straighten by extending toward the water. In the same motion, the chest and head rise slightly to allow the body to completely straighten for an entry slightly short of vertical.

REVERSE SOMERSAULT, ONE TWIST - PIKE
(Free Position) (One Meter) 5322D

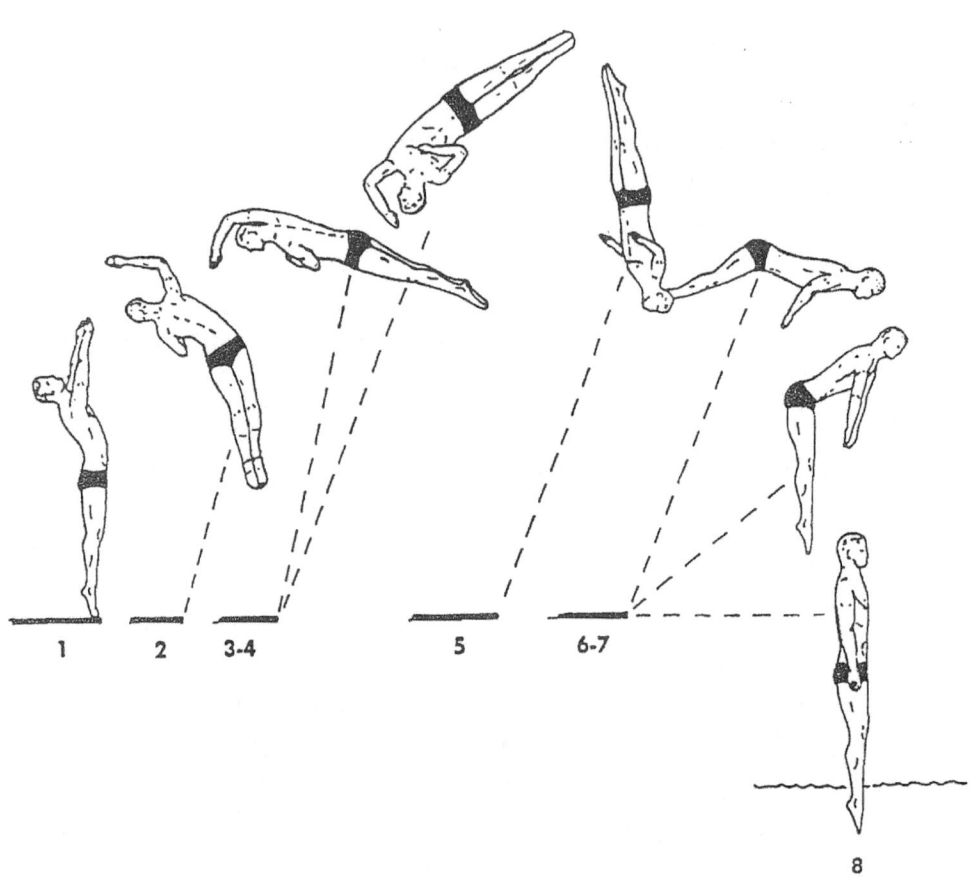

REVERSE SOMERSAULT, ONE TWIST - PIKE
(Free Position) (One Meter)

1. The take-off is made with the arm rising overhead and the head tilted upward with the eyes looking in the direction of the hands. The chest is raised to form a high arch in the back.

2-3. As the diver leaves the board, the legs move upward, and the twist is started immediately. The twist is made by pulling back and down with one arm bent at the elbow while the other arm pushes forward and in front of the head.

4. The arms then change position with the lower arm lifting laterally over the head and the upper arm dropping down and across the chest.

5-6-7. The water can be sighted as the full twist nears completion and the body approaches three-quarters of a somersault. At this moment, the arms extend and move to the level of the shoulders as the body bends at the waist to assume a pike position, which is facilitated by pulling the legs down toward the water and pulling the chest toward the legs. The diver has the option of grabbing the legs in the pike position or leaving the pike open.

8. The body straightens, and the arms drop to the sides as the diver approaches the water for a vertical entry. The head is erect and in line with the body at the entry.

REVERSE SOMERSAULT, ONE TWIST LAYOUT (Free Position) (One Meter) 5322D

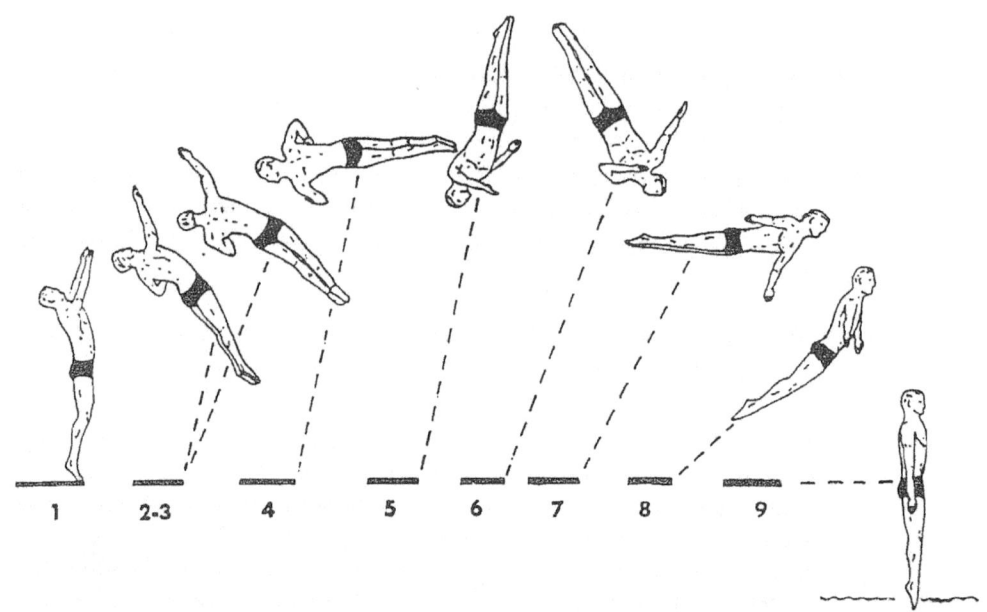

REVERSE SOMERSAULT, ONE TWIST LAYOUT (Free Position) (One Meter)

1. Before the feet leave the board on take-off, the arms swing upward over the head as the legs, ankles and toes extend. The head looks up at the hands once the arms are overhead.

2-3. With the legs moving upward, the twist is made by pulling one arm back and downward while the other arm moves forward and in front of the head.

4-5. The arms then begin to change position with the lower arm moving upward over the head while the upper arm bends, and moves across the chest.

6-7-8. The twist is completed as the diver approaches three-quarters of a somersault. At this time, the arms extend laterally to the level of the shoulders. This stops the twist and places the body in a position where the legs can be pulled clown toward the water while the head and chest rise.

9. The arms drop to the sides as the body reaches a vertical position for the entry into the water.

REVERSE SOMERSAULT, 1 ½ TWISTS - TUCK
(Free Position) (One Meter) 5323D

REVERSE SOMERSAULT, 1 ½ TWISTS - TUCK
(Free Position) (One Meter)

1. The take-off is initiated with the forceful raising of the arms, chest, and head and the full extension of the legs, ankles, and toes. The body leaves the board with the arms, head, and chest continuing to rise. A high arch in the back is created by this action. The legs move forward and upward as the toes leave the board.

2-3

4-5-6. The twist commences as soon as the body leaves the boa rd. It is started with both arms overhead and moving simultaneously. One arm bends slightly at the elbow and pulls backward to a position be ow the shoulder. The other arm also bends slightly at the elbow as it passes in front of the head and then lowers to press across the body at around the level of the chest. The head turns toward the arm that pulls back. While one arm lowers to press across the chest area, the other arm, which was originally pulled back, is raised overhead, bent at the elbow, and pulls back at the elbow. The body continues to rotate in the layout position during this action.

7-8. The 1 ½ twists are completed as the diver nears three-quarters of a somersault. At this time, the legs bend at the knees and are drawn toward the chest as the arms move toward the legs to form a tuck position. The hands grasp the legs high on the shins and pull the knees in toward the chest. The head remains tilted up slightly so to control the somersault.

9-10. The hands release the legs as the body passes three-quarters of a somersault. The legs then extend and move down toward the water as the chest rises slightly. This causes the body to straighten for a vertical entry into the water.

REVERSE SOMERSAULT, 1½ TWISTS - PIKE
(Free Position) (One Meter) 5323D

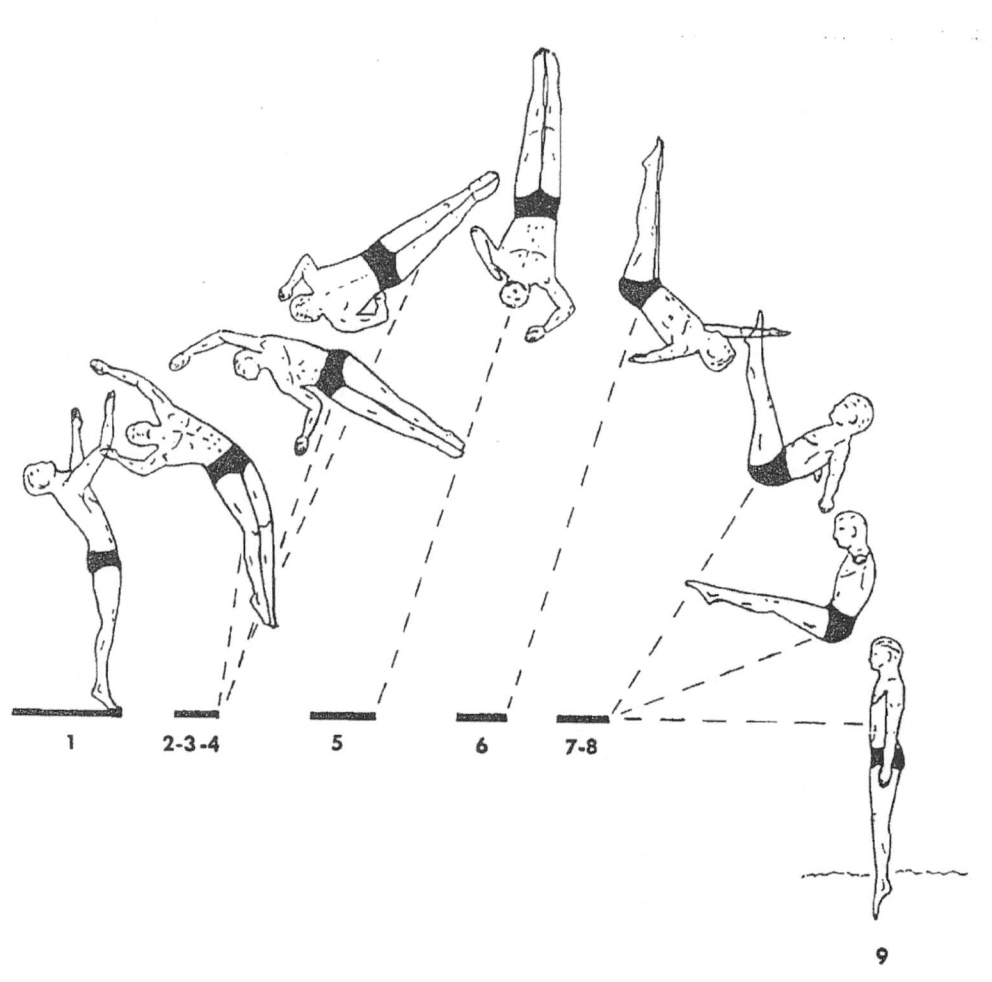

REVERSE SOMERSAULT, 1 ½ TWISTS - PIKE
(Free Position) (One Meter)

1. The take-off is made with the arms rising overhead vigorously and with the head and chest rising to form a high arch in the back. The legs extend completely as the diver leaves the board.

2-3
4-5. The legs rise as the diver leaves the board, and the twist is started immediately. With both arms extended slightly behind the head, one arm bends at the elbow and pulls back as it drops down below the shoulder. The other arm passes in front of the head. The arms then change position with the lower arm lifting overhead, still bent at the elbow, while the upper arm bends, and moves downward across the chest. The head follows in the direction of the newly established upper arm. In other words, the head turns in the direction of the twist.

6-7-8. The twisting action is stopped by extending the arms near the completion of 1½ twists. The arms are then placed in a lateral position as the body bends at the waist, with the chest pressing toward the legs to form an open pike position. The head is held erect to control the somersault.

9. The legs are then forced down toward the water, and the chest is raised slightly to straighten the body for a vertical entry. The arms are placed at the sides as the body straightens for the entry.

REVERSE SOMERSAULT, 1 ½ TWISTS - LAYOUT
(Free Position) (One Meter) 5323D

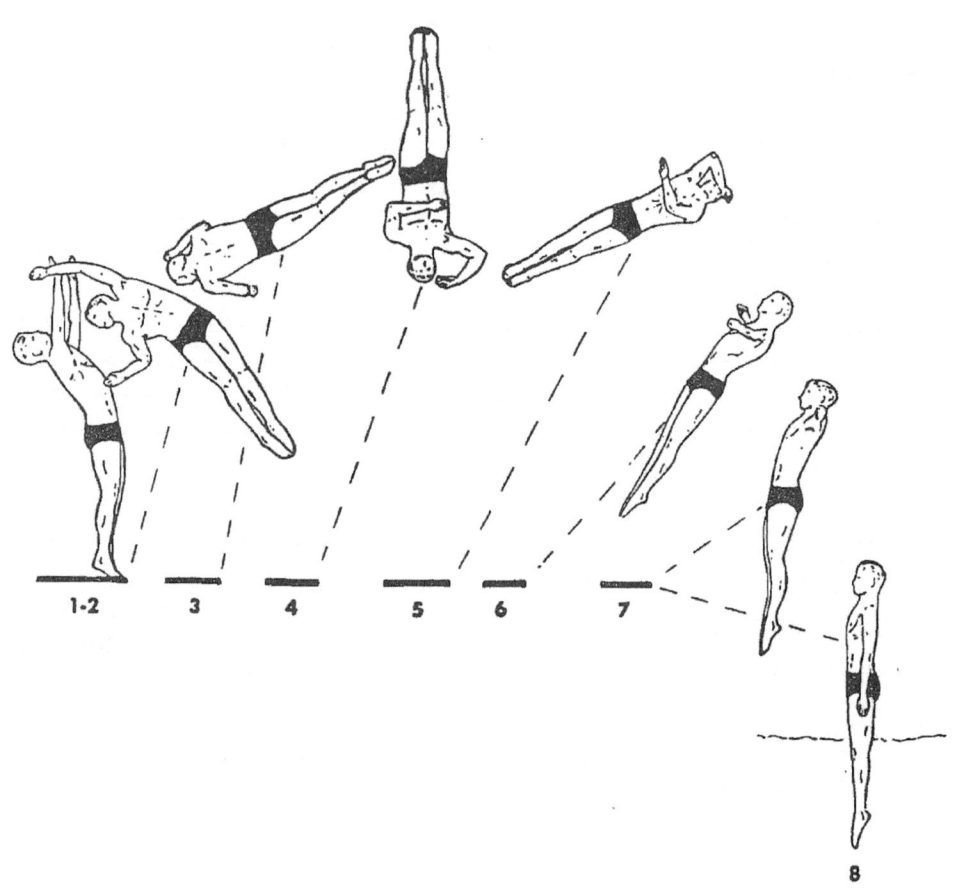

REVERSE SOMERSAULT, 1 ½ TWISTS – LAYOUT

(Free Position) (One Meter)

1. The take-off is made with the arms forcefully rising over the head and with the chest and head rising in the same motion to form a high arch in the back.

2-3
4-5. The legs move upward from the board and the body starts to rotate with the arms spread above the head. The twist starts immediately with one arm pulling back and downward, bent at the elbow, while the other arm moves in front of the head. The arms then change position with the lower arm lifting above the head and pulling back at the elbow while the other arm bends at the elbow and pulls down across the body at chest level. The head turns in the direction of the twist.

6-7. The 1½ twists are nearly completed as the diver finishes three-quarters of a somersault. The twisting action is stopped by extending the arms to a lateral position at right angles to the body. The head is held erect so that the body may remain in a layout position.

8. The arms drop to the sides as the diver approaches the water for a vertical entry.

REVERSE 1 ½ SOMERSAULTS, HALF - TWIST - TUCK
(Free Position) (Three Meter) 5331D

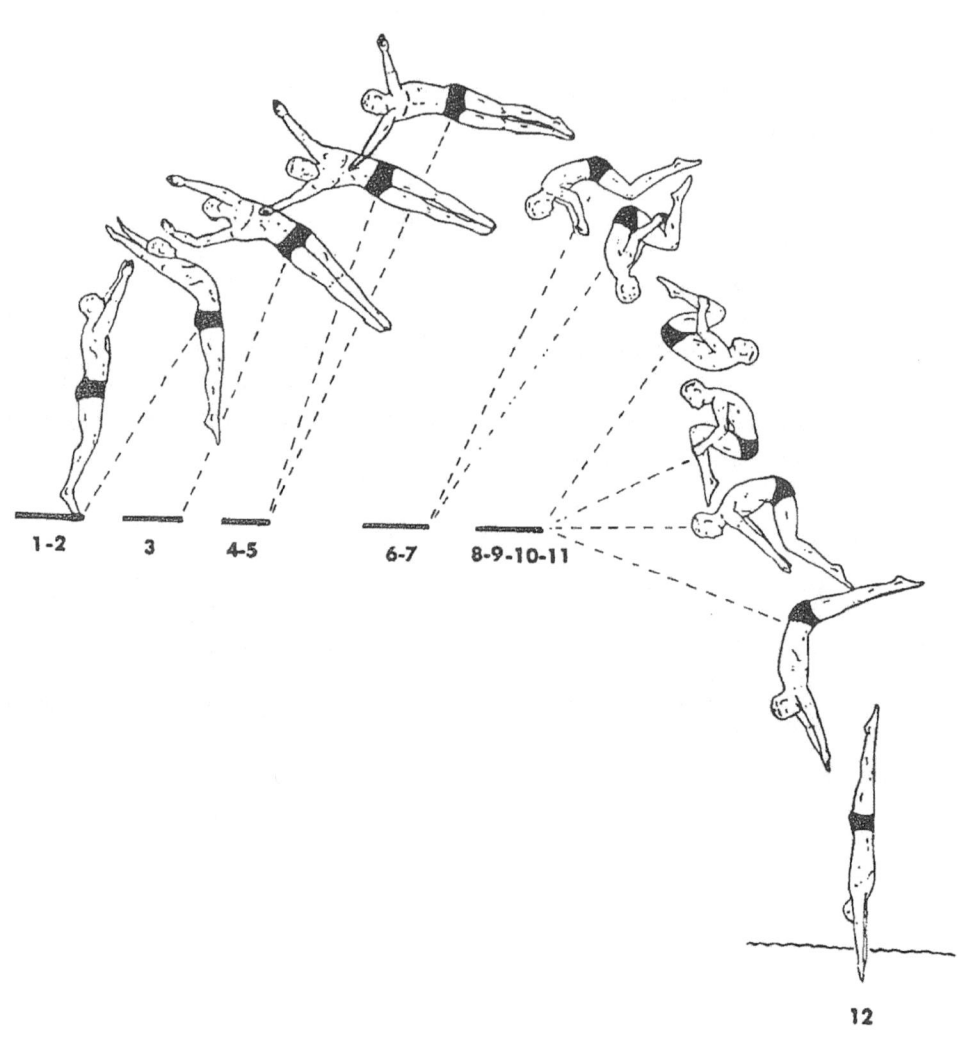

REVERSE 1½ SOMERSAULTS, HALF - TWIST - TUCK
(Free Position) (Three Meter)

1-2. The take-off is made with the diver reaching straight overhead with the arms. The head and chest rise along with the arms, and the eyes look up in the direction of the hands.

3. The twist is started soon after the feet leave the board and the legs begin to move upward. The arms and head continue to rise and pull back to create a high arch in the back.

4-5. The twist is made with one arm pulling down and back while the other moves forward. The head and body turn toward the arm that is pulled back. The water may be sighted as the diver completes the half-twist, which is controlled and stopped by pulling the arms to right angles near the level of the shoulders. The legs continue to rise as the half-twist is completed.

6-7. On reaching the peak of the dive with the half twist completed, the diver starts into the tuck by moving the arms toward the legs while bending at the waist. The legs bend in the same moment and the knees draw toward the chest with the head pulling inward.

8-9. The hands grasp the shins and pull the knees close to the chest to form a tight tuck position.

10-11. The hands release the legs as the diver passes three-quarters of a somersault. The eyes sight the water as the legs are released. The legs straighten and move upward as the arms begin to extend overhead.

12. The body straightens completely as the near vertical entry is made.

REVERSE 1½ SOMERSAULTS, HALF - TWIST - PIKE
(Free Position) (Three Meter) 5331D

REVERSE 1 ½ SOMERSAULTS, HALF - TWIST - PIKE
(Free Position) (Three Meter)

1. The diver takes off from the end of the board by reaching straight overhead with the arms. The head also rises with the eyes looking upward in the direction of the hands. The legs extend with force, and the chest rises, creating a high arch in the back.//
2-3. The twist starts as soon as the diver leaves the board. The twist is initiated by pulling downward and behind the body with one arm while pushing upward with the other. The head turns in the direction of the arm that is pulled back.
4. The legs of the diver continue to rise as the half-twist is completed. The diver stops at a half-twist by extending the arms in a lateral position, with the eyes spotting the water.
5. While the legs continue to move upward, the diver momentarily holds the swan-dive position before the pike into a somersault. The pike movement is started by moving the arms toward the legs and bending at the waist. The head ducks during this action.
6. The arms continue to chase the legs until the hands clasp the legs behind the knees.
7. The pike is tightened by drawing the chest toward the legs, with the elbows close to the sides of the body.
8-9. The water comes into view at the completion of one somersault. At this time, the hands release the knees and the eyes spot the approximate point where the body will enter the water.
10. The legs rise toward the vertical, after the release of the knees, and the arms extend over the head for the entry, which is vertical, with the body straight.

REVERSE 1½ SOMERSAULTS, 1½ TWISTS - PIKE
(Free Position) (Three Meter) 5333D

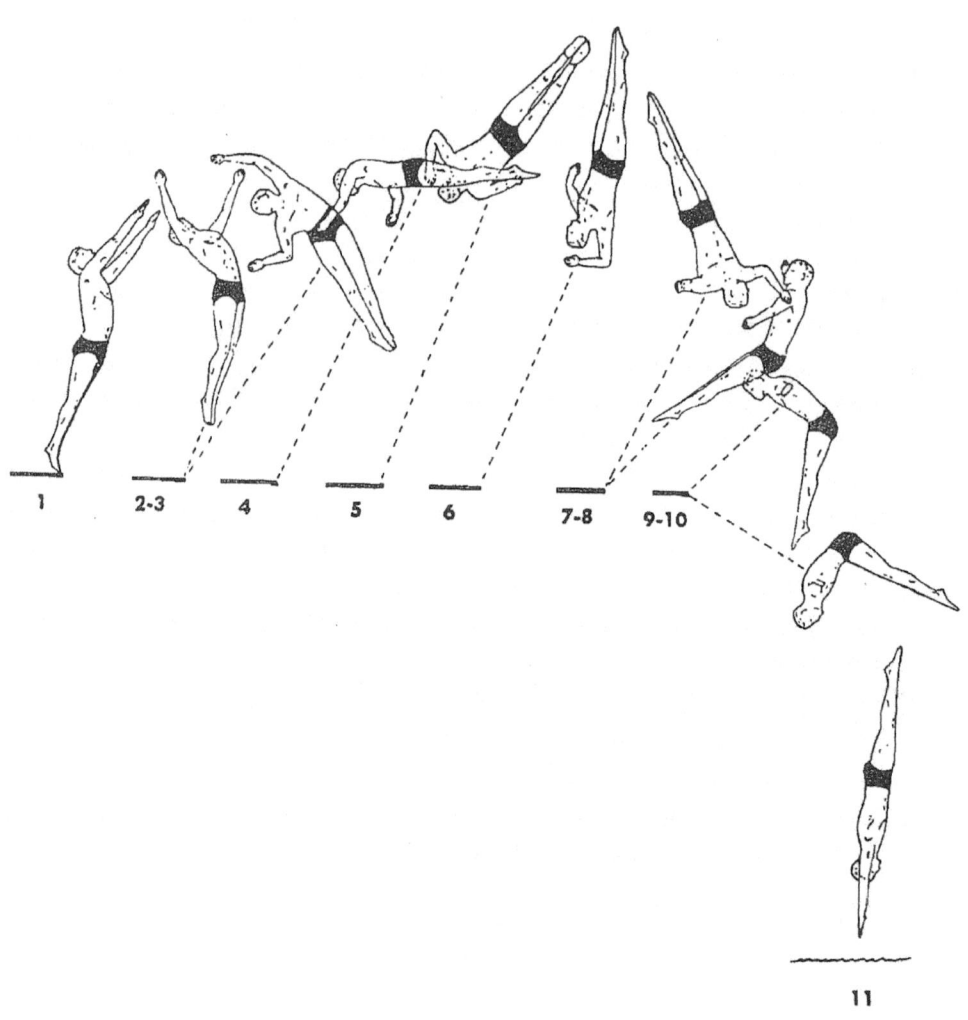

REVERSE 1½ SOMERSAULTS, 1½ TWISTS - PIKE
(Free Position) (Three Meter)

1. The take-off is made with a forceful raising of the arms, chest, and head and a full extension of the legs, ankles, and toes. The diver leaves the board with the arms, head, and chest continuing to rise, which forms a high arch in the back. The legs move forward and upward as the toes leave the board.

2-3

4-5-6. The twist starts with the arms overhead and moving simultaneously. One arm bends slightly at the elbow and pulls backward to a position below the shoulder. The other arm also bends slightly at the elbow as it passes in front of the head and then lowers to cross the chest. The head turns in the direction of the twist. While one arm lowers to press across the chest, the other arm, which was originally pulled back, is raised overhead bent at the elbow. e legs continue to rise during the twisting action.

7-8. The arm held close to the chest rises and assumes the same position as the other arm when the 1½ twists near completion.

9. The arms then move to right angles of the body at shoulder level as the diver pikes at the waist. The chest presses toward the legs, and the head ducks so that the diver can sight the water as the body pikes.

10. The legs press down past the vertical at this point and then up behind the body while the arms reach down toward the water.

11. With the eyes spotting the water, the arms extend over the head and the legs rise to a vertical position. The entry into the water is vertical, with the body straight.

REVERSE 1½ SOMERSAULTS, 2½ TWISTS - PIKE
(Free Position) (Three Meter) 5335D

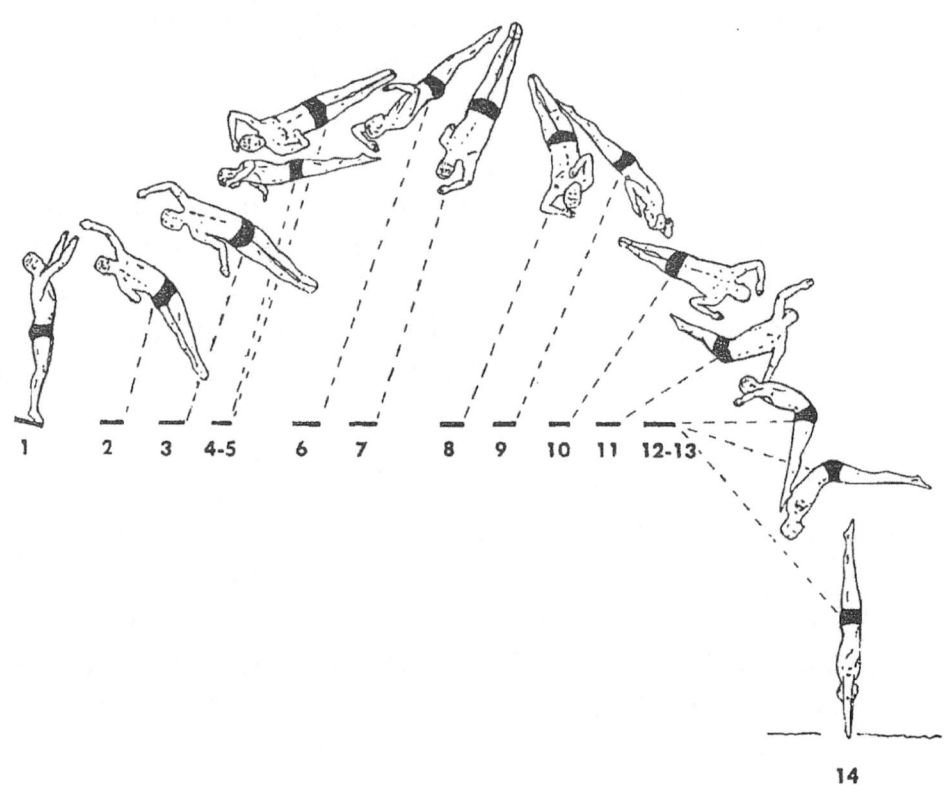

REVERSE 1 ½ SOMERSAULTS, 2½ TWISTS - PIKE
(Free Position) (Three Meter)

1. Prior to the take-off from the board, the arms sweep forward and upward with the head and chest rising as the arms pass the shoulder level and the legs extend. The arms, head, and chest continue to rise as the diver leaves the board and the legs completely extend.

2-3

4-5. The twisting action is started as soon as the legs begin to move upward. With the arms extended behind the head, one arm bends at the elbow and pulls down and back while the other arm moves forward in front of the head. The lower arm then lifts upward to a position overhead while the upper arm pushes down and across the chest. The head moves in the direction of the twist.

6-7

8-9. The body continues to twist while the diver concentrates on pulling back with the upper arm and pushing across with the lower arm. Control of the twist can be maintained as long as the legs remain straight and together. The head remains tilted back slightly during the twist.

10-11. The twist is stopped near the completion of 2 ½ twists, when the diver has executed about 1¼ somersaults. This is accomplished by extending
the arms outward at shoulder level and piking the body by pulling forward and downward with the head and shoulders.

12-13. The water is spotted as the diver assumes the open pike position. He then starts to reach down for the water as the legs move upward.

14. The arms extend over the head as the legs reach a near vertical position, to place the body in a straight position for the entry into the water.

REVERSE 1½ SOMERSAULTS, 3½ TWISTS - PIKE
(Free Position) (Three Meter) 5337D

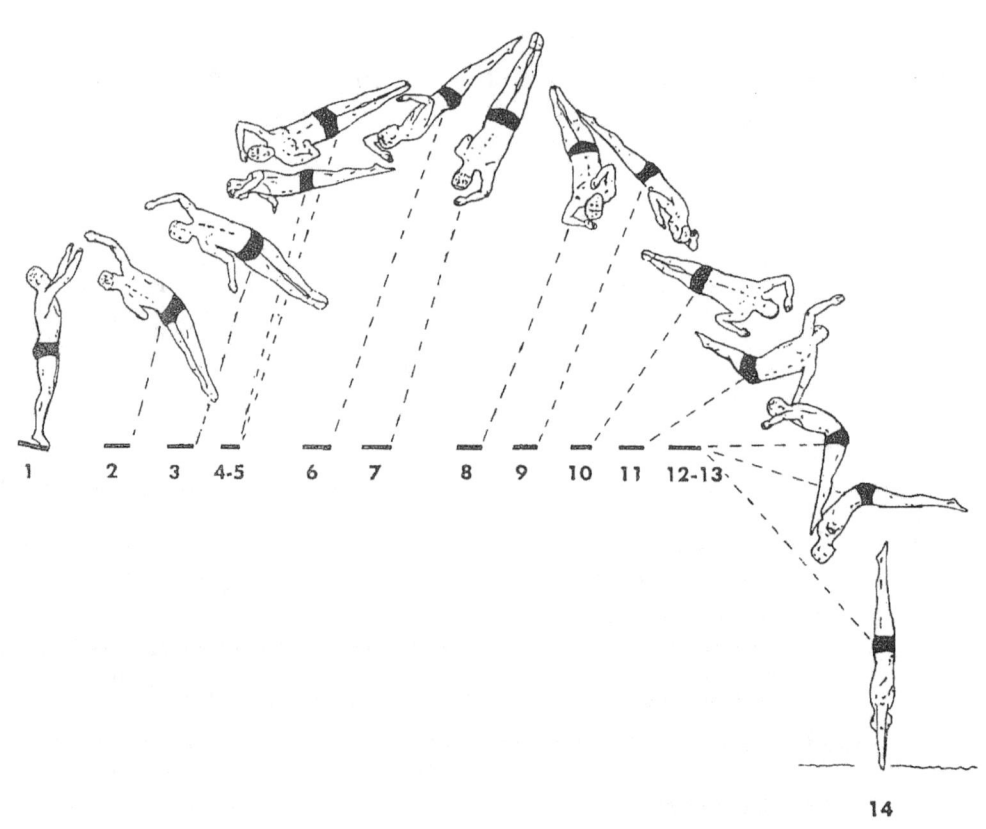

REVERSE 1½ SOMERSAULTS, 3½ TWISTS - PIKE
(Free Position) (Three Meter)

1. The take-off from the board is with the arms swinging overhead as the legs, ankles and toes extend.

2-3
4-5. In coming off the board, the arms continue to pull back in the direction past the head. The twist is then started by pulling one arm-which bends at the elbow-and shoulder down and back while the other arm moves forward, crossing the head. At this point, the lower arm lifts to a position above the head while the upper arm continues to move in front of the body and down across the chest.

6-7-8-9
10-11-12-13. The diver maintains the twisting position while pulling back with the elbow of the upper arm and pushing the lower arm across the body. The head is held erect and turns in the direction of the twist.

14-15
16-17. Near the completion of 3½ twists, the diver pulls the top arm down as the lower arm lifts to place both arms at a shoulder level position at the sides of the body. This action aids in the diver piking at the waist, at which time the water can be sighted. The arms then extend overhead as the body straightens for a vertical entry.

INWARD DIVE, HALF - TWIST - PIKE
(One Meter) 5411B

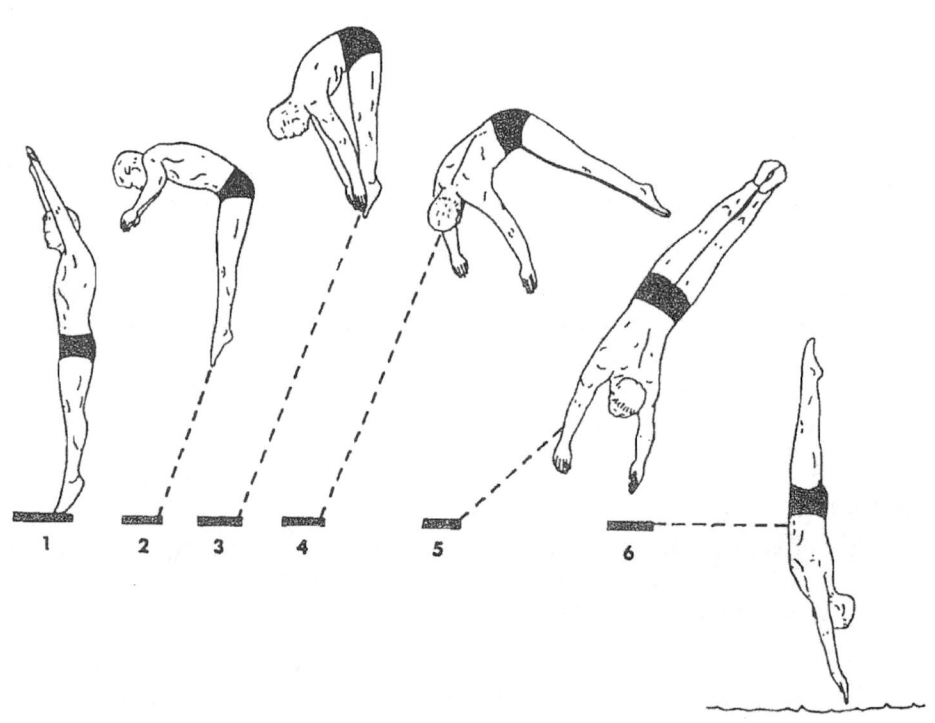

INWARD DIVE, HALF - TWIST - PIKE

(One Meter)

1. The take-off is made with the arms reaching over the head, which is held erect. The legs extend with the weight of the body over the feet.

2. The diver rises from the board by extending the legs, feet, and toes and lifting the hips nearly straight up as the body begins to bend at the waist. As the body bends, the arms move down, within the width of the shoulders, toward the feet. The diver can easily see the water as the body begins to pike.

3. The hands touch the feet, with the legs in a vertical position at the peak of the dive. The head remains in line with the body.

4. The body begins to straighten as the diver drops from the peak of the dive. The twist is started at this time by pulling back slightly with one shoulder while pushing the other shoulder forward. The head and body turn toward the shoulder that is pulled back. The body continues to straighten, with the legs rising and the arms reaching toward the water.

5. The body straightens before the half-twist is completed, and the diver continues to execute the half-twist in the layout position. The legs are nearly straight overhead as the half-twist is completed. The arms begin to close over the head when within reach of the water for the entry.

6. The entry is made in a vertical position with the arms extended over the head in line with the body.

INWARD DIVE, HALF - TWIST - LAYOUT
(One Meter) 5411A

INWARD DIVE, HALF - TWIST - LAYOUT

(One Meter)

1. The take-off is made with the arms rising straight overhead with the head held in line with the body. The weight of the body is held directly over the balls of the feet.

2. The legs, feet and toes fully extend, and the arms forcefully move down laterally before the feet leave the board. The head remains in line with the body. The body pikes very slightly as the hips and legs begin to move backward and upward.

3. The arms pull down laterally to a swan position and the head remains erect with the eyes sighting straight behind the board. The legs continue to rise, and the back then arches a little.

4. The half-twist starts just before the body attains the swan position. The half-twist is done by pulling down with the arm and shoulder of one side while lifting slightly with the arm and shoulder of the other side. The head remains up until the peak of the dive when the head tilts down and looks over the shoulder at the water.

5. The half-twist continues as the diver drops from the peak of the dive. The diver continues to spot the water as the legs continue to move upward.

6. The legs are nearly vertical as the half-twist is completed. The arms then begin to close over the head.

7. The arms extend completely over the head and reach for the water as the body straightens with little arch in the back. The entry is vertical.

INWARD DIVE, ONE TWIST - PIKE
(One Meter) 5412B

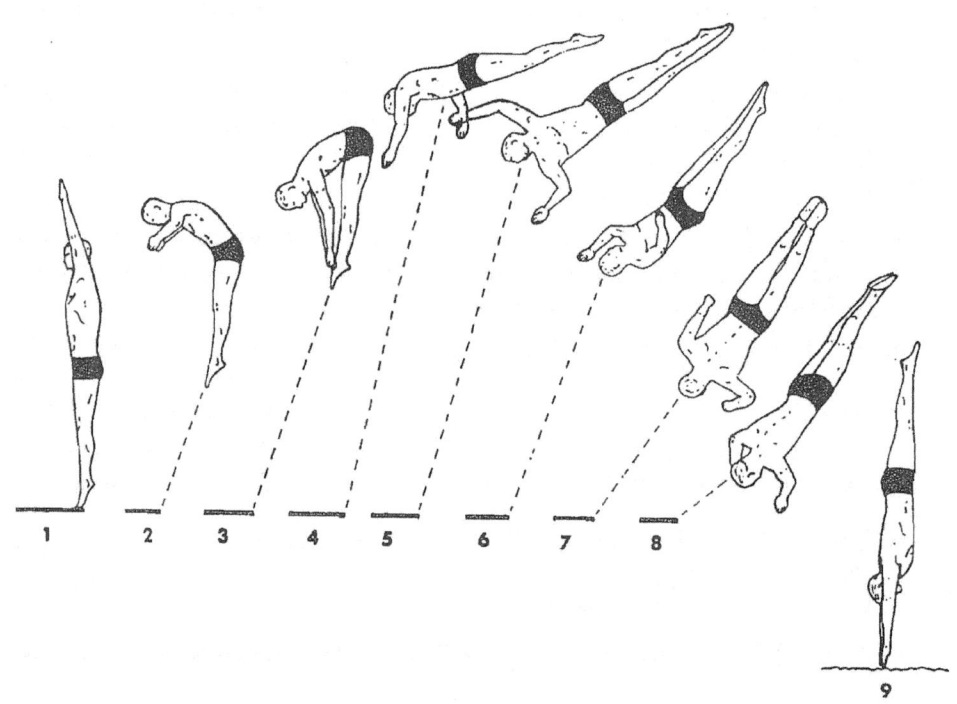

INWARD DIVE, ONE TWIST - PIKE

(One Meter)

1. The arms rise above the head, which is in line with the body as the legs extend to push the diver upward from the board. The weight of the body is held directly over the balls of the feet as the take-off is executed.

2. The hips drive straight up as the legs, feet, and toes extend. In the same motion, the body begins to bend at the waist and the arms move down toward the feet within the width of the shoulders and with the head still in line with the body.

3. The hands touch the insteps at the peak of the dive, with the legs in a vertical position. The head remains in line with the body at this time, and the water can be sighted.

4-5
6-7. The twist is started as the diver passes the peak of the dive and the body begins to straighten. The twist is executed by crossing one arm in front of the body at waist level while raising the other arm above the head, keeping it bent at the elbow. The head and body turn toward the arm that is above the head. The legs continue to move upward during the twist.

8. The water comes into view near the completion of the twist. The arms are then brought together at around shoulder height.

9. The arms extend over the head in line with the body as the diver approaches the water for a vertical entry.

INWARD DIVE, ONE TWIST - LAYOUT
(One Meter) 5412A

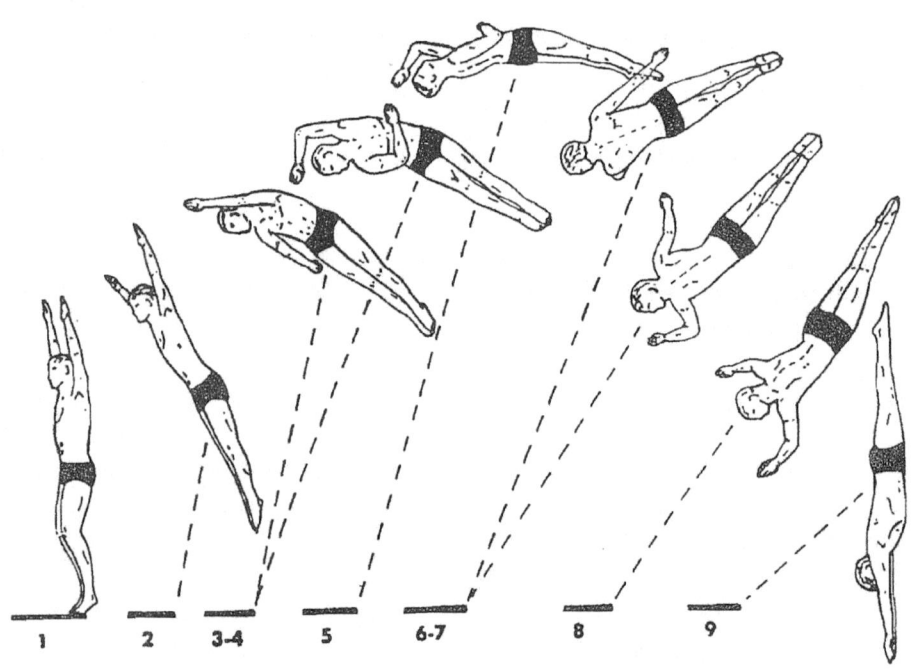

INWARD DIVE, ONE TWIST - LAYOUT

(One Meter)

1. The arms rise overhead with the head erect before the take-off. The arms then start to forcefully pull down laterally while the legs, ankles and toes extend before leaving the board.

2. The legs extend completely, as do the feet and toes, when the diver leaves the board. The arms continue to pull down laterally with force, and the legs start to move upward behind the body. The head remains in line with the body.

3-4
5-6. The twist is started as the legs continue to move upward with the head in line with the body. The twist is made by crossing one arm in front of the body at waist level while lifting the other arm overhead and pulling back with it. Both arms bend at the elbow during the twisting action. The head and body turn toward the arm that is above the head.

7-8. The arms spread laterally at head level as the twist nears completion. The water is sighted as the legs approach a vertical position.

9. The arms are extended overhead for a vertical entry into the water, and the head is in line with the body, with the eyes sighting the point of entry.

INWARD SOMERSAULT, HALF – TWIST - TUCK
(Free Position) (One Meter) 5421D

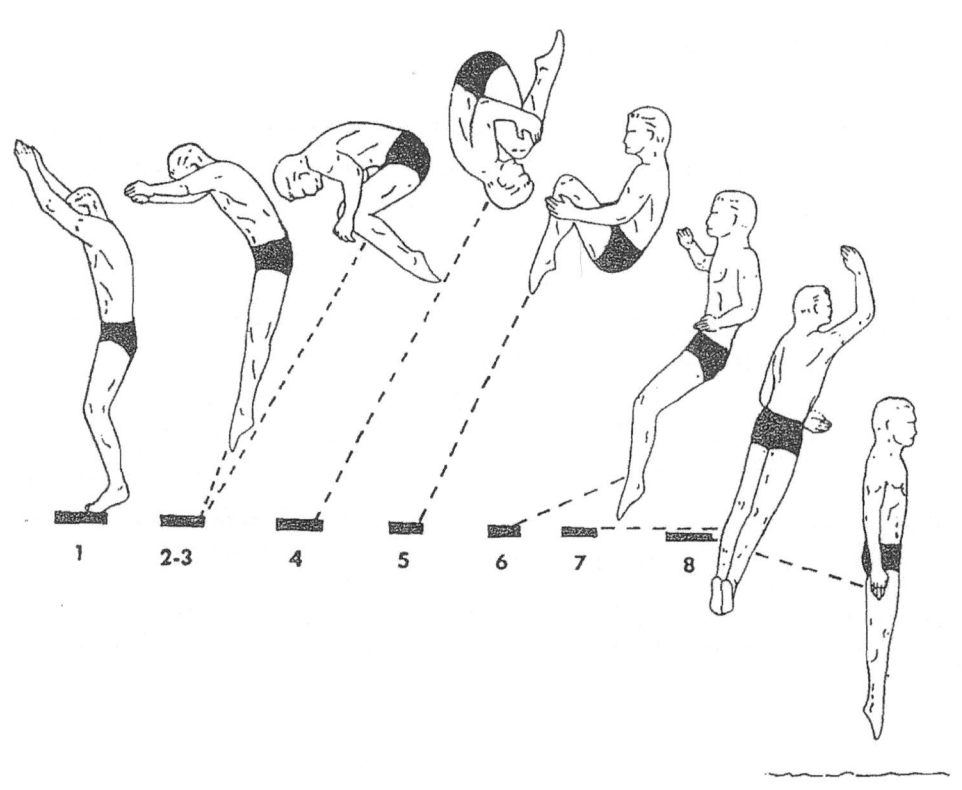

INWARD SOMERSAULT, HALF - TWIST - TUCK
(Free Position) (One Meter)

1. The arms rise over the head, which is in line with the body at the take-off from the board. The weight of the body is held directly over the balls of the feet.

2. The diver rises from the board with the extension of the legs, feet, and toes. The body bends at the waist as the hips drive nearly straight up. In the same motion, the arms are thrown clown toward the legs and the head is pulled down toward the chest.

3-4. The legs bend as they are drawn toward the chest. The hands grasp the shins and pull the knees in tight.

5. As the diver completes three-quarters of a somersault, the hands release the legs and the body begins to straighten by extending the legs toward the water and by a slight rising of the chest.

6. The half-twist is started as the body straightens. The half-twist is made by having one arm, bent at the elbow, cross in front of the body while the other, also bent at the elbow, is lifted over the head and pulls back. The head and body follow the arm that pulls back above the head.

7. When the half-twist is completed, the arms move toward the sides of the body to stop the twisting and to move into position for the entry.

8. The entry is vertical, with the arms at the side, the head erect, and the body straight.

INWARD SOMERSAULT, HALF - TWIST - PIKE
(Free Position) (One Meter) 5421D

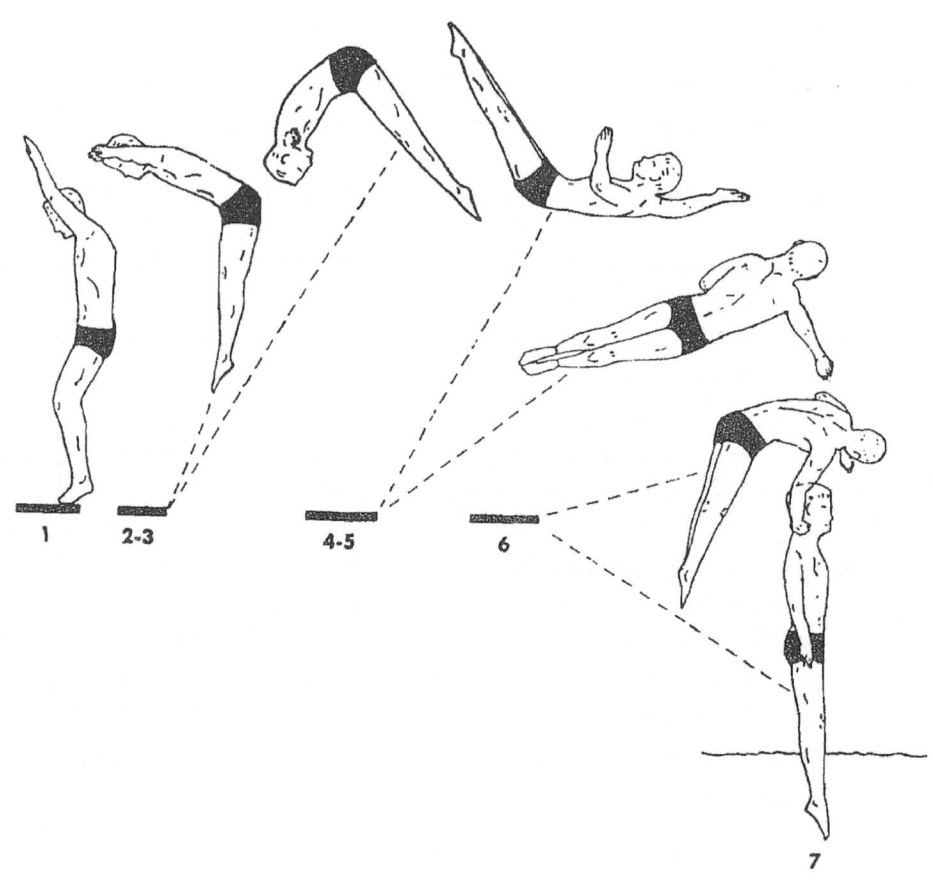

INWARD SOMERSAULT, HALF - TWIST - PIKE

(Free Position) (One Meter)

1. The take-off is made with the arms extended over the head, the weight of the body over the balls of the feet, and the head tilted slightly.

2-3. The legs, feet, and toes fully extend as the diver leaves the board, and the hips rise straight up as the body bends at the waist. As the body begins to pike, the arms move laterally with force to a position level with the shoulders. The head continues to pull down during this action.

4-5. The half-twist, which is started as the body passes the peak of the dive, is made by bending one arm and pulling it across the chest while lifting the other arm and pulling it back. The body turns toward the arm that pulls back.

6. As the half-twist is completed, the diver straightens the body by pulling up with the head and chest while pushing the legs toward the water. The arms move toward the sides of the body to stop the twisting.

7. The body straightens for a vertical entry with the arms at the sides and the head erect.

INWARD SOMERSAULT, ONE TWIST - PIKE
(Free Position) (One Meter) 5422D

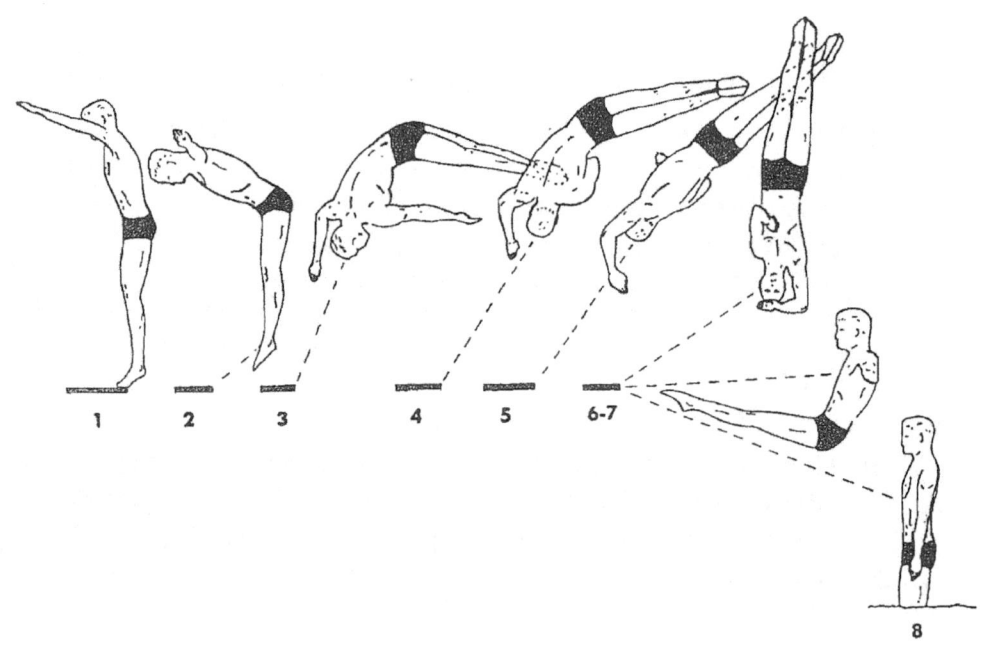

INWARD SOMERSAULT, ONE TWIST - PIKE
(Free Position) (One Meter)

1. Prior to the take-off, the arms rise overhead with the hips and shoulders directly over the end of the board. The eyes sight the other end of the board, which helps to keep the head erect.
2. As the diver leaves the board, the arms are pulled down laterally to shoulder level while the legs extend, and the hips are pushed upward. The body bends at the waist to assume an open pike. The head and shoulders pull down with the arms.

3-4

5-6. The twist is started, as the legs approach a horizontal level, by lifting overhead one arm (bent at the elbow) while the other is moved across the body in front of the chest. The diver pulls back with the elbow of the upper arm as he continues to push across the body with the other arm. Meanwhile, the body straightens to permit an easier twisting action.

7. At the completion of one twist, the arms are extended to the sides at shoulder level to stop the twisting. The completion of the twist is usually reached just as the diver approaches three-quarters of a somersault. As the arms extend out to the sides, the body again pikes at the waist, which allows for control of the legs, in preparation for the entry into the water.
8. The entry is made by pushing the legs down at the water as the head and shoulders remain upright. The arms drop to the sides, close to the thighs, to allow for a vertical entry without the back arching.

INWARD 1½ SOMERSAULTS, ONE TWIST - PIKE (Free Position) (Three Meter) 5432D

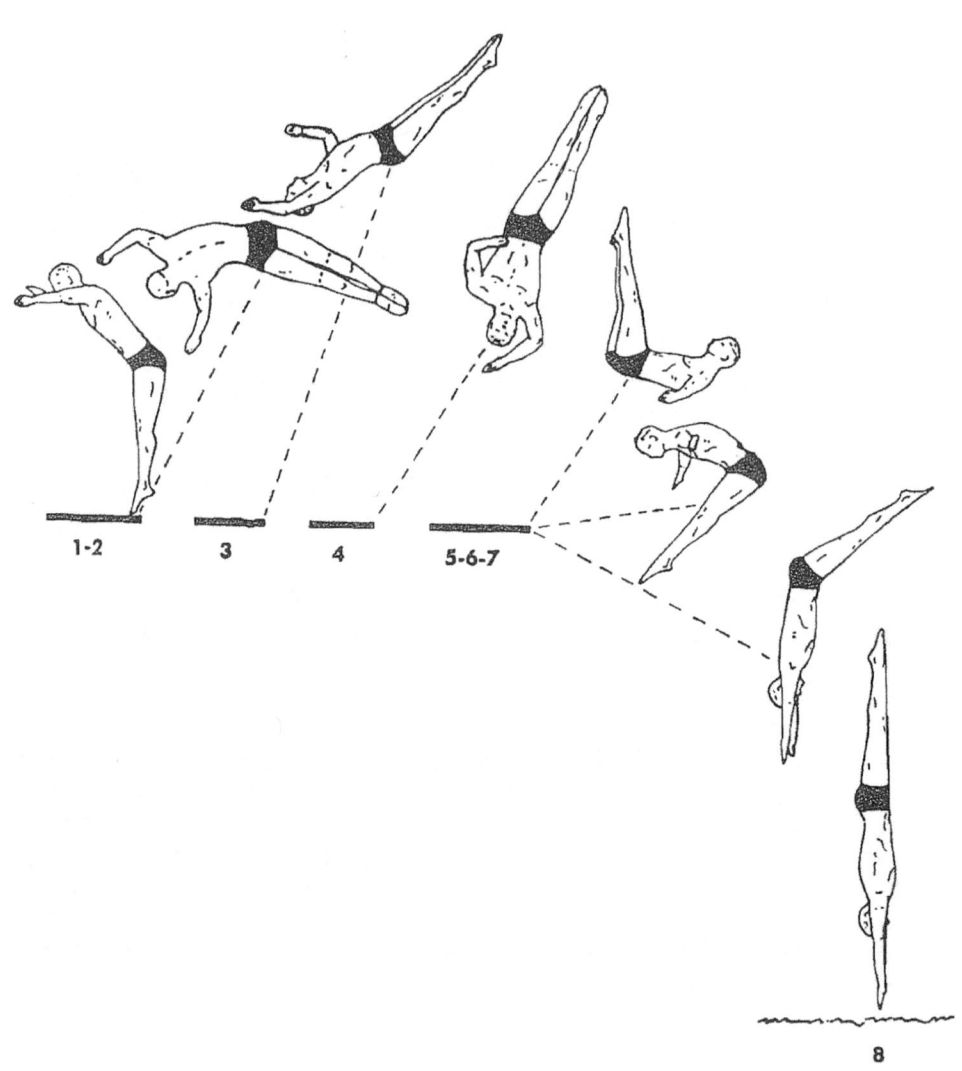

INWARD 1½ SOMERSAULTS, ONE TWIST - PIKE (Free Position) (Three Meter)

1. The diver takes off from the board, with the arms pulling down in front of the body. The legs completely extend, and the hips drive upward. The head and shoulders drive downward in the same motion, to aid in the somersaulting action.

2-3. The twisting action starts as soon as a definite pike position is established. The twist is executed with one arm overhead and bent at the elbow while the other, also bent at the elbow, thrusts across the body in front of the chest. The body straightens during these actions to permit a fast twist.

4. A smooth twist is obtained by pulling back with the elbow of the upper arm while pushing farther across the chest with the lower arm. The head attempts to turn in the direction of the upper arm.

5-6. The twist is completed at approximately three-quarters of a somersault. The arms extend laterally to shoulder level at this time, and the head and shoulders move down toward the legs to form a deep open pike position. The water can be sighted at this time, which aids the diver in lining up the dive for entry into the water.

7. The diver reaches for the water as the legs pass the horizontal at 1¼ somersaults. The body begins to straighten as the diver reaches overhead and the legs continue to rise toward a vertical position.

8. The diver enters the water in a vertical position with the arms in line with the body.

INWARD 1½ SOMERSAULTS, DOUBLE TWIST-PIKE (Free Position) (Three Meter) 5434D

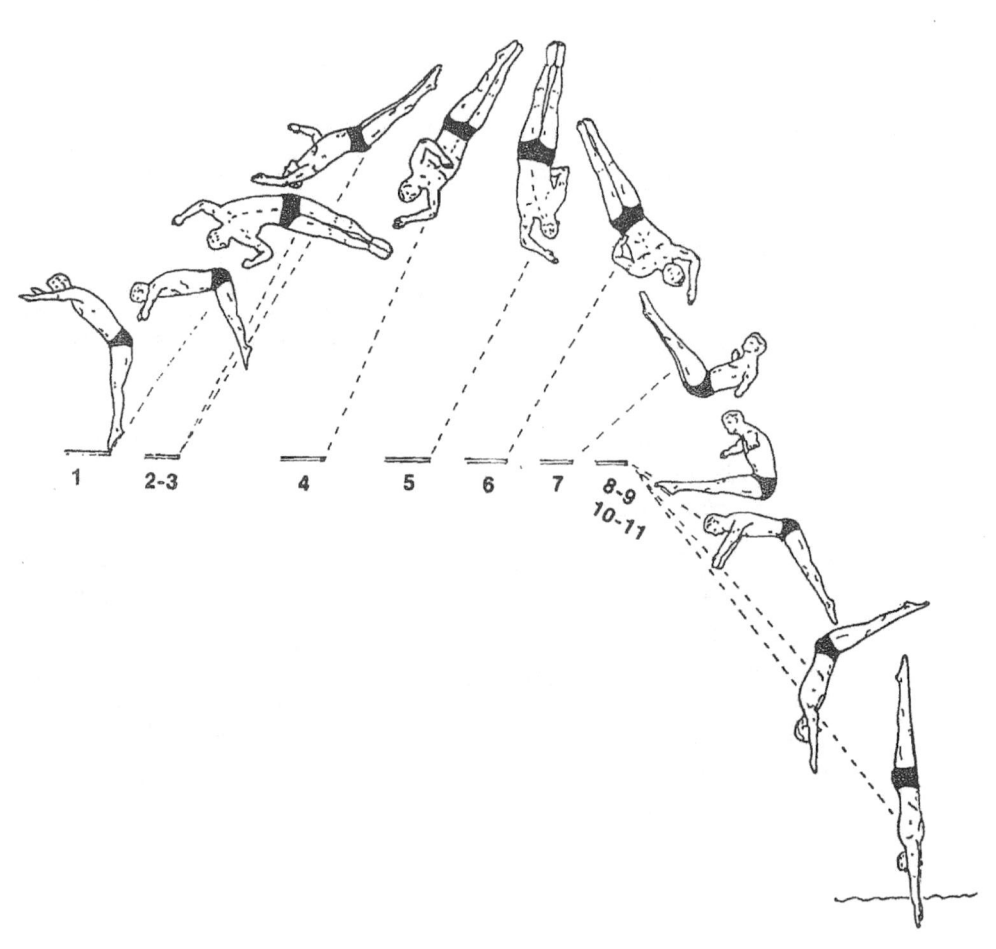

INWARD 1 ½ SOMERSAULTS, DOUBLE TWIST - PIKE (Free Position) (Three Meter)

1-2. The diver takes off from the board by forcefully pushing the arms, head and shoulders forward and downward while the legs, ankles and toes extend. On leaving the board, the body bends at the waist, pushing the hips upward.

3-4

5-6. As the body begins to rotate, the diver starts the twisting action by bending the arms at the elbow with one arm pulling across the chest while the other arm lifts above the head and pulls back at the elbow. The body straightens as the arms move into position. The head also moves in the direction of the twisting action.

7-8. As the diver nears the completion of two twists, the top arm pulls downward and the lower arm lifts to a position at right angles to the body and at shoulder level, which allows for the diver to assume an open pike position.

9. The body continues to pike downward with the diver sighting the water.

10-11. Keeping the point of entry in sight, the diver extends the arms overhead and the body straightens for a vertical entry.

GROUP VI - TOWER DIVING

INTRODUCTION

Tower diving presents one of the most thrilling and breathtaking experiences found in any sport. Diving from the height of ten meters requires an abundance of courage, self-confidence, strength, body control, agility, desire and coordination. A poorly executed dive from this height can result in a serious injury to the diver from landing on the surface of the water. It is highly recommended that the diver first become somewhat proficient on the three-meter springboard and the lower platforms that range from one meter to 7½ meters before attempting the dives from a level that is over three stories high.

When learning to tower dive, the diver should first try to make a mental and physical adjustment to the added height from which he may be diving. The beginner should realize that the body is traveling at approximately 32
miles an hour when hitting the water from ten meters high. It must be recognized that the impact on hitting the water from this height is much greater than when diving from the three-meter springboard. The diver must learn the different platform approaches and take-offs and adjust to the lift from a solid and immobile surface.

Nearly every diver will agree that, when first learning, the most difficult part of tower diving is to stand on the ten-meter platform and look down at the water and the surrounding area. However, once the diver learns some dives, the tower no longer seems so high. Whether the diver is experienced or a beginner, it is always a challenging experience when learning a new dive from the top. Actually, the time the diver is in the air when diving from the ten-meter platform is nearly the same as when diving from the three-meter springboard because the diver springs higher from the point of take-off on the springboard than from the tower.

The execution of the dive from the ten-meter platform is basically the same as from the three-meter with these exceptions: The take-off differs because there is no spring on the platforms, the timing of the dives differs due to the differences in height, and the impact on the surface of the water differs with height. It must also be understood that some dives that are easy to perform on the springboard are not easy to execute from the high platforms and vice versa.

When learning to tower dive, most divers prefer to try the dive or the lead-up dive from a lower level before trying the dive from the ten-meter platform. This is almost mandatory in learning some dives. However, when the desired lower platform is not available, the diver normally chooses to either chance doing the dive or postpone learning it until a desired height is available. In the case where the higher platforms are not available, the diver can learn only those dives that can be executed from the lower platforms.

It is very important that when learning to tower dive, the diver have an experienced coach and/or experienced diver present to offer protective guidance. It must be noted that persons who have little or no background in tower diving should not attempt to learn, coach or teach beginners on the tower since their lack of knowledge could easily result in an injury to the learner. With regards to safety, most complexes that have diving platforms now have bubbler systems which greatly reduce any chance of injury when learning new dives from the different platforms.

TOWER APPROACHES AND TAKE-OFFS

Because of the solid platform that offers no spring, the tower diver uses several approaches and take-offs that differ from those used on the springboard. Since it is not possible to jump as high from a solid platform as it is from a springboard, the diver finds the platform more reliable for take-off action than the unpredictable springboard. However, in some cases, the diver may use a similar approach or take-off from the tower as is used on the springboard. The diver often has more than one choice in the kind of approach or take-off that can be used to execute certain dives when diving from the tower. The approach and take-off most desirable are that which will give the maximum lift, control and consistency in executing the dive.

The rules governing the approach and take-off from the platforms are not quite as rigid as those from the springboard, but they do require the diver to make as smooth and natural movements as possible. It may be safe to say that, if the action on the approach and take-off contribute to a successful execution of the dive, then the action is permissible. The beginner should execute fundamental dives when practicing the different approaches and take-offs from the tower. This will ensure safety to the diver and permit him to concentrate better on the desired actions. The approaches and take-offs most commonly used when diving from the platforms are explained on the following pages.

STANDING FORWARD TAKE-OFF

The diver walks to the edge of the platform and stands near the end with the feet together and the toes on or curled over the edge. The arms are raised in front of the diver in a position shoulder width apart and at shoulder level. The diver then takes off from the platform in one of the following ways.

Figure A. - Version 1
(used mainly in performing standing front and reverse dives)

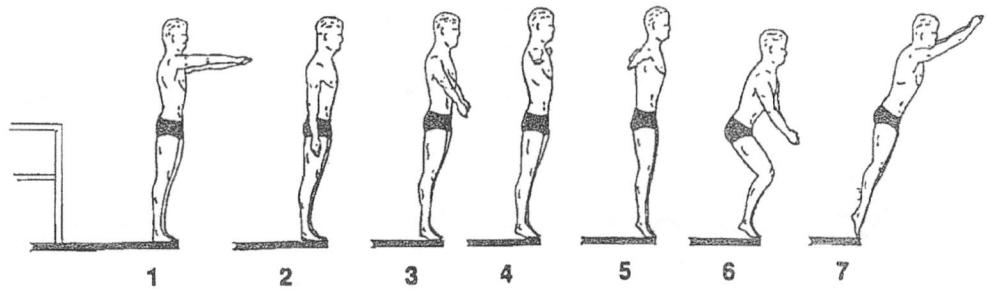

1-2. The arms drop slowly to the sides of the diver by pulling them down in front or pulling them back to a position at right angles to the body, then down to the sides where they remain stationary for a moment to permit the diver to concentrate on the movement required for the dive.

3-4. The arms then lift upward, slightly in front of the body, and spread to a right-angle position at shoulder level.

5-6-7. The arms continue to circle back and down behind the diver as the knees flex and the upper body and head remain in a near erect position. The arms then pass close to the hips and swing forward and upward, about shoulder width apart, in front of the body and overhead, as the legs, ankles and toes extend.

STANDING FORWARD TAKE - OFF

Figure B. - Version 2
(used in performing forward somersault dives,
and also the front dive tuck, pike and layout)

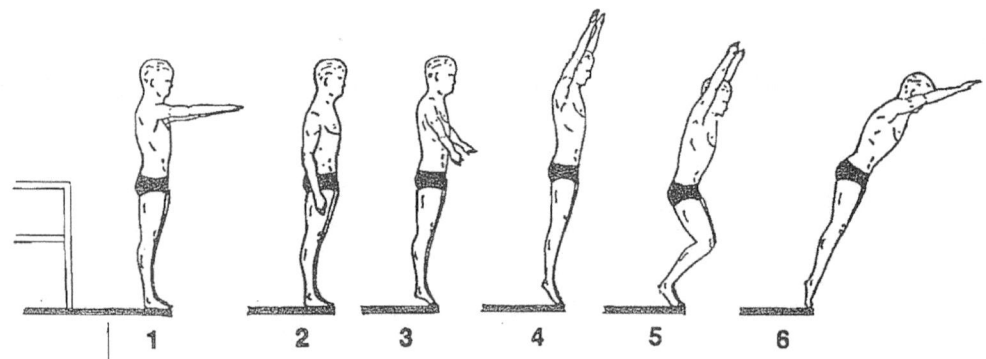

1-2. From the stance with the arms in front, the arms drop to the sides either in front of the body or by pulling the arms back to the shoulders, then down to the sides.

3-4. The arms then lift overhead by moving them in front of the body or laterally.

5-6. The arms normally pause for a moment before they move forward and downward as the knees flex, then extend before the feet leave the platform.

RUNNING AND WALKING FORWARD TAKE - OFFS
RUNNING APPROACH, TWO FOOT TAKE-OFF

Figure C. - Version 1
(used in performing forward dives)

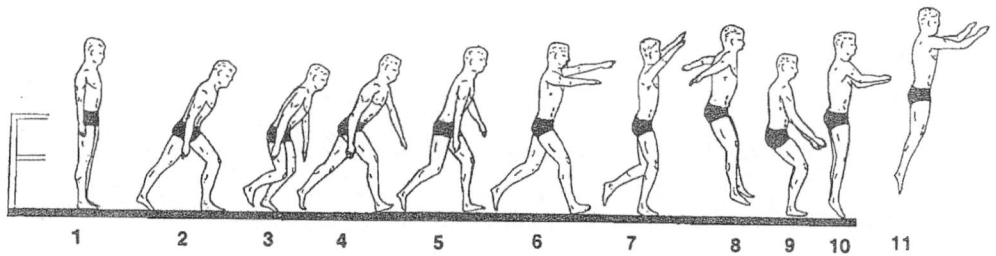

1-2-3

4-5. The diver runs easily but forcefully toward the end of the platform. The arms swing normally in the first few steps of the run, then both arms move forward and upward just above head level. The arms then continue to swing upward outside the width of the shoulders.

6-7. The diver then springs forward from one foot while the arms continue to swing forward and upward.

8-9. The arms circle back and down behind the body and pass the hips when both feet land on the end of the platform.

10-11. The arms then move forward and upward overhead as the diver jumps from the platform.

RUNNING AND WALKING FORWARD TAKE-OFFS

RUNNING APPROACH, TWO FOOT TAKE-OFF

Figure D. - Version 2
(used in performing forward dives)

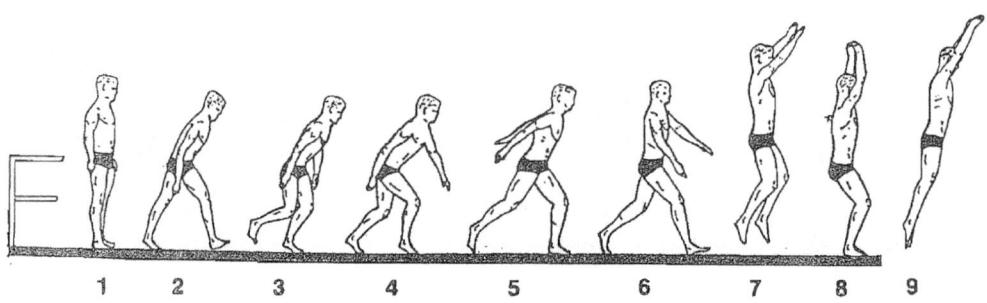

1-2
3-4. The diver runs forward with a natural swing of the arms and sighting the end of the platform. The speed of the run depends on the dive to be performed. Normally, easy dives require a walk or slow run while difficult dives require a faster run.

5-6-7. While on the run and approaching the end of the platform, the diver springs forward from one foot into a low hurdle. A low hurdle is used in tower diving because the platform offers no spring. The arms swing overhead while the diver is still in the hurdle. ***NOTE-*** The diver has three choices on how to lift the arms above the head in the hurdle: 1. Swing the arms upward in front of the body; 2. Lift the arms overhead laterally; 3. Lift the arms laterally to shoulder level during the run, then drop them down and across the front of the body in a crossing motion. The arms then move laterally over the head from the crossed arm position as the diver springs from one foot into the hurdle.

8-9. The diver lands on the end of the platform flatfooted or on the balls of the feet with arms extended overhead before jumping from the edge.

WALKING APPROACH WITH ONE FOOT TAKE-OFF

Figure E -
(used in performing reverse dives)

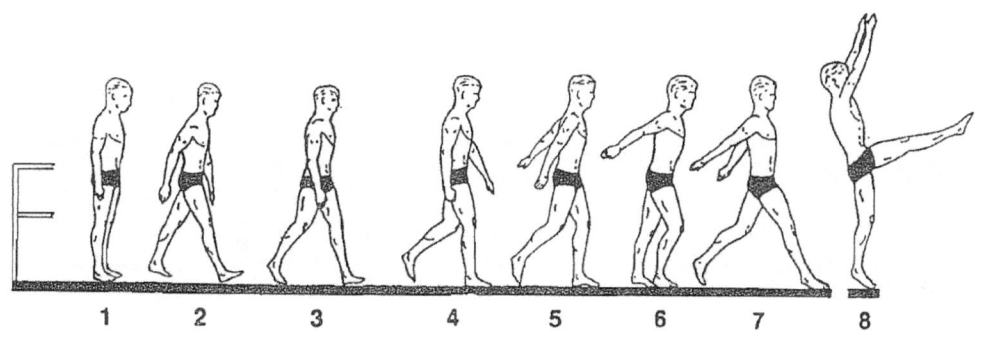

1-2
3-4. Starting from the stance, the diver walks normally toward the end of the platform.
5-6
7-8. After two or three steps, the arms drop behind the diver on the second from the last step, then swing forward as the last step is made with the foot planted near the edge of the platform. The other leg swings forward and upward along with the arms.

WALKING APPROACH WITH ONE FOOT TAKE - OFF

Figure F. - Version 1
(used in performing reverse dives)

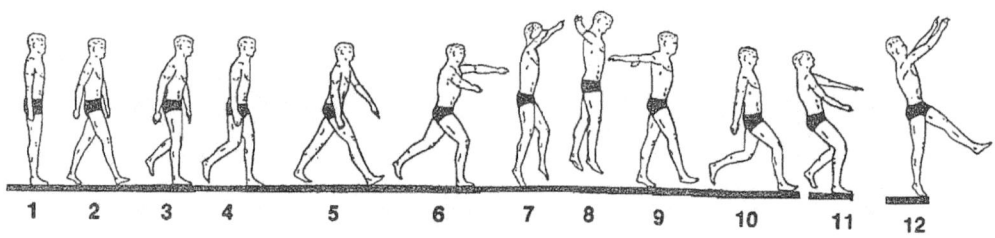

1-2-3
4-5. The diver walks toward the end of the platform in a normal fashion.

6-7-8. Still walking forward, the diver lifts the arms semi-laterally or laterally to a position slightly over the head. The diver then jumps from one leg with the other leg moving forward, bent at the knee. The forward leg then pulls back behind the jumping leg.

9-10
11-12. With the arms continuing to circle behind the body, the forward leg that was pulled back lands on the ball of the foot on the platform and the jumping leg moves forward and is planted at the end of the platform. This complete movement is performed in the form of a "hop." The back leg then swings forward and upward, along with the arms, as the leg on the end of the platform extends to lift the diver from the platform.

WALKING APPROACH, SKIP STEP, WITH ONE FOOT TAKE-OFF

Figure G - Version 2
(used in performing reverse dives)

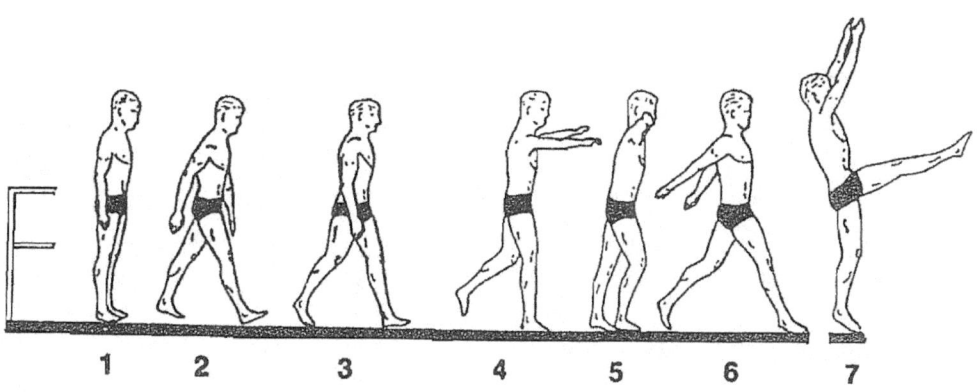

1-2-3. The diver walks in a normal fashion toward the end of the platform.

4-5

6-7. Still walking forward, the diver lifts the arms forward, or laterally, above the head with the weight planted on the forward step. The back step then moves up to the heel of the front foot where the weight is shifted lightly to the ball of the back foot. The front foot then takes a short step forward to the end of the platform where the body weight is again placed on the forward step. The arms continue to move in a backward circle during this skipping action. With the forward step planted on the end of the platform, the back-leg swings forward and upward, along with the arms, as the diver jumps from the platform with the leg planted on the end.

BACKWARD TAKE-OFF

Figure H. -
(used in performing all dives in backward direction)

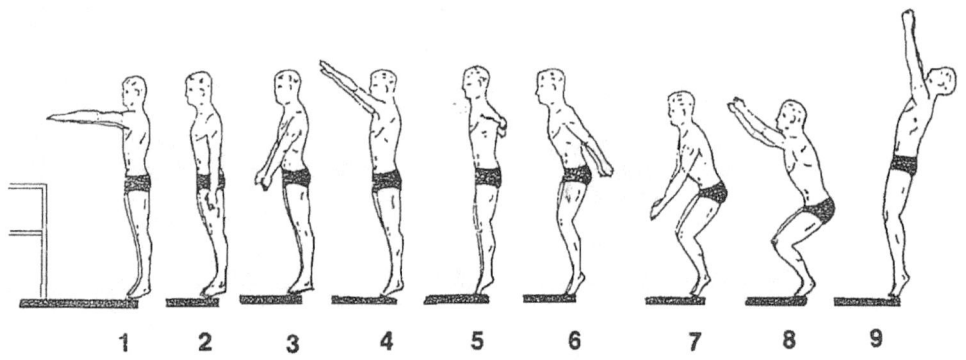

1-2. Standing backwards with the arms elevated at shoulder level and shoulder width apart, the diver drops the arms to the sides in any manner desired or spreads the arms to a swan position.

3-4
5-6. From either of these two positions, the arms lift overhead and circle behind the body. As they pass the shoulder level, the legs begin to flex with the body remaining in a near vertical position and the head held erect.

7-8-9. The arms continue to circle as they pass the hips and move forward and upward. The legs extend as the arms swing upward.

INWARD TAKE-OFF

Figure I. -
(used for all inward dives)

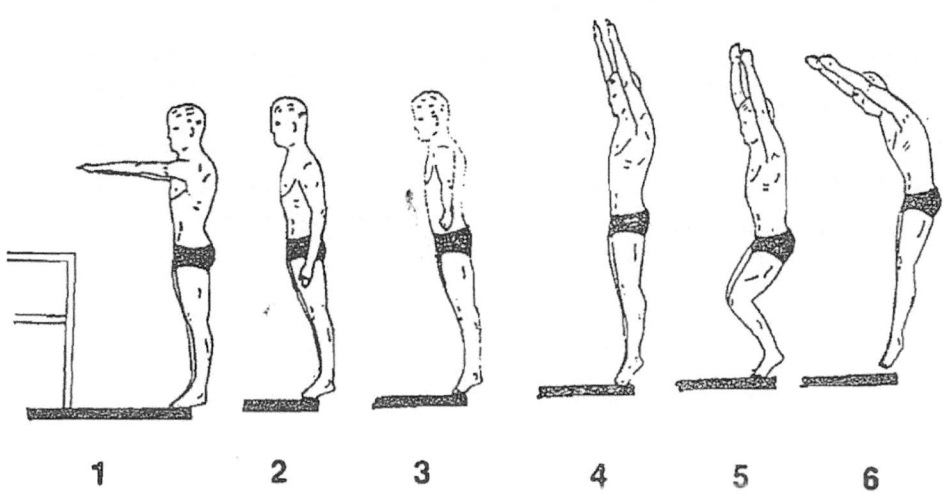

1-2
3-4. From the back-stance position with the arms extended in front at shoulder level and shoulder width apart, the arms can move in two directions. Either they drop to the sides and lift overhead, or they move overhead without dropping them to the sides.

5-6. From an upright body position with the head erect, the arms, head and shoulders move downward as the legs bend slightly, then extend to push the hips upward before the diver leaves the platform.

ARM STAND APPROACHES AND TAKE-OFFS

In all arm stand dives, the head is in a position where the eyes can sight the water throughout the execution of the arm stand. Some divers prefer to place the fingers, up to the first joint, over the edge of the platform when executing the arm stand. Other divers prefer to place the whole hand on the surface of the platform near the edge.

The arm stand must be held for at least three seconds to exhibit control before the diver can begin the execution of a dive from this position. Once the arm stand is assumed, the legs must be straight and together with the feet extended, the toes pointed, and with little or no arch in the back. Some of the ways of approaching the platform to perform the arm stand are explained on the next several pages.

ONE LEG KICK UP

FIGURE J

1. The diver kneels and assumes a "track start" position with the arms spread about shoulder width apart, the shoulders leaning forward, and the eyes sighting over the edge of the platform.

2. The body lifts up by slightly extending the front leg while the back leg straightens as it kicks upward from the platform.

3-4. The back leg continues upward over the head as the forward leg also pushes from the platform and moves upward. Both legs continue to move upward in a "V" position until the diver is in balance.

5. The legs then slowly close when they are directly above the head and the diver's body is perfectly straight with little or no arch in the back.

  Note. Some divers perform the one leg kick up by starting a step or two back on the platform, then walk up to the edge, plant the hands on the edge and in a continuous movement kick up to the handstand using the same motion as used in the "track start" approach.

PRESS UP IN TUCK POSITION

FIGURE K

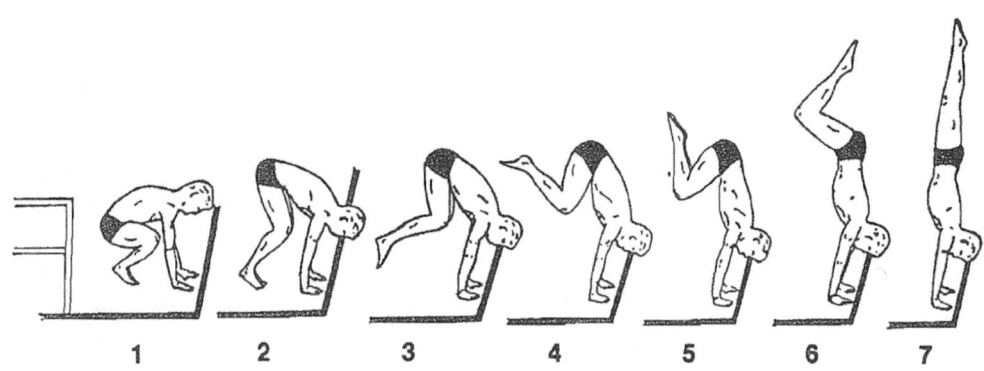

1. The diver stands near the end of the platform and bends over to a squat position. The hands are placed on the edge of the platform at about shoulder width apart.
2. The seat is then lifted by slightly extending the legs with the shoulders leaning forward and the eyes sighting over the edge of the platform.

3-4

5-6. Keeping the shoulders forward, the diver gives a slight push from both feet, keeping the knees drawn in toward the chest. With the strength from the arms, the legs slowly rise to a vertical position, staying in the tuck position.

6. Once the diver is in balance with the legs in a vertical position, they extend and place the body in a straight vertical position with little or no arch in the back.

PRESS UP IN PIKE POSITION

FIGURE L

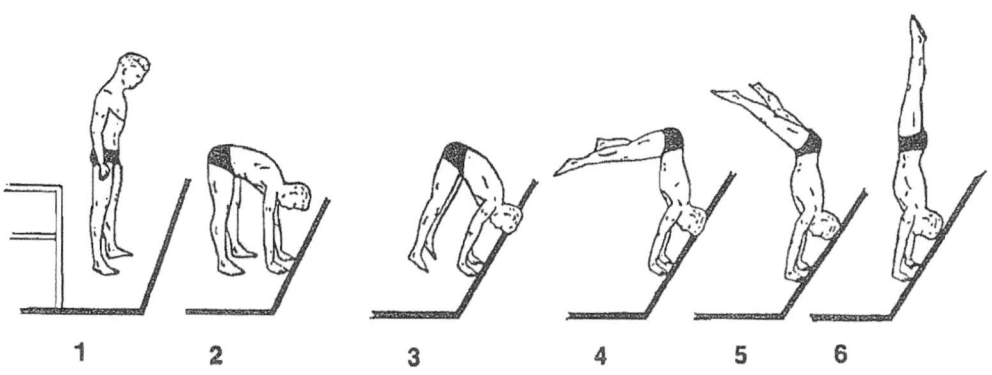

1-2. Standing near the edge of the platform with the legs slightly spread apart or with the feet together, the diver bends over and places the hands on the edge of the platform about shoulder width apart.

3-4-5. Keeping the legs straight, the diver leans forward with the shoulders over the edge of the platform and the eyes sighting the water. Using the strength of the arms, the diver slowly lifts the legs upward from the tip of the toes. The legs are slowly brought together when they reach a vertical position if the diver started the arm stand with the legs apart.

6. The diver then holds the body in a straight and vertical position with little or no arch in the back and with the eyes sighting over the edge of the platform.

BASIC TOWER DIVES

A beginner on the high platform should learn certain basic dives before attempting some of the more difficult dives. The advantages of learning basic dives first are quite obvious. First, the diver can adjust easier to the take-off from the solid platform by doing dives that are relatively easy. And second, the diver can adjust easier to the different heights on a tower if he/she learns dives that are considered basic. This approach to tower diving can greatly reduce the chance of injury.

Many of the preliminary dives can be learned by first attempting them on a lower platform, such as the five-meter, then attempting them from the higher platforms, like the 7½ meter or ten-meter. However, there are certain basic dives that are actually easier to perform from the ten-meter platform than from the lower platforms.

Some of the basic tower dives performed from the ten-meter platform are described on the following pages.

RUNNING FRONT 1½ SOMERSAULTS, OPEN (OR CLOSED) PIKE
FIGURE A 103B

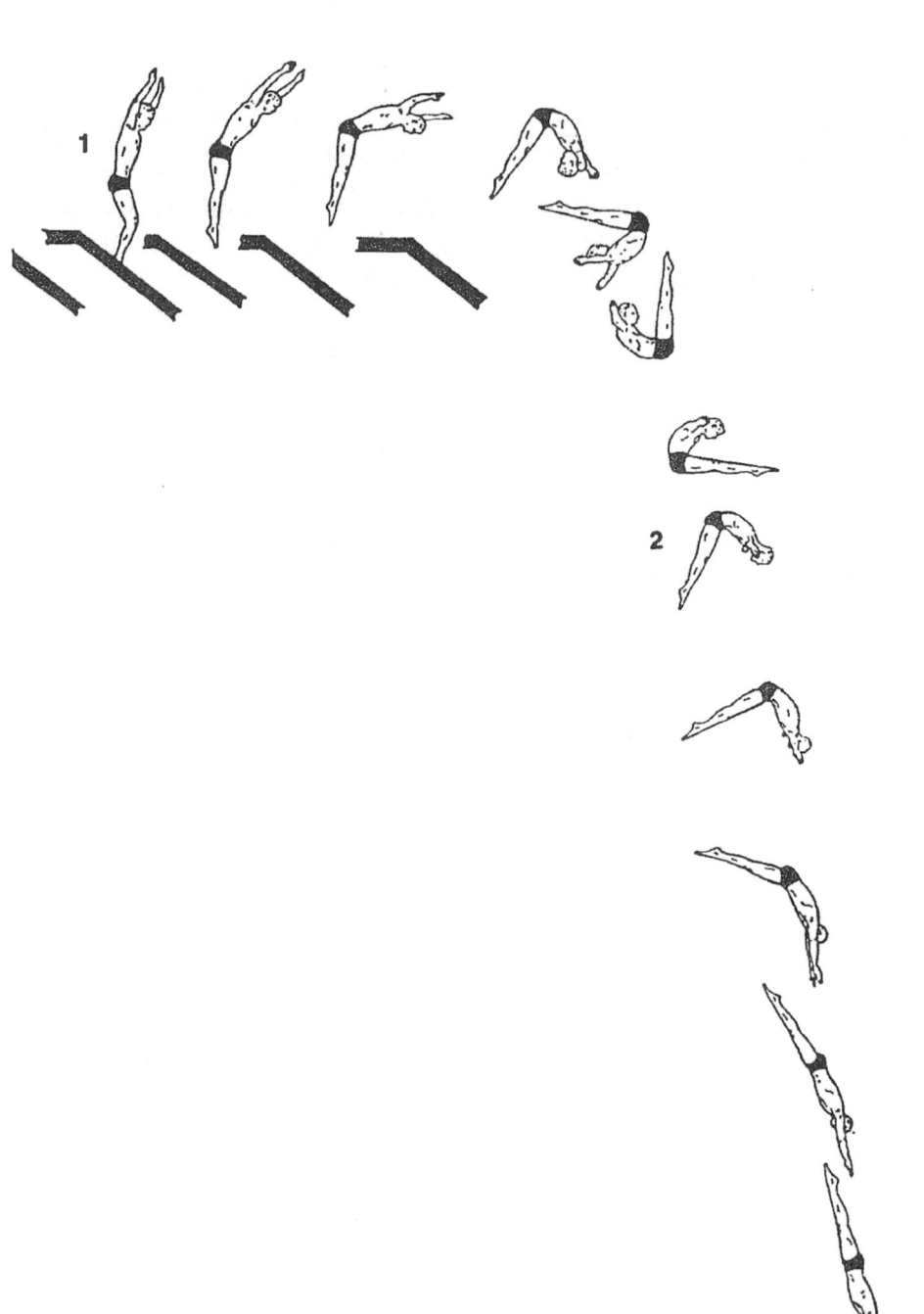

RUNNING FRONT 1½ SOMERSAULTS, OPEN (OR CLOSED) PIKE
FIGURE A

The diver may attempt this dive using a walk or slow running approach with a two-foot take-off from a standing position (Figures B & E - Tower Approaches). Whatever way, the diver prepares to leave the platform with the arms extended overhead and head erect. As the diver jumps from the platform, the arms push forward and downward with the hips rising and the eyes sighting the water.

1. Once off the platform, the arms may pull laterally to a position level with the shoulders as the body bends at the waist to form an open pike position or the arms may push forward and downward to grasp the legs behind the knees in a deep pike position. The diver remains in either of these positions until he/she completes about three quarters of a somersault, at which point the water comes into view.

2. If the diver is in a closed pike position, the legs are released and the arms circle slightly outside the width of the shoulders while extending them toward the water. If an open pike position is used, the arms begin to reach overhead in a lateral motion in the direction of the water for the entry. At this moment, the diver begins to extend the arms overhead, laterally adjusting the timing, so the hands clasp together at a point just slightly in front of vertical for the entry. The body straightens during this action.

STANDING FRONT DIVE, LAYOUT
FIGURE B 101A

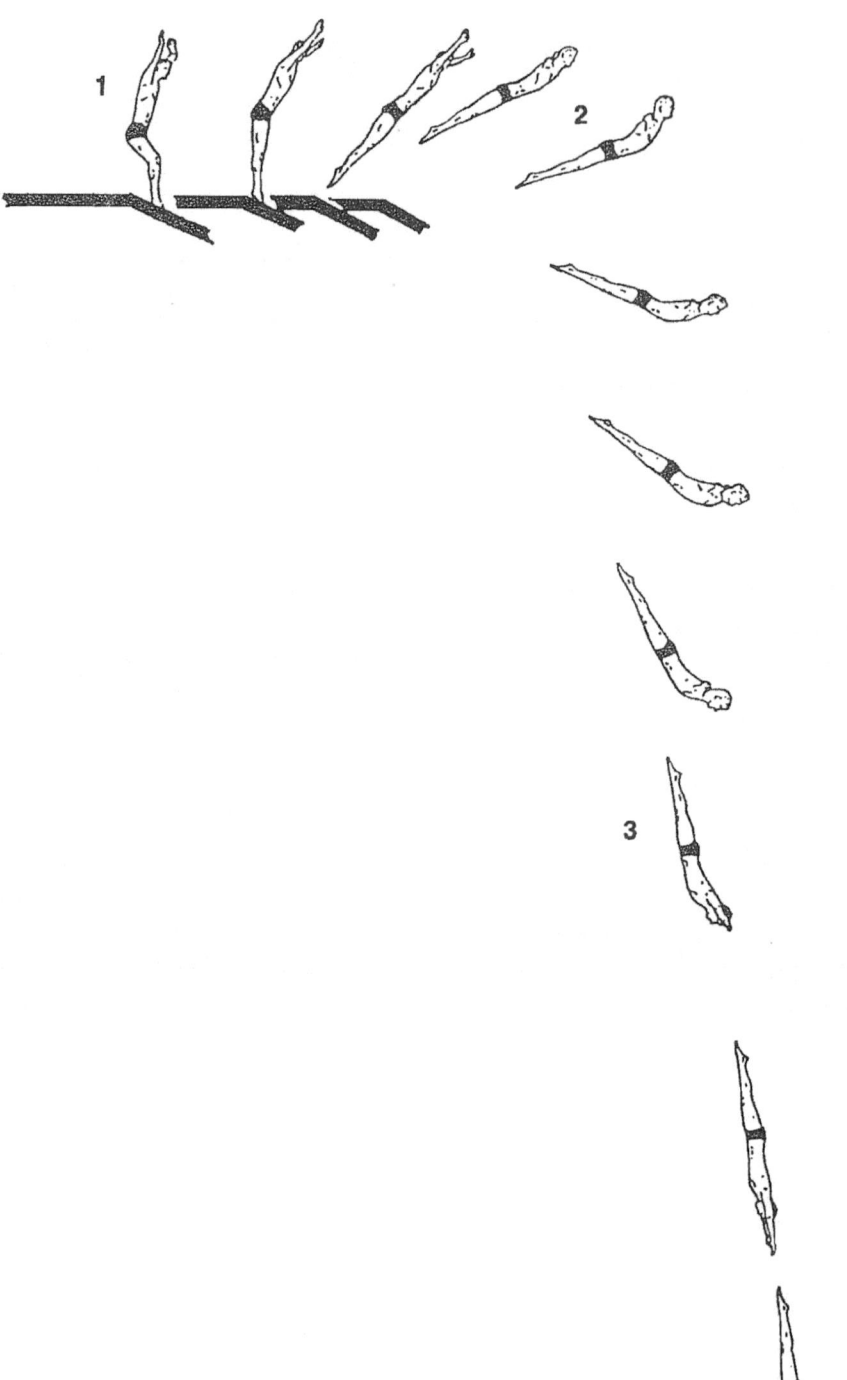

STANDING FRONT DIVE, LAYOUT
FIGURE B

1. The diver assumes a stance on the end of the platform and uses either take-off action explained Figures A & B -Tower Approaches. In either case, the diver's arms extend overhead on the edge of the platform prior to the take-off. As the diver prepares to jump from the platform, the arms pull down laterally to a position at shoulder level with the head held erect.
2. The arms remain in a fixed "swan position," with little arch in the back, until the diver approaches the water. The diver may find the dive easier to control if the head tilts down to sight the water just as the body passes the edge of the platform on its downward flight.
3. When the diver approaches the water, the arms extend overhead in a lateral motion and reach for a point of entry slightly in front of vertical.

INWARD DIVE, PIKE
FIGURE C 401B

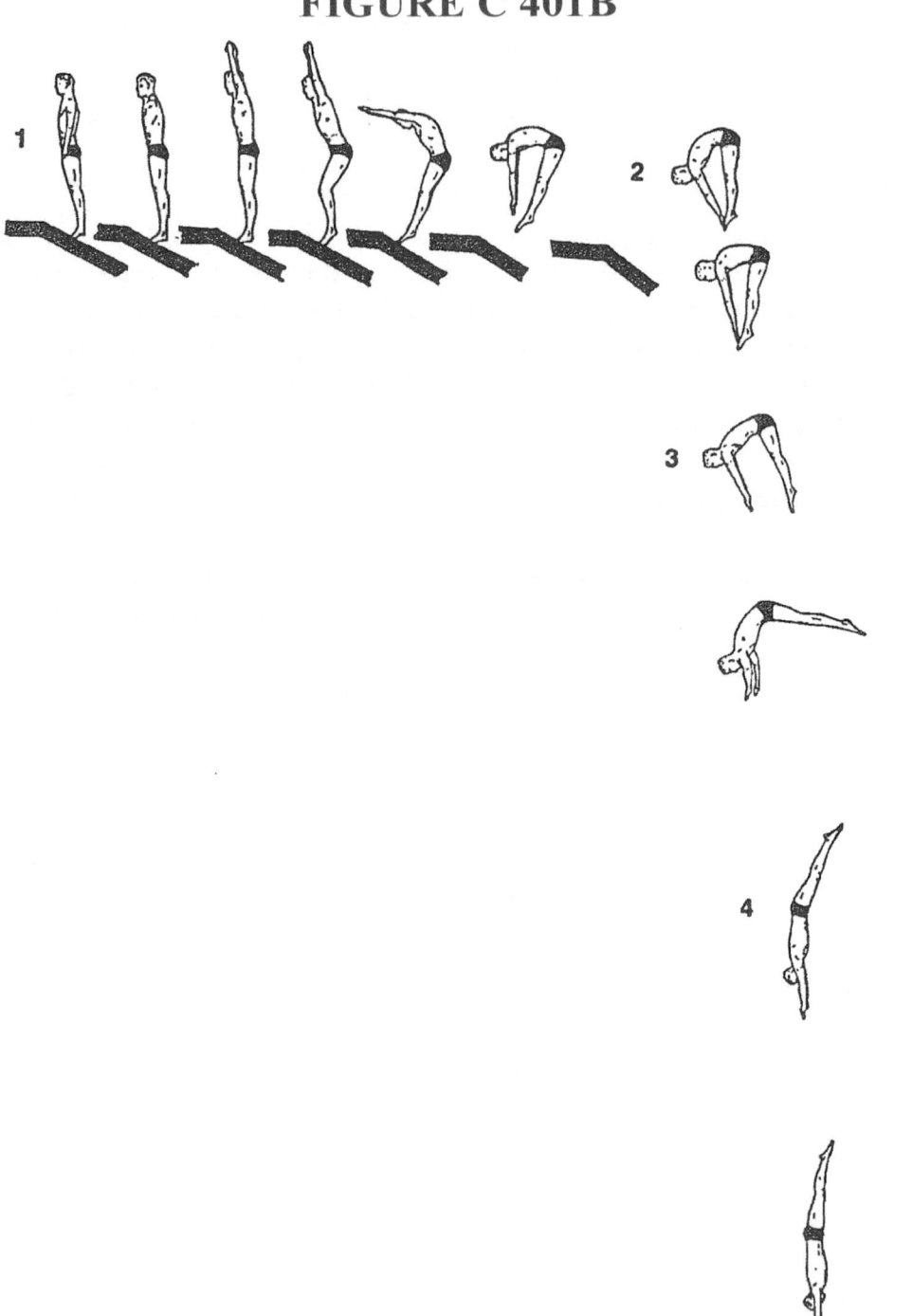

INWARD DIVE, PIKE

FIGURE C

1. Standing on the edge of the platform with the back to the water, the diver lifts the shoulders laterally overhead in a vertical position (Figure I-Tower Approaches). As the diver jumps slightly backward from the platform, the hips push upward, and the arms, head and shoulders push downward, allowing the diver to bend at the waist. The legs remain straight.
2. The hands touch the feet near the peak of the jump with the legs vertical and the eyes sighting the water.
3. Following a soft touch of the feet, the arms extend toward the water by circling just outside the width of the shoulders and the legs move upward as the body starts to straighten.
4. The hands clasp just before the entry into the water with the body straight and the arms extended over the head in line with the body.

BACK DIVE, PIKE
FIGURE D 201B

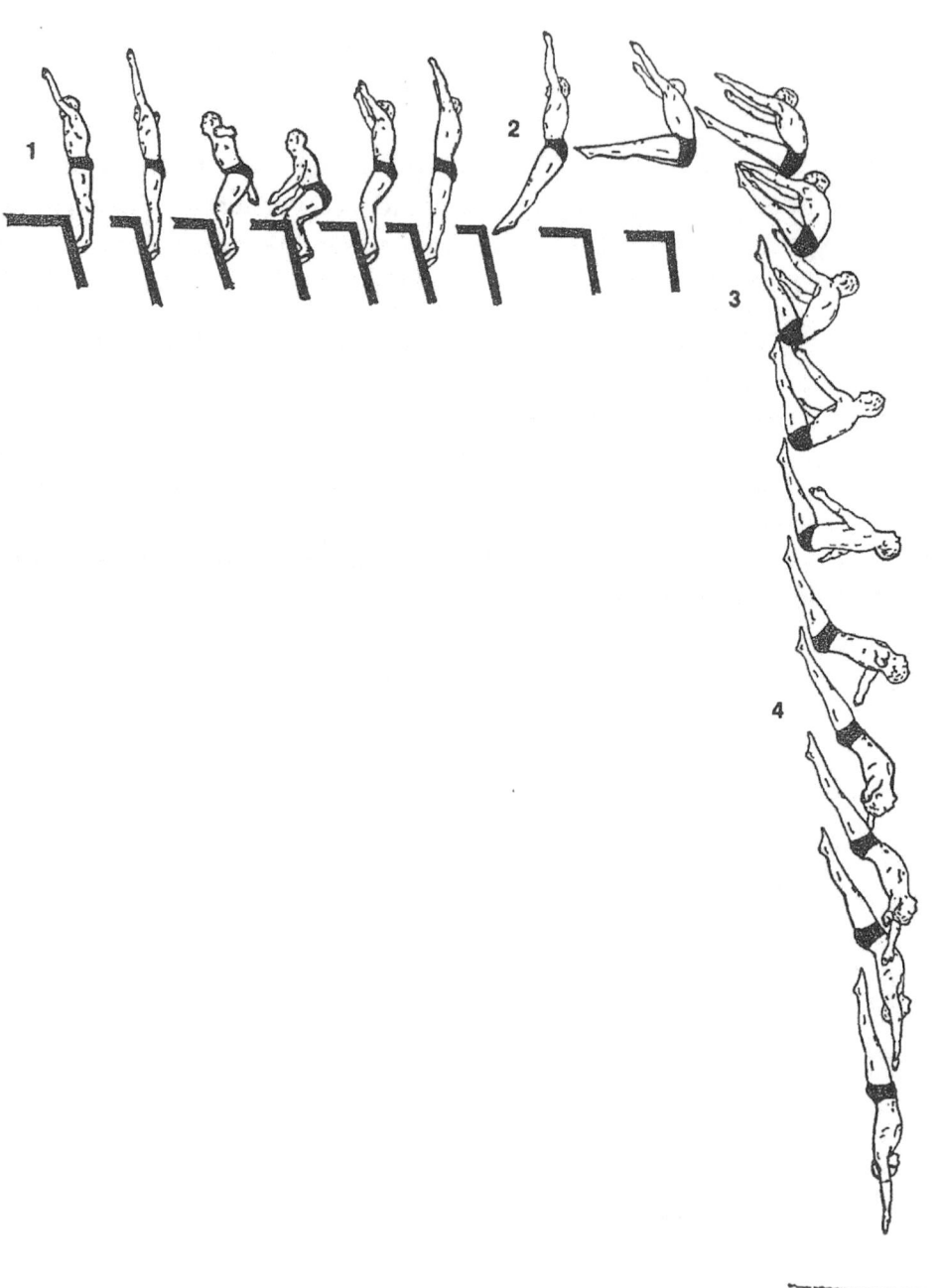

BACK DIVE, PIKE
FIGURE D

1. Standing on the edge of the platform with the back to the water (Figure H-Tower Approaches), the diver lifts the arms overhead, then circles them back behind the body, down past the hips, and forward and upward while the hips drop back slightly from the platform. During this motion, the legs bend, and the body remains upright with the head erect.
2. With the arms overhead in a vertical position and the body and head erect, the diver extends the legs, feet and toes to jump upward from the platform. Once in the air, the legs immediately lift toward the arms which move slightly forward to touch the feet with the hands. The eyes can sight the hands as they touch the feet.
3. With the touch of the feet, the upper body then begins to drop away from the legs with the arms extending laterally over the head toward the water. The head drops back to sight the water before the arms pass the level of the shoulders to control the dive action. The arms and head movement also cause the legs to remain in a fixed near vertical position.
4. The head continues to look back to sight the water as the diver nears the entry. The arms close overhead just before the entry with the body slightly short of vertical and with the arms extended overhead in direct line with the body.

REVERSE DIVE, PIKE
FIGURE E 301B

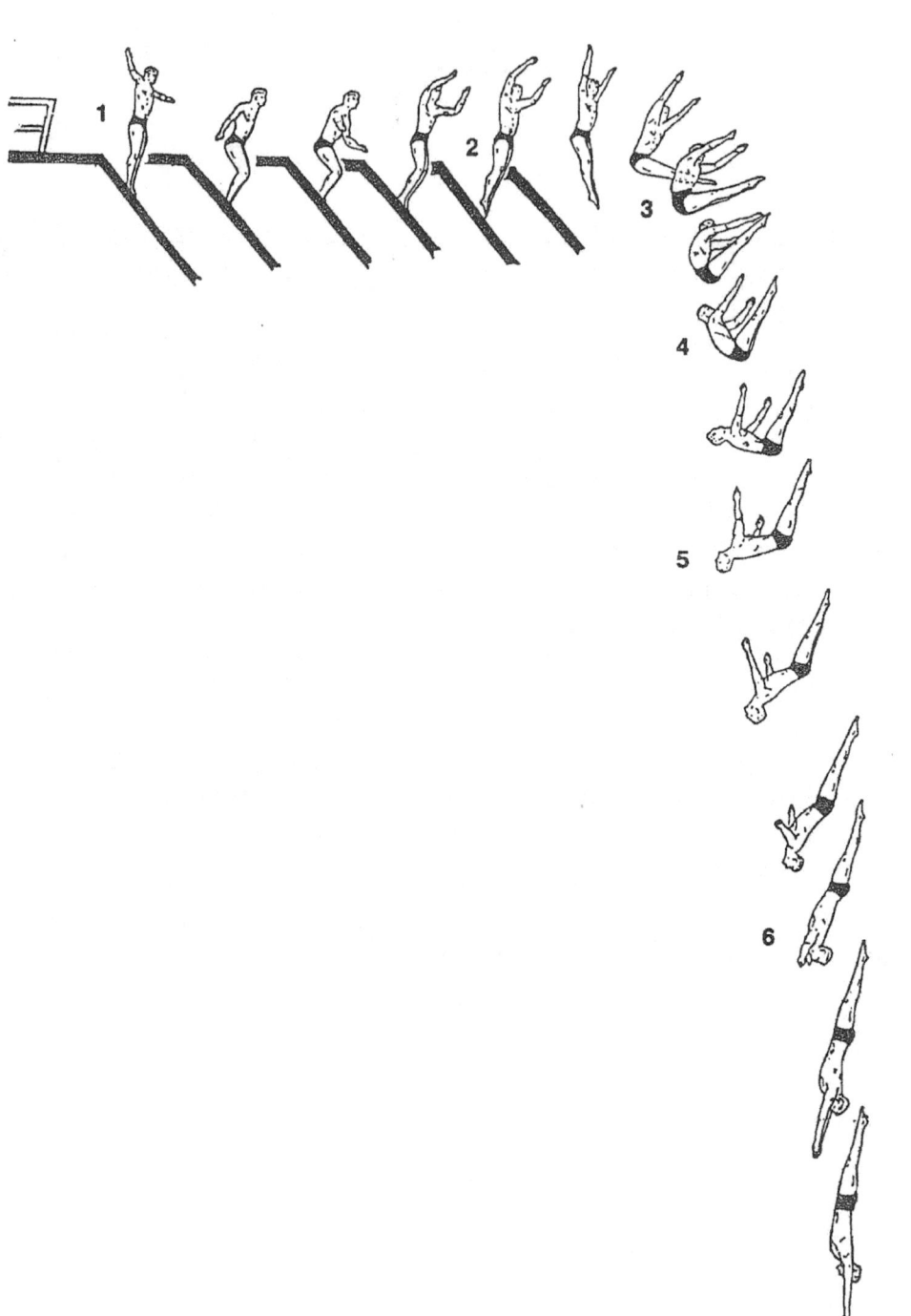

REVERSE DIVE, PIKE

FIGURE E

1. The diver stands on the edge of the platform facing the water (Figure A-Tower Approaches). From shoulder level, the arms swing back behind the body, downward past the hips, then forward and upward as the legs bend prior to the take-off.
2. The arms continue to swing upward to a vertical position over the head as the legs, feet and toes extend and the diver jumps from the platform. When the feet leave the edge of the platform, the body bends at the waist as the legs lift upward in the direction of the arms. The head and upper body remain in an erect position.
3. The arms move forward a short distance just before the touch of the feet is made with the hands.
4. Following the touch, the upper body begins to drop back and away from the legs along with the arms, which begin to spread in a lateral direction.
5. The body continues to straighten while the legs remain in a position just short of vertical. The arms also continue to extend over the head. The head then drops back insight of the water before the arms pass the level of the shoulders.
6. The legs remain in a fixed position, the eyes look back and sight the point of entry, and the arms extend overhead in direct line with the body with the hands clasping just before a vertical entry is made.

HANDSTAND, CUT THROUGH, TUCK
FIGURE F 631C

HANDSTAND, CUT THROUGH, TUCK
FIGURE F

1. The diver stands near the edge of the platform and assumes a handstand (Figures J, K & L-Tower Approaches) and holds the position for at least three seconds.
2. Looking over the edge of the platform, the diver moves the body slightly forward, pushes from the platform with the hands, and draws the legs in toward the chest to form a tuck position.
3. Once the tuck position has been defined, the diver releases the legs and extends them toward the water. The eyes sight straight ahead as the release of the legs is made. The arms move laterally to the level of the shoulders to form a "swan position."
4. The arms drop laterally to the sides of the body, which enters the water vertically in a straight upright position with the eyes looking straight ahead.

FORWARD FLYING 1½ SOMERSAULTS, PIKE
FIGURE G 113B

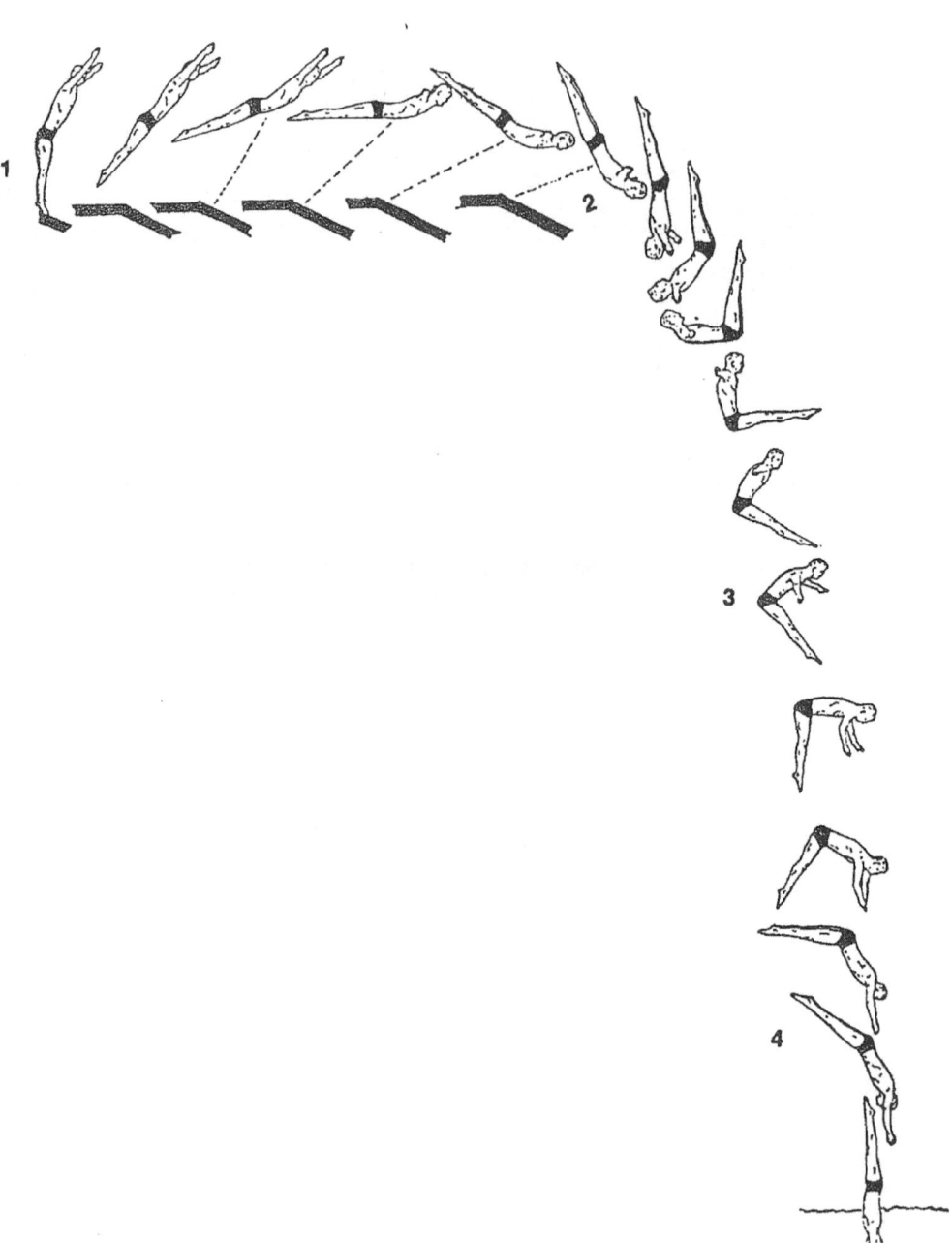

FORWARD FLYING 1½ SOMERSAULTS, PIKE

FIGURE G

1. The diver runs toward the edge of the platform (Figure D - Tower Approaches) and lands with the arms extended near vertical overhead. On leaving the platform, the diver leans forward and immediately pulls the arms down laterally toward the level of the shoulders and leaves the head up to allow the legs to lift upward.

2. When the body rotates to a near vertical position, the body bends to form an open pike position by pulling the head inward and pulling the chest in toward the legs. The arms remain in a fixed position.

3. The diver remains in the open pike position until over three quarters of a somersault is completed. The body then begins to straighten by extending the arms laterally over the head as the diver sights the point of entry.

4. The arms extend completely overhead with the hands clasping as the diver enters the water in a position slightly short of vertical.

REVERSE SOMERSAULT, LAYOUT
FIGURE H 302A

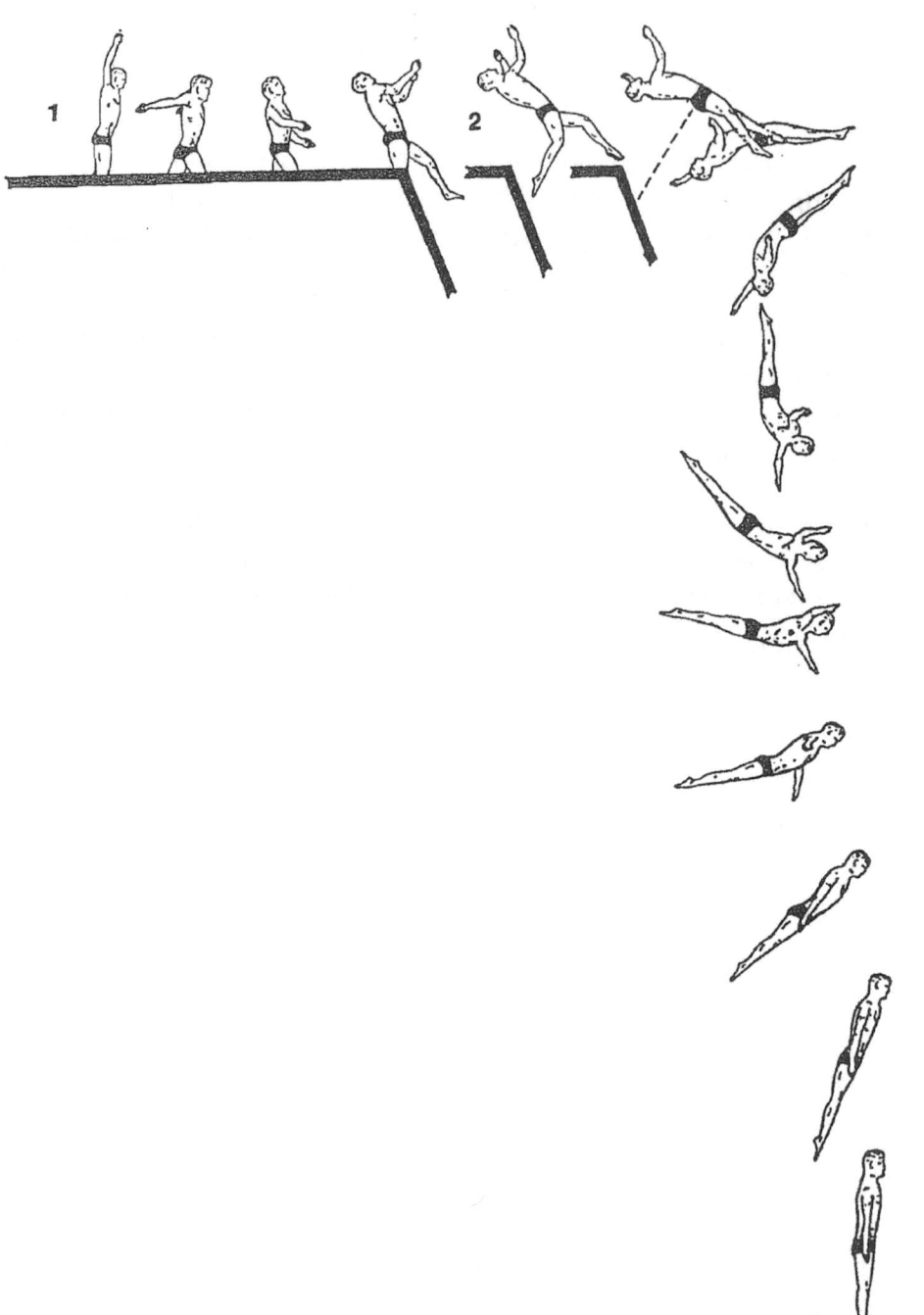

REVERSE SOMERSAULT, LAYOUT
FIGURE H

1. The diver approaches the edge of the platform on a slow run (Figures E, F & G).
2. The arms swing overhead, the chest lifts upward, the head drops back, and the back arches as one leg swings forward and upward upon leaving the platform.
3. Keeping the head up, the arms pull down laterally to a position at shoulder level as the diver somersaults. The diver can sight the water as the legs pass the vertical plane.
4. The arms remain at shoulder level for over three quarters of the somersault, at which time the arms then drop laterally to the sides of the body as the diver nears the water in a near vertical position. The diver enters the water with a straight body and the head erect.

INWARD 1½ SOMERSAULTS, PIKE
FIGURE I 403B

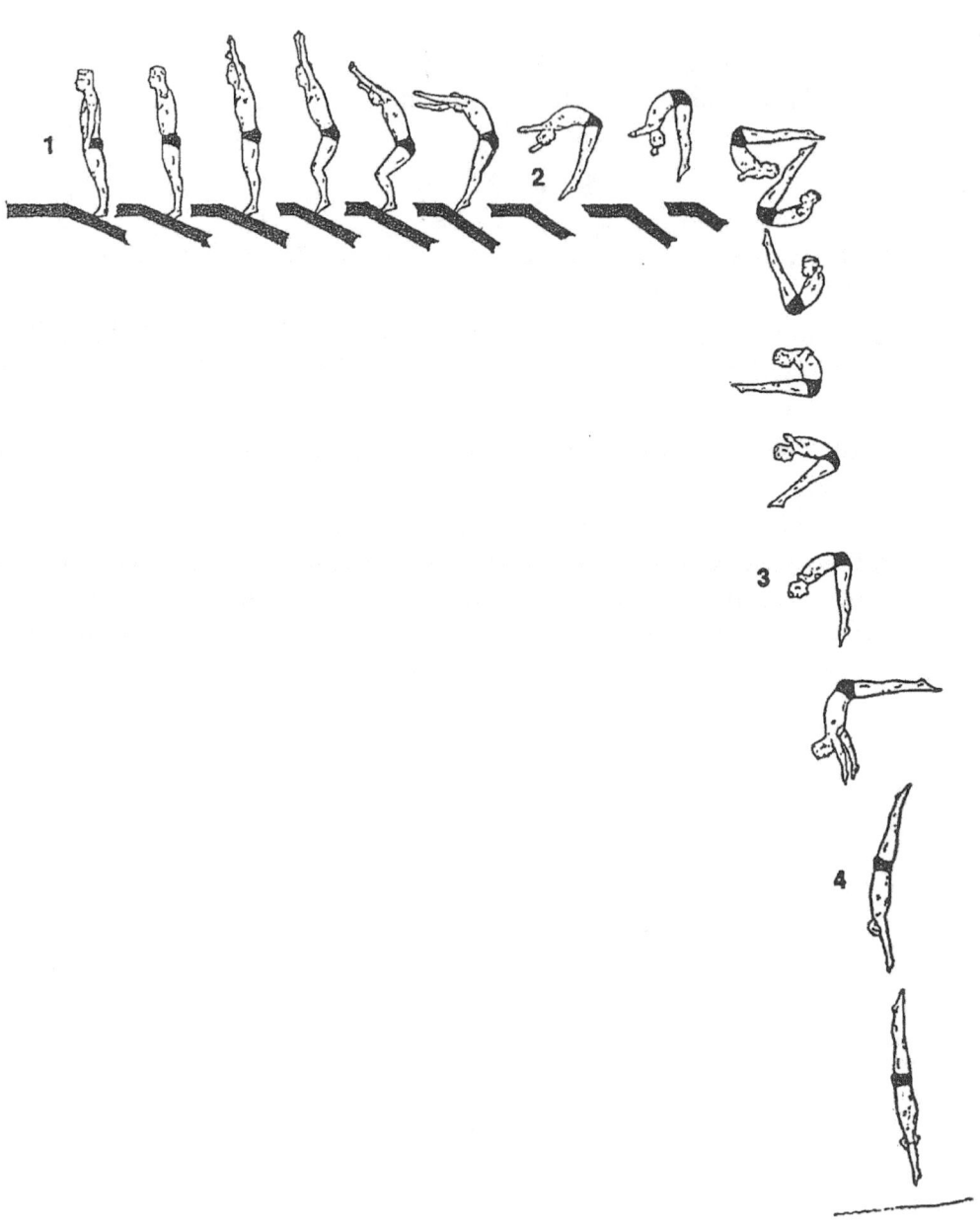

INWARD 1½ SOMERSAULTS, PIKE

FIGURE I

1. Standing on the edge of the platform with the back to the water, the diver extends the arms overhead and jumps back from the tower while lifting the hips upward and pushing the arms, head and shoulders downward (Figure I - Tower Approaches).
2. The body bends at the waist with the legs straight and the arms extending to a position at shoulder level to form an open pike position.
3. The diver can sight the water near the completion of one somersault, at which time the arms begin to extend laterally over the head and the body begins to straighten.
4. The arms extend overhead in direct line with the body and the hands clasp just before the entry, with the body completely straight and slightly short of vertical.

THINGS TO REMEMBER WHEN TOWER DIVING

1. Warm up with some exercises and practice some dives from the three-meter board before diving from the tower. This will help prevent injury.

2. Be sure to start with the more basic dives before trying the more difficult dives. This could prevent the tear of muscles and other connective tissue.

3. Concentrate on the dive to be performed before making an attempt, and don't change your mind once the dive has been started.

4. Make sure the hands are close together when entering the water head first.

SAFETY HINTS FOR TOWER

1. Swimmers should be kept out of the diving area when tower is in use.

2. A diver should always check the diving area beneath the tower before executing a dive. Caution should be given to those on other platforms of your intention to dive.

3. The depth of the water should be checked, and the type and shape of the pool bottom should be explored before diving from platforms when in a strange pool.

4. Divers should not linger in the water after the execution of a dive but should swim immediately to the sides of the pool.

5. Diving platforms are much too dangerous for horseplay.

6. The diving platforms should be roped off with signs posted when not in use.

7. A diver should never practice tower diving unless a lifeguard, coach or other qualified person is present.

8. The diving area should be roped off from the swimming area when the facilities are all in the same pool. This will prevent a swimmer from accidentally swimming into a dangerous area.

9. Allow only the more experienced divers to perform from platforms above five meters.

10. Do not practice tower diving just after eating. This could make a diver quite ill.

www.ingramcontent.com/pod-product-compliance
Lightning Source LLC
Chambersburg PA
CBHW060418010526
44118CB00017B/2265